James Baldwin

James Baldwin

Escape from America, Exile in Provence

Jules B. Farber
Foreword by Jack Lang

PELICAN PUBLISHING COMPANY
GRETNA 2016

The word "Pelican" and the depiction of a pelican are trademarks of Pelican Publishing Company, Inc., and are registered in the U.S. Patent and Trademark Office.

ISBN: 9781455620944

E-book ISBN: 9781455620951

Cover photo of James Baldwin in Saint-Paul de Vence Copyright © Cinquini. Photo portfolio researched and developed by the author.

Printed in the United States of America

Published by Pelican Publishing Company, Inc.
1000 Burmaster Street, Gretna, Louisiana 70053

For my wife Barbara, who was at my side, assisting in all phases of preparation and realization of this book.

My son, Mark, who helped me see the trees from the forest in his merciless editing.

And to Yannick Farber, my young grandson, who was an untiring computer aide-de-camp.

I remain most grateful for their encouragement and support.

This book is based on interviews with some seventy Baldwin friends who recalled being "at home with Jimmy" or who dined at his "Welcome Table" in Saint-Paul de Vence. They included Harry Belafonte, Sidney Poitier, Angela Davis, Caryl Phillips, Henry Louis Gates, Jr., George Wein, Bill Wyman, Maya Angelou, Cecil Brown, Wole Soyinka, Nicholas Delbanco, Nikki Giovanni, David Leeming, Quincy Troupe, Jr., Herb Gold, James Campbell, among others.

Contents

Acknowledgments

This was one man's personal determination to further contribute a well-deserved homage to the important American writer, James Baldwin, during his Saint-Paul period. I am more than grateful to all the institutions, publishers, biographers and many individuals who knew and loved Jimmy that made this odyssey possible.

Very special thanks to Gloria Baldwin Karefa-Smart, Jimmy's step-sister, who gave me introductions to her brother's friends from all over the world who had visited him in Saint-Paul and was so helpful in answering my many queries.

The Roux family — François, Hélène and Pitou — proprietors of *La Colombe d'Or* who had welcomed Baldwin like a "brother."

Nicole Sobié of the Saint-Paul de Vence Tourist Office, who identified all kinds of locals who had had a relationship with Jimmy that I otherwise never would have found and Christophe Messineo who was extremely helpful with photo images. Sandrine Léonard, director of the tourist office, who gave her enthusiastic support.

Philippe Bébon, Jimmy's secretary, always available when I was seeking missing details or more of his unending leads.

Of the many people in town or direct vicinity who were extremely helpful, particular thanks to: Bertrand Mazodier, Heidi Widenfelds, Dr. Véronique Larcher, Nelly Poirier, Nall, Wanda van Dijk, Henri Baviera, Xavier Huvelin, Josette Bazzini, Pierre Fouques, Michole Cohen, Gilles Quenaou, Marc Bosco, Jill Hutchinson, Jacques Simonelli, René Vialatte, Denise Mache and Doctors Roger Boizard, Christian Camel, and Joseph Benichou, as well as René Pesce and Nejib Ammar of the Café de la Place.

Much further afield, I continued searching for men and women who shared Jimmy's hospitality or were important in their contributions to his Saint-Paul saga. There were early contacts with Lucien Happersberger, biographer-friends, David Leeming and James Campbell; Colm Toibin, David Linx, Carole Weinstein, Daniel Baldwin, Corice Canton Arman, Alain Cinquini, Engin Cezzar, Ekwueme Michael Thelwell, Rosa Bobia, Quincy Troupe, Jr., Nicholas Delbanco, Jeffrey Robinson, Kalamu ya Salaam, Nikki Giovanni, Henry Louis "Skip" Gates, Jr., Joanne Kendall, Wole Soyinka, Maya Angelou, Annie Terrier, Bill Wyman, Jean Ferrero, Philippe and Denise Durand-Ruel, Jack Lang, Stéphanie Busuttil, Peter Murphy, Dr. Jean-Claude Bertrand, Sol Stein, Herb Gold, Lynn Orilla Scott, Harry Belafonte, Sidney Poitier, Pat Mikell, Roy Betts, George Wein, Jean-Louis Prat, Patrick Poivre de la Freta, Annie Cohen-Solal, Richard A. Long, Miguel Gomez, Cecil Brown, Angela Davis, Cassandra Shaylor, Bettina Aptheker, Christine Bunting, Quincy Jones, Ted Jones, Rodolfe "Rudi" Ankaoua, Robert Wildau, Akiva Potok, Adena Potok, Alain Sapin, Nicole Siccardi and Corinne Brethes of *Nice Matin* Documentation; Helen Wilson and Rebecca Gibbs at Guardian News and Media Limited.

If, inadvertently, I missed one or another of the many who readily aided me, my apologies.

Likewise, my sincere appreciation and gratefulness to Caryl Phillips, professor of English at Yale University. He was a regular guest at the Baldwin house, who filmed Jimmy on his sixtieth birthday for a BBC documentary, wrote the introduction to the *Giovanni's Room* paperback reprint edition (2001), referred to him in his books and essays — and knew him well as a trusted friend. Most importantly for me was his willingness, as the first professional, to read the manuscript. He took the text with him on a lengthy flight to South Africa where he further persisted reading in his hotel room in Durban until he had turned the last page. I sensed immediately from his incisive commentaries and positive appraisal that he had indeed lent a knowing eye.

Special appreciation to Mark Mathes, the Pelican editor who proficiently guided the development of this work with friendly enthusiasm and encouragement.

Thierry Rostang, a very creative Provençal photographer, who enthusiastically did "facelifts" to all sorts of old, faded pictures of James Baldwin with his closest friends, bringing them up to printable form.

Foreword

My first encounter with Jimmy Baldwin was well after he had finished the long odyssey that had taken him in 1948 from Harlem to Paris. For me, that felt more like a reunion than a first encounter.

For so long I had admired the talent, courage and generosity he mobilized in his fight for equality and racial harmony, but also his unfailing commitment to post-war social causes, and more particularly to the defense of homosexuals. As much as his public involvement with figures such as Medgar Evers, Malcolm X and Dr. Martin Luther King, Jr., I would mention but these three publications, *Go Tell It on The Mountain, Giovanni's Room* and *The Fire Next Time*, succeeded in making him one of the greatest voices of tolerance and progress. These works inevitably also made Jimmy a target. And as early as 1948 he was forced into exile, choosing for Paris, and again in 1970 when he settled in Saint-Paul de Vence— opting to come again to France, a choice that honors us.

I had great respect for James Baldwin with whom I became acquainted soon after he arrived in Paris the first time. He was relatively unknown in France and was struggling to survive. I provided encouragement on a number of occasions to support his literary efforts and tried, unsuccessfully, to get one of his books published in French. It was of great esteem to have a writer of this remarkable calibre come to our country.

Jimmy and I spoke with some regularity early on and again later when he had taken up permanent residence in Saint-Paul de Vence. Naturally, I had read all of his books. He was generally adored by the French intelligentsia and particularly by writers like Marguerite Yourcenar, though I wonder if the French literary world wasn't very slow in recognizing his talent.

It is regrettable that a man with his intellectual capacity and moral fiber should have been so badly treated in the United States. He was a martyr. For me he was a great humanist for whom I had always had the highest regard. He fought anarchy and was a victim of his tireless struggle to defend civil rights. It was with pride that as Minister of Culture I could propose James Baldwin to be recognized and honored by France. He was inducted as Commander in the Legion of Honor by President François Mitterrand in 1986.

UNESCO paid an international homage to James Baldwin in Saint-Paul in November 1998 on the 150th anniversary of the abolition of slavery. For that occasion, I was requested to send a message to be read expressing my respect of this great man.

His courageous campaign as a witness and spokesman in the civil rights struggle to free the blacks in America from second class citizenship, to achieve their equal rights, was an important contribution to the metamorphosis in the United States. In my opinion, his dauntless efforts, which were severely criticized by blacks as well as whites, paved the way over the past decades for an evolution that made it possible in America for the emergence of brilliant, deserving leaders like Barack Obama to be recognized.

His destiny, his career path, have always been emblematic for me: born in poverty, as a teenager he chose the career of a preacher, until his unique gifts brought him the world-wide recognition that put him on the cover of *Time* magazine and a stamp made in his effigy. But the finest testimony to his greatness as a man and to the magnitude of his work is to be found in the scope of the numerous contributions assembled here.

No, Jimmy Baldwin has not been silenced. Jimmy Baldwin will never be silenced.

—Jack Lang

About Jack Lang

Although I didn't know Jack Lang personally, like everyone living in France I was very aware that he had been a prominent, flamboyant, two-term Minister of Culture among numerous other key government responsibilities. During my research, I discovered that he was a great admirer and early supporter of James Baldwin in France.

I phoned Mr. Lang at his Paris office in the *Assemblée Nationale*. He was a member of the National Assembly for a total of fourteen years, first as a député from the Loir-et-Cher region and later as a député from the Pas de Calais region and a member of the Commission of Foreign Affairs in the National Assembly. Currently he is president of the Association for the Development of the Centre Pompidou and president of *l'Institut du Monde Arabe* [Arab World Institute], both in Paris.

Earlier, he had also served as Minister of State for Education. He had functions in the European Parliament; was chairman of the Bicentenary of the French Revolution; and was sent by President Nicolas Sarkozy on a mission to Cuba "to open a new page" in relations between Paris and Havana, where during a six-day mission he met with Raoul Castro.

Mr. Lang, immediately amenable to talking about his longtime friendship with James Baldwin, gave me an appointment which resulted in the Foreword to this book.

—Jules B. Farber

Prologue: *Searching for Jimmy in Saint-Paul de Vence*

Long before moving to Provence, whenever my wife and I came to the south of France, we generally took a side trip to Saint-Paul deVence to see the invariably superb exhibitions in the family modern art collection of the Fondation Maeght; lunch, whenever possible in sunny weather on the shaded terrace of the iconic *La Colombe d'Or* restaurant/hotel; and wander the cobble-stoned, pedestrian-only narrow streets along the cheek-and-jowl houses of this walled-in village that traces its origins back to around the year 1000 AD.

Depending on the hour we would start with coffee or *pastis* at the Café de la Place, the town's social center, which has always drawn its share of bold face names along with *La Colombe d'Or* across the street.

Besides the convivial waiters, we were always amused by the enthusiastic yelps of joy and the moaning, depressive grunts coming from the teams on the adjoining *jeu de boules* [pétanque] field. During a stop at the café, some years back, my wife remarked "this is right out of a French movie." Indeed it was! Suddenly, to our amazement and delight, we identified the team captain who stood out in his bellowing commands to fellow players and exaggerated movements while gesticulating with such bravado. It was Yves Montand, the movie star, who owned the café.

On a visit, I met Nadine Vivier, who, aware of my curiosity about the town's architectural heritage, mentioned an intriguing citation from her late partner, the poet/artist Verdet. "Once upon a time there was a handsome old stone village shaped like a boat. Its name in Provencal was *Saint Paou* — Saint-Paul." Nadine also told me that the cemetery I planned to visit was the "prow" of Saint-Paul.

This has remained one of the most picturesque and seductive hamlets in southern France, long reputed as the gathering place, a mecca, for great painters, literati, movie stars, musicians, *bon vivants* and VIPs of all shades.

Droves of the Hollywood crowd discovered this unspoiled, medieval enclave starting in the mid-1940s soon after the Cannes International Film Festival was inaugurated and they still come in droves every July. Roger Moore, among the many early regulars, ended up living there for some time. Nowadays, among the well-known residents are the film producer Claude Lanzmann *(Shoah)*, philosopher/author Bernard-Henri Lévy and Bono, the Irish singer and guitarist leading the U2 rock group. All of them were drawn here for the serenity and seclusion of this mystical setting. There is still the same old magic in the air despite throngs of tourists searching the multitude of art galleries and design shops.

Marc Chagall had his atelier and home here from 1966 until his death in 1985. He and his wife, Vava, are buried on the "prow" close to the entrance of the small cemetery set in a bucolic plateau high above the sea. Their memorial plaque, decorated with a simple bouquet of thyme, is always covered with small stones placed on it in the Jewish tradition by visitors. Chagall's paintings often depicted embracing couples and floral bouquets flying high in a peaceful blue sky over the village of Saint-Paul, which is perched 150 meters high on a hill between the Alpes Maritimes and the Mediterranean.

Delving into local history, I learned that it has been inhabited since antiquity and had struggled through Greek, Roman, and Moorish occupations before devastation by the plague. When Provence was liberated with the expulsion of the Saracens in 972 AD, a chapel dedicated to Saint Paul was built high on that hill, followed by an *oppidium* [fortress] and some houses next to it, leading to the start of a village which took the name of the chapel: Saint-Paul.

Towering stone ramparts, constructed in the 1540s as protection against belligerent forces, still stretch out for 800 meters with the old village nestled within its bastioned walls. There are also two towers, including the town's northern gate, remaining from the earlier destroyed fourteenth century ramparts. And, dating from even earlier times, is the *donjon* of the twelfth century château—not a dungeon but a "keep" or tower—which survived the castle's destruction, along with its bell, dated 1443, bearing the inscription,

"*Hora est jam de sommo suggere.* [Roughly translated, "The hours invite us to dream right now."]

It was around the count's castle high on the so-called *Passe Prest* Hill where the population huddled to avoid the cranky, unaccommodating lord's threatening vindictiveness if they came too close. *Passe Prest* in modern French is *Passe Vite*, pass quickly.

Since the eighteenth century the tower has served as the town hall and witnessed many celebrity marriages, including Rolling Stone guitarist Bill Wyman, movie star Gene Wilder, and others.

From the Middle Ages onward, Saint-Paul became an affluent town of merchants and craftsmen.

Right up to the eighteenth century, the leading families built imposing houses on a former Roman road, the *rue Grande*, which was then — and still is today — the main shopping street. Butchers, bakers, shoemakers, candlestick makers, and craftsmen had their shops and ateliers on the ground floor of these impressive residences.

In the center of the *rue Grande*, on the *Place de la Grande Fontaine*, an imposing fountain, erected in 1850 in the heart of the medieval market place, is one of the most famous in France. Behind the fountain under the vaulted arch is the cavernous, old washhouse where the women did their laundry. A curiosity, a few steps from the fountain, is the *pontis*, a bridge crossing that links two houses on either side of the street.

Someone told me, "A village is, first of all, a church tower." It is presumed that the first stones of the Collegiate Church were laid in the fourteenth century, dedicated to the conversion of Saint Paul. In a dominant position overlooking the town, it reflects four centuries of building from Romanesque to Gothic to Baroque styles.

On a route leading out of town, among four chapels built from the Middle Ages onward, is the baroque Saint-Clément Chapel from 1680 and the Holy Cross Chapel of the White Pénitents, also seventeenth century, with a surprising three-sided bell tower and modern mosaics, stained glass windows, sculptures and frescoes created by the Belgian artist Folon. The penitents served soup to the poor.

The Fondation Maeght, situated a few kilometres outside the center of Saint-Paul, is always a must on our visits. Some fifty years ago, Aimé and Marguerite Maeght, having discovered fallen stones in the ruins of a small votive chapel dedicated to Saint Bernard, decided to create an art center in the imposing vast wooded nature as a memorial for their loss of a young son whose Christian name was Bernard.

The renowned Catalan architect Josep Lluis Sert was commissioned to harmonize architecture with the arts and nature, with painters and sculptors integrating monumental works into the building and gardens.

Georges Braque, Fernand Léger, Alberto Giacometti and other artist friends of the Maeghts encouraged them to proceed and created *in situ* works in the complex. Among the highlights are the Giacometti courtyard, the Miro labyrinth filled with sculptures and ceramics, Chagall's and Tal-Coat's mural mosaics, Braque's pool and stained glass window, as well as Bury's fountain.

Since its opening in 1964, the foundation has presented over one hundred thematic or monographic exhibitions and attracts annually close to 250,000 visitors. The collection of twentieth century paintings, sculptures, drawings and graphic works — now with more than 6,000 works offering a panoramic overview of modern and contemporary art — is one of the most important in Europe. Likewise, its library has become a major resource for twentieth century art research.

During a morning visit a few years ago to an indoor exposition at the Foundation, we skipped our usual saunter over the terraces and in the gardens with their towering sculptures in view of the *mistral*, the fierce, biting north wind sweeping over the grounds. We headed back to our car and drove to Saint-Paul for lunch at *La Colombe d'Or* but even the expansive, walled-in patio was too cold for comfortable dining so we went indoors.

While wandering in the narrow halls, I spotted a portrait of Picasso, which was not surprising since he was a habitué and friend of the owners. Further on, a photo of James Baldwin caught my attention.

With a few questions to our waiter, I discovered that Jimmy was considered like "one of the hotel family," completely integrated into the village. He seemingly knew everyone and everyone knew him and frequented the Fondation Maeght, whose director, Jean-Louis Prat, was a good friend.

Baldwin had been one of my literary heroes. My admiration for not only his writing but for his intellectual battle against racism had never dimmed. I knew he had spent time in Paris back in 1948. I was not aware that he had later made his home in this village. I was curious to know what people thought of him, this black stranger, and what effect this new life had on his writing.

What better way than to research firsthand recollections about the kind of man Baldwin truly was and how he fitted in? I sought a variety of people from all walks of life who knew him. Friends, lovers, doctors, café owners, barmen, writers, artists, taxi drivers, chauffeurs, mailmen—anyone who could provide insight to the real Jimmy. There could not be anyone of a certain age still living in Saint-Paul who did not know and love Jimmy.

It soon appeared that many of those I encountered who claimed "close friendship" turned out to be no more than very casual contacts who Jimmy would always greet in passing, invite for a drink or to come home for dinner or a party. During several dozen meetings with locals, I was always fearful I might miss one or another genuine account or anecdote. Finally I had to whittle out many vapid recollections. I did find a good number who truly knew Baldwin well and could contribute to his Saint-Paul portrait.

My objective was to locate those people who played a meaningful role in his life—and Jimmy in theirs. Their remarks always revealed mutual love and respect.

Curiously, I never heard a bad word, a sly innuendo, a sarcastic remark about Jimmy—which I certainly was not looking for—but I wanted honest, objective recollections. He emerged as a "great black idol" who everyone respected.

In essence, there was a large and faithful Baldwin fan club with a virtual unanimity in terms of endearment.

I heard an occasional reference to his unreliability in keeping appointments, always arriving late, money problems, not paying back loans and his being over-generous to a fault, making it easy for people to take advantage of him while feigning friendship.

The criteria for those qualified to provide first-hand memories always required a Saint-Paul link. After starting with locals, I would go further afield to find others who had shared Jimmy's life there in some manner or other, from working for him, dining with him at the "Welcome Table," socializing regularly within his inner circle of intimates, interviewing him, dropping in, coming as house guests — or making love with him.

The wonderful upside was that once reached everyone was happy to talk about Jimmy and took lots of time to do so as they reminisced about the charismatic figure in Saint-Paul who they admired.

During four years, I was able to realize some seventy interviews, which were further enriched by numerous writers' willingness to grant permission for my citing from their work about Jimmy.

Selected recollections have been inserted amidst excerpted highlights from biographies of Jimmy's life; quotations from articles, essays and novels he penned; critical reviews and interviews he gave during his seventeen years in Saint-Paul; and other relevant information researched as a backdrop for the people who still remember James Baldwin's life in Saint-Paul.

I discovered that Jimmy — or at least his spirit — was still very much alive among everyone who had known him and had never forgotten his impact on the place or on them.

The high ramparts of Saint-Paul seem protective in enclosing this Baldwin country, his fiefdom, his literary legend and his humanity, while the winding cobblestone streets still echo his legend.

This book, about the man called the "Henry James of Harlem," is an homage to the important, often controversial, African-American writer, James Baldwin, who traded Harlem, New York for the medieval Provençal village of Saint-Paul de Vence in southern France for the final period of his life.

But its significance should be recognition of the importance of Baldwin in terms of his literary production in objective retrospect, despite the facile criticism of his being an "out of touch" writer living abroad; as well as his own development and discoveries in an European culture clearly not his own; his contribution to the French literary scene; his influence on developing young black American writers; his warm gentleness; and, most significantly, why this period in Saint-Paul reveals so much of his unheralded greatness.

—Jules B. Farber

The Importance of Being Baldwin

Jimmy, as he was known to everyone, was important in his last seventeen years spent in France. No longer a spokesman in the civil rights strife, he shed his earlier fiery, angry tone of the sixties, replacing it with a more nuanced position on the white/black debate in the US, despite ongoing attacks from an upcoming younger generation of black writers, the black press and other African-Americans.

He was able to take distance and become more complex and humane with a more lucid vision of race relations, human tolerance, and understanding. He was far ahead of the time. Through his novels, essays and other lesser-known writings and interviews, he expounded new perspectives on bigotry, homosexuality, and exile.

Henry James was clearly Baldwin's role model and literary mentor who epitomized the need to go into exile. James's philosophy, frequently quoted in prefaces to Baldwin's books, decidedly influenced his writing. Baldwin had acknowledged that the nearest thing he could find "for the means to order and describe something that happened to me in the distance — America — was James."

Early on, in his escape to Saint-Paul from the turmoil in America, he made it clear that he was not running away.

Baldwin was trying to be a writer. In America, he could not find the support or encouragement he sought. No one had ever told him that Alexander Dumas was a mulatto or that Pushkin was black. As far as he knew, there had never been a reference to anything called a black writer.

On the other side of the ocean, Baldwin could not call himself an expatriate. He insisted that only white Americans could consider themselves expatriates. He brought his home and his heritage with him. Never would he be able to escape the fact that he was the grandson of a slave.

As the first black in this all-white French enclave with a conservative, agrarian population, initially he encountered the same racism he knew in the States and had experienced during an earlier period in Paris. But with his wide, toothy smile and gregarious, outreaching personality exuding genuine love, he warmed the hearts of everyone he met. Before long this small, ugly, gay, black American — as he liked to describe himself — was accepted as "one of us" in the provincial community.

Settling into French life, he realized, and cherished, how American he actually felt. And with this awakening he became a more complex person who, with a new peaceful detachment, continued to have an important impact on the literary world and public opinion in the United States and France.

This was a difficult period in his life, with recurring bouts of anxiety, self-induced collapses, alcohol abuse and writing blocks. Baldwin's sporadic literary production frequently was subjected to mixed American critical reviews. In some one could sense a subtle, resentful judgment of an American author writing about American life from a distant land. But there was also a good share of praise, particularly for his essays.

He did produce some dozen works — including novels, essays, collaborations, poetry, scenario, children's story and an adaptation for presentation on the Public Broadcasting System — and continued right up to his deathbed when he was editing his final play, *The Welcome Table*. Besides his books, there was other writing, numerous articles and frequent interviews. All had a profound influence on upcoming authors. His work was food for thought among his intellectual peers on both sides of the Atlantic.

During the last decade of his life, his yearning to connect with young people led him to venture from Saint-Paul for a semester every year to lecture at American universities on literature and the history of civil rights, as well as to lead seminars in creative writing. His discourses, though not written, were scrupulously noted by students hanging on his every word.

Exemplifying Baldwin's very significant influence was his mentoring Lori Parks who would win the Pulitzer Prize for drama. Toni Morrison, a close friend who stayed with Jimmy in Saint-Paul, acknowledged that his texts about Black English, among others, had been very important to her. As an homage, this great African-American author would, in 1998, edit two extensive volumes of his literature and essays for the prestigious Library of America.

Though Baldwin often suffered disparaging reviews for his late work, in recent years there has been a rehabilitation of his literary reputation from that period. This enlightened research unveiled his daring experimentation in treating sensitive issues of racial identity, social justice, and sexuality. While many scholars had earlier segregated his literary prowess into a fiction or nonfiction box, current evaluation positions him as one of the twentieth century's most complex writers and thinkers.

Baldwin had critical success in France among the most intensely studied of the postwar group of African-Americans since Richard Wright, owing to ongoing French translations right up to his demise. While he was nominated for diverse prestigious literary prizes—but always lost out—he remained a beloved, respected writer and celebrity.

French critics acknowledged that Frenchmen could not comprehend the black Americans' soul and struggle without reading James Baldwin.

Adopted by the French, he was decorated by President François Mitterrand with the distinction as Commander in France's Legion of Honor, the highest recognition of service to the country.

While Baldwin couldn't live in the United States, he couldn't live—and write—without the United States. He found his salvation in France. Saint-Paul was the bridge between the two worlds.

—J. B. F.

Introduction: *Escape (Again) from America, 1970*

James Arthur Baldwin — African-American author, essayist, poet and playwright — suffered a mental and physical breakdown in 1970. It had all become too much for him. He was haunted by the assassinations of black protest leaders and distressed by the setbacks in the Civil Rights Movement, which he feared might erupt into violence as the only route to justice. He was also wounded by the criticism and attacks levelled against him especially from within the black community, and angered by the FBI's malicious scrutiny.

During his thirteen years back in the United States after a nine-year stint in Paris, Baldwin had become more famous as a celebrity-spokesman than as a writer. The unceasing public recognition, combined with his inability to concentrate, added to his insecure, dispirited state. He became dependent on tranquilizers, washed down with bottles of whiskey, punctuated by incessant chain smoking.

Jimmy had been demoralized by the sad state of his fellow blacks in the United States. As in earlier years when he had fled to Paris, his need to escape was building up again. He felt an oncoming collapse, albeit, perhaps self-induced.

He was targeted by the African-American community which asserted that he taken a position as a self-glorifying "mouthpiece" rather than as a witness. Baldwin, while insisting that his mission was "to bear the truth," rebuffed the label of "spokesman" for the Civil Rights Movement: "A spokesman assumes that he is speaking for others. I never assumed that I could. What I tried to do, or to interpret and make clear, was that no society can smash the social contract and be exempt from the consequences, and the consequences are chaos for everybody in the society."

He experienced betrayal by black writers who unloaded their venom on him. One was an ex-friend, turned adversary, Amiri Baraka (known earlier as LeRoi Jones), the new star of the Black Arts Movement. He called Baldwin the "Joan of Arc of the cocktail party," and insisted that "his spavined whine and plea was sickening beyond belief."

The young Ishmael Reed referred to him as "a hustler who comes on like Job." Others dubbed him "Martin Luther Queen."

According to Gore Vidal, a Kennedy intime, Jack and Bobby frequently argued about which one of them had been first in referring to James Baldwin as "Martin Luther Queen."

Black Panther Minister of Information Eldridge Cleaver—while still in Folsom Prison in 1965 for the rape of several white women, assault with intent to murder, drug and theft charges—authored *Soul on Ice*. It's a book portraying America as a treacherous cauldron of racism, which was published in 1968. This coincided with the ending of the civil rights struggle in the South. In it he lauded his own love of white women and brandished black homosexuals' frustrations, coupled with an alarming homophobic attack on Baldwin for his way of life and his presumed role supposedly as spokesman for the movement.

Cleaver wrote, "There is in James Baldwin's works the most grueling, agonizing, total hatred of the blacks, particularly of himself, and the most shameful, fanatical, fawning, sycophantic love of the whites that one can find in the writings of any black writer of note in our time." Baldwin's sexuality was also attacked: "Many Negro homosexuals are outraged because in their sickness they are unable to have a baby by a white man. . . Jimmy was engaged in a 'despicable underground guerrilla war, waged on paper, against black masculinity.'"

In referring to Baldwin's best-seller, *Another Country*, in which the black hero, Rufus, is characterized as self-destructive and violent, Cleaver said that Baldwin was "a pathetic wretch who indulged in the white man's pastime of committing suicide, who lets a white homosexual f--- him in the ass, and who took a Southern Jezebel for his woman."

Baldwin found the vitriolic attacks particularly painful coming from a "brother." Besides also being ridiculed as the "African Queen," there were death threats and he was convinced that his life was truly in danger.

He faced still another dilemma: writer's block. "Any writer, I suppose, feels that the world into which he was born is nothing less than a conspiracy against the cultivation of his talent—which attitude certainly has a great deal to support it," he said. Certainly the untenable climate of racism was smothering his creativity. And being constantly shadowed by the FBI worked on his nerves and his boundless paranoia.

"To save myself," he remarked in 1970, "I finally had to leave for good. . .One makes decisions in funny ways; you make a decision without knowing you've made it. I suppose my decision was made when Malcolm X was killed, when Martin Luther King was killed, when Medgar Evers and John Kennedy and Bobby Kennedy and Fred Hampton were killed. I loved Medgar. I loved Martin and Malcolm. We all worked together and kept the faith together. Now they are all dead. When you think about it, it is incredible. I'm the last witness—everyone else is dead. I couldn't stay in America. I had to leave."

In total despair, he again sought asylum in France, where he had first found refuge in 1948 from the bigotry prevalent in the United States. Actually, though his first period in Paris was a psychological break, it was not a bed of roses. Marked not only by poverty, there was at least one suicide attempt, demeaning treatment by certain visiting white Americans and constant police harassment. He was stripped of his belt and shoelaces and locked in a jail cell for unknowingly accepting a hotel bed sheet stolen by a friend.

There were clashes with Africans—primarily Algerians—and African-Americans. Baldwin had compared the systematic control of black lives in Paris with that of blacks in America, concluding that his adopted country was no less racist than his land of birth. His experience in the French capital underscored for him how irrevocably American he was. And he admitted feeling a closer kinship with some white Americans than with the African blacks, whose culture he had never shared.

At the age of forty-six, he left the hostile atmosphere in America, returning to France to start on the third and final act of his literary career. He arrived in Paris as the world's most revered black author and sought-after personality. *Time* magazine had spotlighted him on a cover. Press reviews of his best-selling books translated into French had appeared in major national media. His global reputation preceded him. He picked up contacts with old friends among expatriate black writers like Richard Wright, artists, musicians and entertainers who he idolized, along with leading white personalities in the arts, music, literature, theatre, and motion pictures.

But his well-being was short-lived. He suffered from exhaustion and depression, fearing he would become insane like his stepfather, a painful memory which never left him.

"When I came back to Paris, I collapsed again. Friends then shipped me, almost literally, out of the American Hospital to Saint-Paul, a little lofty village near Nice in the south of France," Jimmy had recounted. Actually, it was his friend and new agent, Tria French—an African-American woman living in Paris and working as a talent scout for Warner Brothers—who brought him there for his convalescence. Baldwin had encouraged Tria French to open an agency in Paris in 1971 to promote black artists, with his financial backing. It closed in late 1972 when she died of a heart attack.

Baldwin had escaped the racial strife and turmoil, as well as the terror of his suspected own assassination and the FBI surveillance in the United States, for the peaceful shelter of Saint-Paul.

—J. B. F.

Chapter 1

Open House: *A Racist Landlady*

Simone Signoret and her husband Yves Montand — guests with separate rooms many months of every year in Saint-Paul's iconic hotel La Colombe d'Or — ran into James Baldwin in the hotel's bar soon after his arrival in late 1970.

Following his release from a Paris hospital for mental and physical illness, Baldwin was booked for his convalescence in the inexpensive Hôtel le Hameau on the road leading down from the historic center. But it quickly became apparent that he couldn't afford to continue paying the modest rates for all the family, friends, hangers-on, and visitors who came to see him and, naturally, accepted his hospitality often for weeks on end. Other lodgings had to be found.

Simone had become friends with him during his May 1968 visit and was particularly influential in charting his further stay in France, urging him to remain in the village after his recuperation.

Signoret checked out possible quarters in a rooming house across from the hotel owned by an elderly spinster, *Mlle.* Jeanne Faure, a *pied noir* — a reference still used today for repatriated Frenchmen expelled from Algeria during the country's war of independence, which ended in 1962. Having been born in Oran to a wealthy French family living there for many generations under French colonial rule, *Mlle.* Faure carried a resentment all her life for dark-skinned North Africans who had forced her departure, though she was only two years old when her family had to leave.

Mlle. Faure kept part of the large house for herself and her brother, renting rooms in the other part on a weekly basis. Known for being violently opposed to people of color, she was very frightened of the prospect of someone with whom she associated her banishment coming into her home. Signoret—aided by Baptistine "Titine" Roux, who with her husband Francis owned the Colombe d'Or— persuaded *Mlle*. Faure to rein in her prejudices and accept Baldwin as a tenant. He moved from the hotel to the Faure estate.

While Baldwin was settling in, *Mlle*. Faure imposed her personal form of "apartheid." She blocked the door leading to her part of the house with a heavy, wooden wardrobe while openly expressing her anxiety about having a *"neeger"* under her roof.

Though Baldwin was relegated to a basement flat in the old stables, accessible through a small, narrow passage under the kitchen, he kept "buying" rooms he needed to provide a place for everyone invited to stay, as well as those who just showed up and expected—and got—shelter for extended periods of time.

As time passed, *Mlle*. Faure became charmed by Baldwin's elegant manners, and her racism evolved into a strange, loving friendship. She allowed him to continue "purchasing" rooms with the intention that one day the whole house would be his. (Though Baldwin, as well as others, often talked about his purchasing more space, the transactions were generally agreements sealed with IOUs, a payment method which eventually resulted in a prolonged legal battle over the house's ownership after his death.)

Pierre Fouques, an attorney in nearby Vence and *Mlle*. Faure's first cousin, told me, "Jeanne was old and needed love, affection. As time went on, she told Jimmy he could live in the house as long as he wanted. She had her office on the ground floor where she wrote history books, while she and her brother had rooms upstairs. They had money and didn't have to work but rented out rooms anyhow to augment their income."

Fouques further said, "Jeanne was *trés à droite*, very rightist in her thinking. She was, one would say, in reality a monarchist, while Jimmy was clearly progressive, but always extremely courteous to his older hostess. Jeanne would go on about the horrors of the French Revolution while Jimmy talked passionately on a high intellectual level about the poor blacks and racial inequality in the United States.

"They had a mutual respect for each others' beliefs. I observed the development of harmony and an exceptional friendship. On one side was this black writer, a diamond of intelligence and sensitivity with origins in misery; while, in reality, she was a *paysanne* [peasant] but also cultivated and friendly. Each of them, Jeanne and Jimmy, in 'their house' read a lot and wrote. One was recording the history of our village, while the other was preoccupied with his message of fraternity which was his *raison d'être*.

"Jimmy was frequently invited to dine in her part of the house and she accepted dinner invitations in his segregated part. This old maiden, who wrote a history, *Saint-Paul, Une ville royale de l'ancienne France sur la Côte d'Azur [Saint-Paul, A Royal City of Old France on the Côte d'Azur]*, was intrigued by Jimmy's literary skills."

Fouques recalls attending dinners at the house with the Faures and Baldwin.

"The meal was always served in a dining room that was from another époque with antique furniture, silver service, embroidered napkins—a Provençal dream for Jimmy. The four walls had been painted by Italian Renaissance artists who came to the village to decorate the great houses in the center and along the ramparts.

"The floors were covered with *tomettes*, hexagonal red tiles typical of this region, and there were deep-piled carpets in the two main downstairs reception rooms. White ivory basins were used to wash one's hands before going to the table. There were beautiful Provençal *bahuts*, sideboards for storing her antique chinaware and crystal glasses. This sprawling eighteenth-century house, with twelve vast rooms, original frescoed walls and rough beamed ceilings, is in the most fashionable quarter, named *Les Fumerates*, since there had been *fontaines murées*, walled fountains, everywhere."

Bertrand Mazodier, a native villager whom I visited in his antique jewelry boutique, *la Balance*, in the historic center, filled me in on his recollections of Jeanne Faure and on the situation in Saint-Paul before Baldwin arrived.

"Almost everyone here was National Front, very right wing. Even though *Mlle.* Faure was brought here from Algeria by her family as a child, she still had fixed notions of imperialistic superiority and was prejudiced against people of color. She was like a French Nazi, a World War II collaborator with a huge Pétain portrait on her wall.

"Just as most of the people here, *Mlle.* Faure lived in the baptism basin of the church. We called them *grenouilles de benitier* [holy water frogs]. Everyone was constricted by the church, holy rollers, afraid of what their neighbors would think if they strayed. But, to their credit, since they were all good Christians, they helped the Jews during the war. The straight-jacket conservatism changed in May 1968 with the protest marches and student strikes. Suddenly, people dared to come out, to be free."

Undiplomatic in his directness, Mazodier continued, "It was well known in the village that she was very mean, greedy. She earned money from her big garden with flowers for the perfume makers in Grasse, besides olive and orange trees, vineyards, thyme, myrtle, citrus fruits. There were rumors that she sold her vegetables on the black market during the war. When she took in children as wards after the war, at Easter time she gave each of them half an egg.

"But she changed when she got close to Jimmy. It became a kind of 'last love' for her but for him, too. She didn't like anyone except Jimmy. Can you imagine that this dyed-in-the-wool racist was in love with a black? Jimmy dedicated his last work to Jeanne. At her funeral, he wore a boat-shaped astrakhan hat and was visibly shaken up."

I was surprised when I asked Mazodier about his recollections of Baldwin to find that he delivered mail every day to the Faure property.

He recalled, "In the early 1970s, when I was sixteen years old, I worked for the local post office. Since I was the only one who spoke English, I took down telegrams for Jimmy that came in by phone, letter by letter, every word spelled out, page after page. His was the last stop on my route, so I always ended up just after twelve noon at his place and was usually invited in for a glass or two of wine. He would come out of the garden, where he was typing on an old Remington, and make small talk.

"Although I had read French translations of his books—there weren't many yet at that time—I never dared discuss them with him. My English wasn't good enough to be intelligent. He let me know that it was good for him to be here, to be accepted, with no problem of color, away from the States. It seemed that writing was difficult for him, but once he got started, he could go on for days. I suspect that he, like most French writers, was on speed, Coryphedrine, and other drugs. Everyone, including myself, was getting it from the drugstore. In the States, it was called Ritalin.

"I can't claim that Jimmy was my friend. He was more like a grandmother to me, kissing me—and I'm not gay! This was in sharp contrast to the cool stance of his assistant, Bernard Hassell. He was an extremely handsome man, proud to be black, proud to be a good dancer—but a real racist. I was too white for him. He always wanted to be above you.

"Whenever I went there, I was always aware of the very obvious police watch on the house. Their car was parked nearby. Perhaps they were from the *Renseignements Generaux* [Intelligence Service of the French Police] and were authorized to tap phones and read mail. They peered at the goings-on through binoculars and must have thought that Baldwin was some kind of black militant. The French government was controlling everything left wing. I suppose there was also governmental surveillance. People in town were also suspicious. For a long time, there was hate mail for him coming into the post office every day, all kinds of wild things.

"Jimmy was vaguely aware that the cash drawer was always empty, causing him to borrow regularly, constantly putting him in debt. He was very laid back about it, leaving Bernard to handle the finances. Since Jimmy wanted to be loved by everyone, he invited all kinds of people, even casual acquaintances, to his house. Often there would be a motley assembly of people who were not of his intellectual level or even stimulating conversationalists. But there were also many well-known authors who stopped by. Once Simone brought Françoise Sagan to the house—both of them were bitches—as well as Françoise's brother, who supposedly wrote Françoise's second book."

Mazodier continued, "Jimmy may have been ill and depressed when he came to live in Saint-Paul, but he was not unknown. He was a famous black writer much admired in France. Even though only a handful of locals might have read his books, or any books at all for that matter, no one could ignore his fame and celebrated literary stature. This was quickly buzzed through town."

Hélène Roux of the La Colombe d'Or family reflected her own astonishment in saying, "The most remarkable situation was Jimmy's relationship with Jeanne Faure. He was like a son and a lover to her. She totally adored him. She discarded all her rigid, opinionated bigotry to protect this black, gay guy. We children in the village were afraid of her. She was a terror, always screaming at us if we made noise on the street while playing or ran too fast. She bitched at everyone. But she loved having Jimmy in her house and she wanted him to have the house. *Mlle.* Faure said he can pay whatever he can and that's what he did all along, all through the years. When she died, she had two pieces of paper with the amounts Jimmy still owed attached with a safety pin to her bedclothes."

Xavier Huvelin, director of the Hôtel le Hameau when Jimmy Baldwin stayed there, had a theory that "Jeanne liked having personalities in the house. After the painter, Georges Braque, she rented rooms to Michel Droit, then Henri-George Clouzet's brother and, lastly, to Jimmy. This made her feel more important, that she was being recognized because of her association with these well-known people."

Huvelin went on to say, "Jeanne always wanted to be near Jimmy. It was obvious that she was in love him. She treated him like a god. He was supposed to pay her rent but more often than not, he did not have any money. Although she loved money, she let him get away with all his sweet promises."

As the oldest, largest house and property close to the village on the route de la Colle sur Loup, now lined with chic, modern villas, the mansion survived in its derelict, faded glory. Almost all the other houses on this route have names. Jeanne Faure's house, a "no name" place, almost with a disdain for the *nouveaux riche* neighbors, was simply known as the *propriété* Faure. Nearby residences were visibly protected like small fortresses with burglar alarms, high fences topped by electric shock systems, and ferocious dogs, while at Baldwin's place the iron gates were often wide open and the front door left unlocked. With literary license, Baldwin placed this house "at the side of a mountain. . .at the edge of the sea."

Currently at this point on the route, there is a relatively new red and white sign marking the town limits of Saint-Paul as if the municipal fathers want the outside world to know that a famed American writer once lived there. It is the boundary line of a royal settlement founded in the year 1009. Perhaps the gesture was a late twentieth-century bow to their beloved "adopted son." While he was living there, one could regularly hear the guides as the tour buses passed en route to the Maeght Foundation: "There is the house of two blacks — the famous American author, Mr. James Baldwin, and his assistant."

Coming from the coast, Saint-Paul is about twelve miles west of Nice. On the sinuous left fork of the wider road leading to the village one can locate, but not see, the Faure property hidden behind a high wall. It is situated some 400 meters before the old center. Near the house's rusty gate, a small gatehouse served as a garage, above which was an apartment with a tiny kitchen, bathroom, two bedrooms, and a terrace. Further back is an impressive *bastide,* a three-hundred-year-old elegant country house centerpiece of the ten-acre property. It is set in a wide paved alley accentuated with roses, beds of colorful flowers, and an enormous, centuries-old cypress standing almost in salute to this architectural inheritance. Also along the alley were the proprietors' chief source of income — supplemental tourist lodgings, and rows of *bigaradiers,* [bitter orange trees], cultivated for their flowers to be sold to the perfume industry of Grasse.

Among such vibrant flora, Baldwin soon realized that he had found a new home. The gardens had almond and peach orchards, vineyards, fields of wild strawberries and asparagus, centuries-old pines, almond and hazel nut trees, wild thyme, and massive rosemary bushes. There were also olives, figs, bananas, lemons, and pears. Far from the Harlem tenements, this was paradise for Baldwin, who, with childlike glee, wandered barefooted in the groves, picking fruit and nuts.

While at the Faure estate, Baldwin reached the age when "silence becomes a tremendous gift, and the vineyard in which one labours a rigorous joy." When his agent Jay Acton first came to Saint-Paul, he remarked, "It was a beautiful setting with fascinating company. . . the garden wasn't one of Jimmy's interests. He wasn't a gardener. . . but he loved the house. He did everything to protect and keep the house." On a later visit, Acton commented on the beautiful grounds desperately in need of a "haircut."

Baldwin moved into an underground apartment which served as his office, which he called a "torture chamber." This was the same space used earlier as a studio by Georges Braque. On the wall hung three paintings by Beauford Delaney, an African-American artist who was the greatest influence and inspiration in Baldwin's writing. In *The Price of the Ticket: Collected Nonfiction, 1948-1985*, he referred to Delaney as "the most important person in his life" and "one of the greatest men I have ever known." He depicted Delaney as "the first living proof, for me, that a black man could be an artist. In a warmer time, a less blasphemous place, he would have been recognized as my teacher and I as his pupil. He became, for me, an example of courage and integrity, humility, and passion. An absolute integrity: I saw him shaken many times, and I lived to see him broken, but I never saw him bow."

Two of Delaney's paintings were portraits of Baldwin, the other of Foster White, the Franco-American former live-in lover who was chased away from the house, banished for some unforgivable deed which no one would reveal. Also in Baldwin's office was a beautiful Tuscan landscape painting by Yoran Cazac, who co-authored *Little Man, Little Man* with Baldwin and was also his lover.

On another wall, there were lithographs by his very close artist friends César as he was known (born César Baldaccini) and Arman, who worked under this name (born Armand Fernandez). Baldwin worked at a huge desk, always in disorder, backed by wall to wall bookcases and a wood-burning fireplace. Adjoining was a rather modern bathroom.

Just outside, directly below the house, Baldwin had a private terrace. On the terrace was a large round table covered by a huge umbrella and surrounded by rose bushes, cacti, palm trees, and many flower beds. The outdoor table served as his writing desk in the summer. At a still lower level, there were fields with orchards and shacks for the Algerian field workers.

Eventually Baldwin took over the main floor of the barn, which had its own entrance at road level. Baldwin was able to occupy the entire main house, following an attempted break-in which precipitated *Mlle.* Faure, the frightened elderly spinster, to move to the village in 1976. He paid very little attention to décor. Furnishing was sparse but comfortable in those rooms rented out earlier to tourists.

His house was his kingdom with an open gate policy that attracted throngs of visitors of all types. Baldwin's court was centered on several individuals. There was Bernard Hassell, his assistant *à tout faire*, whom he installed in the gatehouse; Valérie Sordello, a woman from the village who came every day for the housekeeping and cooking; Lucien Happersberger, one of his most devoted friends who regularly visited from his home in Switzerland; and his brother, David Baldwin, who left Harlem and appeared overnight in Saint-Paul whenever Jimmy needed help.

Hassell was an African-American dancer brought over from the United States by Charles Trenet in a troupe for the Folies Bergère in Paris. He was considered a "beautiful man" by everyone who knew him. Baldwin and Hassell met in 1952 during Baldwin's first period in France. Their meeting marked the start of a lifelong, deep-rooted friendship that never became sexual. Their relationship became one of the most important in the lives of both men. Hassell became one of Baldwin's most loyal friends and devoted companions.

Hassell's responsibility in the house involved, in effect, taking care of Baldwin and all his needs, and protecting him from intruders, annoyances, and anonymous threats. Furthermore, he had to stock the provisions, tend the garden, and handle anything else that might arise. He was always there when Baldwin entertained at home and accompanied him whenever he was invited to friends' houses. But their own sexual encounters and partners were kept strictly separate. Baldwin's realm was his playground, while

Hassell had unfettered use of his private domain — the gatehouse — for welcoming nocturnal guests.

Valérie Sordello, "*la mama,*" was clearly the heart of the house. Every morning she would arrive on her Mobylette moped, wearing dark wraparound sunglasses Miles Davis had given her, with all the groceries she had picked up en route. She was a wonderful cook, and often when she was just preparing for five people, thirty people would show up and she would produce miracles. Her specialities were *pot au feu* [various meats and vegetables in a strong broth] and *boeuf en daube* [beef stew drenched in wine], as well as Baldwin's favorite Southern-style chicken. As many of those closest to Baldwin have expressed in their recollections, Sordello was an integral part of the family. Loyal to Baldwin, she was with him from soon after his arrival until the end.

Miles Davis wrote in *Miles: The Autobiography* (written by Miles Davis, Quincy Troupe collaborator): "I'd read his books, and I liked and respected what he had to say. When I got to know him better, Jimmy and I opened up to each other. We became great friends. Every time I was in the South of France, in Antibes, I would spend a day or two at his villa in Saint-Paul de Vence. We'd get comfy in this beautiful, big house and he would tell us all sorts of stories. He was a great man."

In my continuing search for people who stayed at the house and enjoyed Sordello's cooking, an unexpected lead came from Robert Wildau, a retired Atlanta attorney now living in Provence. Wildau led me to Richard A. Long, an Atticus Haywood professor emeritus of interdisciplinary studies at Emory University, where he specialized in African-American culture, history and the humanities, and rising movements like Negritude and the arts movement which accompanied them. When I phoned him at his home in Atlanta, he was startled by my out-of-the-blue contact but was immediately amenable to sharing the following account:

"Upon arriving in Paris in early August in 1973, I went immediately to see my friend, the artist Beauford Delaney, at his studio. I was aware that Beauford was having difficulties in managing daily life, but I was quite distressed by the disorder in the studio. The explanation was that his friend, Bernard Hassell, who had checked on him regularly, had moved to Saint-Paul de Vence. I telephoned Bernard to tell him of my concern for Beauford. He immediately consulted Jimmy and told me that they would both be pleased if I would bring Beauford to Saint-Paul. I agreed to do so and convinced Beauford to make the journey.

"After a few days in Saint-Paul, I returned to Paris. Beauford was upset that he could not return with me, but Jimmy and Bernard assured him that they would take him back to Paris very soon. Beauford continued to decline, and some months after he returned to Paris, Jimmy and a number of Beauford's associates arranged for him to go to a hospital for supervised residence. Jimmy remained certain that Beauford would recover and leased an apartment for him in Paris.

"My second visit to Jimmy's home in Saint-Paul occurred after his passing. He had willed the artworks in the house to the of Clark Atlanta University Art Galleries. I came to Saint-Paul to inventory the objects. Bernard was still managing the house. Works by Beauford were in the group. Jimmy's presence could still be felt."

Lucien Happersberger, whom Baldwin always referred to as his "greatest love," was staying at the house early on when Beauford Delaney was there. Happersberger's relationship with Baldwin got started when they met in Paris in late 1949. As a seventeen-year-old aspiring Swiss artist, he was a tall, handsome, slim, debonair man about town—a sharp physical contrast to the short, slight, bug-eyed author. Happersberger, who survived in the French capital by being "kept" by men and women, enjoyed making love with both sexes. Nightly he shared what food he could buy with his "buddy." Though they never lived together, they were lovers. Their relationship lasted until Happersberger's girlfriend became pregnant. On Baldwin's advice, they married and their son was baptized Luc-James, a combination of both of their names. Baldwin became the godfather.

While I spoke with Happersberger at his home in Lausanne, he continued to refute that he was Baldwin's lover through the years, despite Baldwin's dedicating *Giovanni's Room* to him.

"I was very important to him but was not the 'man of his life,' as he often told people. Jimmy wanted—needed—one person to really love. He wanted to settle down with one loving partner in a permanent domestic relationship and fantasized that it would be me." (In the intervening years, Lucien Happersberger had moved on, been married three times—one spouse being the late black singer, Diane Sands—and he had two children.)

"Through the years, we stayed as close as ever. I visited him often in Saint-Paul but didn't stay long, since it was always hard to talk—to find some quiet when he was surrounded by lovers who flocked to him because of *Giovanni's Room*. I remained his true buddy from our early days in Paris until I sat vigil at his deathbed for days, watching silently as he slipped away."

Among others very close to Jimmy was his brother David. Seven years younger, he was always Jimmy's favorite among his eight stepsisters and brothers. Several of the Baldwin novels include relationships which clearly reflect the brothers' real-life relationship. As he grew up, David became Jimmy's closest confidant, his "lieutenant," someone he could always turn to with problems. David was Jimmy's buffer in hiding his homosexuality from his mother and was at Jimmy's side during the confrontational encounter with Robert Kennedy. Jimmy could talk with David, level with him, as with no one else.

While David lived primarily in Harlem, he was always keenly attuned to Jimmy's state of affairs and would fly over to southern France whenever he sensed his brother needed him. Whenever David heard that Jimmy was having problems with writing or being distracted by a surplus of house guests, he would immediately try to put things right. Such was the case in 1971 when Jimmy wrote that he was ill and having difficulty finishing a collection of essays started before Martin Luther King, Jr.'s assassination. David got on the next plane and then returned to New York with the pages of the unfinished manuscript that would be published a year later as *No Name in the Street*. Furthermore, right after Jimmy's diagnosis with cancer, David came to his side and stayed close to him through the ordeal until his death.

David's last partner, Welsh-born Jill Hutchinson, moved into the house with David after Jimmy died. Although Hutchinson never really knew Jimmy Baldwin very well, she provided an intimate insight to his exceptional brotherly relationship with David.

"David adored Jimmy like crazy. He felt his brother was honest, kind, vulnerable—especially in his amorous life. Jimmy never stopped loving Lucien. David, like Jimmy, was always straightforward and could upset people by bringing up things they didn't want to come out. Jimmy spoke fluent French and was fearless. Someone else had to worry about his getting into trouble. That's why David was extremely protective of his brother.

"When they were together here, or anywhere, David always slept on the side of the bedroom nearest the door to protect him. He was concerned when Jimmy smoked marijuana and then would write and write all night long under the influence, only to rip up all the pages the next day."

While I was looking for other people who had visited Jimmy in Saint-Paul, I was put in contact with Gloria Baldwin Karefa-Smart, the sixth of the eight Baldwin children. Despite her initial reticence for an interview, Gloria was extremely helpful in suggesting others to approach and did convey some recollections of her visits to Saint-Paul. She was particularly close to Jimmy, her illegitimate older brother.

When talking about the house in Saint-Paul, she said, "My fondest memory was Jimmy's fiftieth birthday celebration on August 2, 1974. I came over with my sister Paula. David was there with Carole. There were many friends from everywhere. The village had never seen so many lights as Jimmy had strung up in his orange grove. It was a wonderful celebration and a fabulous summer. The only downside was the ruckus when Jimmy fired Bernard, but Philippe Bébon stepped in and was the best secretary ever.

"The last contact that I and my mother had with Jimmy was on Thanksgiving 1987 when we had a long, sad telephone call. We knew he was dying. My mother was afraid of flying and couldn't go over. We would take leave of him a short time later in the cathedral of Saint John the Divine in New York.

"I had problems going to Saint-Paul after Jimmy passed. His spirit was always present. It was difficult to escape in that space. My last visit was in 1991 when Bernard Hassell died, but there were too many bad memories. David also returned to Saint-Paul that year for Bernard's funeral and moved into the house with Jill Hutchinson. After David died from cancer, Jill stayed in the house."

The "Carole" that Karefa-Smart referred to was Carole Weinstein, an earlier partner of David Baldwin's, who was very much present in the house during Jimmy Baldwin's first decade in Saint-Paul. Weinstein, a top educator, consultant, and founder of Learning Works, first spent the summer in Saint-Paul in 1971 with David. When she met Jimmy Baldwin in 1964, she asked to be known as his "sister-*out*-of-law."

"We had a great affinity. I understood what Jimmy was talking about in relation to power, discrimination," Carole remarked. "He would openly discuss his writing and would talk about the challenges in creating a character. What was going on in the world exasperated him. He was occupied with how he could express his anguish. He would work these things out through his writing.

"Most importantly, he felt free and relaxed in France more than anywhere else. He felt a comfort of being home, surrounded by family. This showed in the way he played with my son, Daniel Baldwin. As a self-taught man, he was very concerned about education for young people, especially for Daniel.

"Jimmy made sure that there was always loads of love and joy in the house. There was a fantastic atmosphere day to day, and this became even more festive with regular visits of his many good friends—people like Harry Belafonte, Alex Haley, and numerous other personalities who adored Jimmy. I remember that the great black singer, Nina Simone, came often. It was like being front-row center, enjoying these two celebrities singing, dancing, shouting, and laughing well into the night.

"The only unpleasant experience I can ever remember through all those long vacations there was caused by Jimmy's very obnoxious Parisian lover who wanted to rule Jimmy's life pattern and be the one in charge. He was jealous of everyone in the house and fought with *everyone*. That was in 1976. Jimmy had tried everything to get him out of the house and eventually fled to New York just to get away from him.

"After spending so much time with Jimmy that first summer, I thought I really knew him, but when I came back with Daniel in following years, I discovered Jimmy the family man. He was more than a doting uncle; he was like a father. Jimmy loved being with him and often took him out, walking hand in hand, so that everyone in the village could see Daniel."

Through my contact with Carole Weinstein, I was put in touch with the adult Daniel Baldwin in Providence, Rhode Island, where he works as a sound engineer.

Daniel recalled, "My mother brought me over to spend whole summers there. The house was always filled with lots of hangers-on, gigolos, and, surprisingly, many Algerians because of his sympathy for them in opposition to the French stance concerning the Algerian war.

"There was always music from the record player. Jimmy listened to jazz, gospel, and soul, with lots of Donny Hathaway. Sure, I sang and danced for him on occasion, but it was he who was always full of music, often singing in the house or when he was walking around the property. It was 'cool' to me, his reading stories he wrote. He had a hectic schedule. He would disappear, work for ten or twelve hours, wake up in the middle of the night, and go out.

"For me, a child growing up in this place, it was like my summer home. In 2004, my mother and I returned for the last time. She was trying to interest some universities in buying it as a residence for aspiring writers in honor of Jimmy. We didn't succeed, but in my mind, the house is always there and I'm in it with my Uncle Jimmy."

Daniel recalled that Uncle Jimmy wrote in the rambling house in a study on the lower level. Baldwin described the terrace directly in front of this office, where he could take breaks from his writing, "as an island of silence and peace." Determined to get on with his literary career, Baldwin spent fruitless hours night after night, armed with packs of cigarettes and a bottle of Johnny Walker Black

Label, staring at his old Remington typewriter and struggling to get the prose flowing. In an interview with *Nice Matin*, Jimmy explained that his all-night writing pattern developed after years of spending nights protecting his younger step-siblings from being devoured by rats in the Harlem apartment.

After his new start on his career in different but friendly surroundings, he did everything to forget the civil rights struggle in America. But Baldwin was often depressed, probably psychologically self-induced, and couldn't work.

According to Pitou Roux (Hélène's sister), "Jimmy loved living in the house high on a hill with a dominant backdrop of Saint-Paul and sweeping views of the Mediterranean. He relished welcoming accomplished African-American friends, as well as many white friends, who came from abroad or lived here, like the Hollywood actor, Donald Pleasence, with a house in town, or Dirk Bogarde, who had a place nearby in Châteauneuf de Grasse. Jimmy was at Dirk's fiftieth birthday party at the hotel.

"When Jimmy settled in Saint-Paul, he used to come here in the late evening where he felt completely free, could unwind and drink. Jimmy moved in leftish intellectual circles and always feared he was being watched by the FBI or the CIA. He would discuss literature with my mother. She thought his works were badly translated in French and told him so. She translated a play and then undertook with Simone the translation of a book—I can't remember which one. I used to see them working for hours, looking for the right word, the right expression.

"He was interested in me because I was young. He was curious about young people, what they thought, what they could teach him. When I came home from school and told him we were reading *Blues for Mister Charlie* in our literature class, he was amazed—proud that he was in our local school.

"Jimmy wanted to know all the racist jokes I heard—and he always reacted with great bursts of laughter. When he, himself, was annoyed by other African-Americans, he would say things like, 'Oh, he's just a stupid nigger,' or, 'I'm not the son of my father. My father was the postman.' Or, 'I'm black, Jewish, and homosexual—

everything that's wrong.' Or, 'I have three strikes against me — I'm black, ugly, and gay.' He was always testing me for reactions. I went to the house all the time and even lived in a part of it later for three or four years."

In Paris, I reached Rodolfe "Rudi" Ankaoua, the hard-nosed, voluntary financial administrator who brazenly demanded and succeeded in getting exceedingly high contractural advances and royalty arrangements in his devotion to Jimmy.

With a nostalgic sigh, he recounted, "We passed many evenings together at his house when I stayed over, laughing all the time about small things. He loved recounting stories about Marlon Brando. We talked about politics, literature, music, and all kinds of things. He knew everything about my life, my wives, my sons. We had no secrets from one another. Often we ate strawberries and cream when we got back to the house after dinner."

Dr. Maya Angelou — a celebrated African-American poet, memoirist, novelist, educator, dramatist, producer, actress, historian, filmmaker, and civil rights activist — spoke with me on the phone from her office in Winston-Salem, North Carolina. Baldwin had been instrumental in getting her started on her literary career. There was a giggle in her deep, rhythmic voice as she related, "When we were together in Saint-Paul, it must have been a comical sight, since I'm six feet tall — but he was always my big brother.

"Our bond became closer than ever because of my books. Every time I was in southern France in the '70s and '80s, I went to stay for a few days with Jimmy and enjoyed the warmth of his home. On some of my visits, David was there. That was a good thing since he loved Jimmy, served him, wasn't afraid of him — a great friendship.

"I didn't see much of him during the day when he was going over his writing. Since I wasn't there to work, I would go on nice walks or read in the peaceful garden. We would sit up late, drink Scotch, and talk. Meals were always a great pleasure. Valérie was an incredibly creative cook. We would make bets on what she would prepare without telling her. He always won."

Among those who lived in Baldwin's house was the extremely talented Belgian singer, composer, lyricist and multi-instrumentalist

David Linx, a Zen-spirited, lanky, six feet three inches young man who towered over Baldwin. He arrived in 1983 and remained until Baldwin's death, leaving only on concert tours. During our lunch at the Parisian Left Bank Café Flore, I sensed how much Baldwin meant to him—and he to Baldwin—emotionally as well as musically. The passion in his voice and his way of phrasing what he remembered about life with Jimmy spoke volumes about their relationship.

In explaining how he had come to live in Saint-Paul de Vence, Linx said, "I first met Jimmy when I was sixteen. I was playing drums with a jazz band in Amsterdam when I heard that Jimmy would be giving a lecture the next day organized by his Dutch publisher. I had read all his books. He later told me he saw me as 'a big wild boy crying out for help' and said I could always come to his house if I needed to.

"About two years later, when I arrived in Saint-Paul with two big bags, he didn't question it since the energy was clear. I grew up with jazz musicians, mostly African-Americans. One of my godfathers is Nathan Davis, a black hard bop saxophonist. I never considered myself white or black in that environment when I was a kid. This doesn't mean that I wasn't aware of it all, the friction and the adversity, color and its line. I immediately felt at home there.

"Jimmy changed my life. He was like a father to me. Trusted me, always wanted to protect the ones he loved. I'll never forget him. I couldn't understand why he was called a radical or why he scared people. He was available to everyone but just couldn't fathom anyone who reacted without love. Although he could become angry, rarely was he impatient, letting everyone say his piece. That was the social Jimmy, but he would get into a silent bad mood if someone made stupid remarks like 'things are better for the blacks now.'

"Soon after I moved into his house, I became immediately aware of that strange, warm, wonderful, sweet, welcoming smell in the quarters where he worked and slept. Unforgettable! There was the deep red carpet with the odor of whiskey, cigarettes, and the open fireplace. I had never drunk before until once I decided to drink whiskey with him, feeling like a character in one of his books. But after a few hours, it had gotten so bad that I couldn't understand what he was saying. That was my first and last time. I quit and haven't had a drop since, but I still have the taste in my mouth. Whenever I see Johnny Walker Black Label displayed in airports, I am immediately reminded of Jimmy and all those wonderful evenings in Saint-Paul de Vence.

"Jimmy would wake up late, having written all night, and we'd have lunch in the garden under the grape vines. There would always be guests—could be anyone from a great jazz musician, like his good friend, Miles Davis, to some unknown artist or aspiring writer who just dropped in. It was the same scene at night with lots of people, famous or not, partaking of his boundless hospitality. Jimmy ate very slowly, first cutting everything up into small pieces, putting them back on his plate, then he finally started to eat, all the while listening to people. I used to tease him and try to distract him by eating from his dish.

"After lunch while we rested on the bed, Jimmy would often read to Bernard and me what he had written the night before. He always asked us what we had done, did not comment even though we waited to see the reaction on his face. There would be discussions of published books like *Evidence of Things Not Seen*. He couldn't understand how on earth the critics could think of him as 'bitter' when he wrote about the Atlanta murders. Jimmy was surprised at how others could misconstrue and not recognize that he couldn't be bitter and write at the same time. An artist can't afford bitterness. He was not bitter and always advocated universal love and brotherhood.

"One day he told us about his story line for *No Papers for Mohammed*, based on his gardener being deported to Algeria and his own immigration problems with French authorities, but it was never finished. He was anxious to have his play, *The Welcome Table*, produced to further establish his reputation as a playwright, but, unfortunately, it remained uncompleted.

"It was idyllic being in the house with Jimmy, Bernard, his brother David when he came over from Harlem. But at the same time it was strange living with such a famous personality, seeing so many well-known people coming over the floor — and some weird ones that Jimmy didn't even know. I remember one man showing up who claimed he was a good friend but Jimmy had no idea who he was. He wanted to spread the ashes of a family member on the property. Jimmy very diplomatically told him it wasn't possible but, not wanting to hurt his feelings, invited him to stay for lunch. He ended up staying for a week, I think. He couldn't turn anyone away.

Linx recalled with a smile: "Valérie was a wonderful cook but she always had to call the gatehouse on the interphone for Bernard, who managed the budget and kept just enough food, not more, for her to prepare the meal. Bernard became Jimmy's metaphor for a refrigerator." He would laugh, with his great captivating grin, looking at you, with complicity, checking to see if you were connected. For example, Jimmy never could understand that Bernard named his small dog 'Josephine.' For him, in France there could only be one Josephine — and that was Baker.

"Valérie was a sweetheart, a simple woman with traditional values from this village in southern France, with a strong character, who didn't have it easy running the house with all the comings and goings. She became blasé about all the well-known people who came. She wasn't easily impressed anymore, but remained formally friendly and correct with everyone. She never used the familiar *tu* form for you with anyone and even when I returned from a trip, she greeted me with '*Monsieur* Jimmy will be so happy to see you.'

"Whenever *Mlle.* Faure was invited to dine with Jimmy, I never joined them. They were fighting all the time, a kind of bittersweet, love/hate relationship, and she would say terrible things like, 'Jimmy, you are the only black person I like.' He would roll his eyes in disbelief and then after a few seconds would burst out laughing.

"Once, when Valérie was on vacation for a month, there were only the two of us and Jimmy wanted to cook for me. But after he burned the rice and poured too much olive oil over everything, he became upset and we went to La Colombe d'Or. As someone who grew up in the inner city, he always got a big kick out of picking figs and oranges off the trees and eating them in the garden of this huge property.

"Jimmy warned me not to say too much on the phone, to keep conversations very superficial and short, just what was necessary — like telling him when I would arrive, for instance — but no small talk. There have been a couple of anonymous death threats. He said he wasn't paranoid about being watched, but. . . whenever we left the house to walk up to the village for a period of time, we were aware that a car was always parked at the curb with two men sitting in it."

Someone suggested that I search for Philippe Bébon, who worked in the house for four years as the most faithful, dedicated secretary Baldwin ever had. According to some villagers, he fled the nonstop, demanding job to avoid a breakdown. No one in Saint-Paul was able to give a clue as to his whereabouts except for some speculation that he might have returned to his home in Sauze in the Alpes Maritimes.

After dozens of phone queries in the region around Sauze to *mairies, gendarmeries,* and schools, since someone thought he had gone back to teaching, I found him in a hamlet high up in the mountains and secured his unlisted telephone number. Though surprised by my call more than two decades after Baldwin's death, Bébon agreed to be of assistance. He turned out to be a reliable source of inside information — since he was clearly still very attached to Baldwin.

"I had met Jimmy in Paris in the sixties through my friend, Bernard Hassell. After Bernard completed his dancing role during a successful run of *Hair* in 1971, Jimmy asked him to come take charge of the house in Saint-Paul — work in the garden, order food supplies, manage the finances, and keep people from just barging in.

"I was asked by Jimmy to become his secretary in September 1972 when Tria French passed away suddenly. He needed someone to sort out all his contracts, book proposals and lots of other papers which he had given to Tria. Bernard was installed in the small gatehouse, and I moved in with him when I arrived. There were two small bedrooms, a tiny kitchen, and a bathroom — all above the garage. We slept in one of the bedrooms and the other became my office. The gatehouse, located right on the road, was about twenty meters from the main house. Communication at first was by a bell being rung, and later we had an intercom.

"Jimmy didn't mind that I was Bernard's lover since he and Bernard were just very good old friends. Actually, only once in the seventeen years Jimmy and Bernard were together in Saint-Paul did they have a falling-out. He fired Bernard in 1974, because he was always making trouble with *Mlle.* Faure, who hated him. He talked to her in violent tones, was aggressive in his behavior with her, and had become difficult for Jimmy to deal with because of all this. But the last straw was Bernard hiring a taxi to take him to Paris and back, a trip which cost Jimmy a small fortune. Jimmy was furious when he found out, dismissed Bernard, and sent him away. It was only some time later he was allowed to return.

"Jimmy's letters to his brother David in New York mentioned having trouble working because of all the people crowding him in his house. But, more important, he was nervous about accepting an invitation from his publisher, Rowolt Verlag, for a nationwide book-signing tour in Germany after the United States Information Agency had suddenly and mysteriously pulled out of their sponsorship. Jimmy was convinced that he was being targeted by someone high up in the FBI. David came over, cleared everyone out, and went with us, serving as a bodyguard, which calmed Jimmy's anxiety. The tour proved to be very successful, and Jimmy's popularity in Germany grew significantly.

"My duties were principally handling all the correspondence, being his *chien de garde* [watchdog], answering telephone calls, organizing all the American tours, arranging lectures at universities, preparing programs, and handling all the minutiae. These trips were fatiguing, nerve-wracking, full of tension. I averaged two hours' sleep a night.

"Besides all the well-known people who came, there was a parade of young men whom Jimmy attracted. I remember all their names since they settled in, but that's not important. Most of them were gigolos, like the French painter, the Algerian guy, the American black, the beautiful young boy from Guadeloupe, and many others.

But once they got to know Jimmy, they fell in love and became attached to him—he couldn't get rid of them. There was one he felt really had writing talent, and he tried to help him. He was sentimental about one lover who died and insisted on spreading the boy's ashes on the grounds.

"The routine when I was in the house," Bébon said, "was that I woke him around noon. He would read the English and French newspapers and then we would have lunch around 2 pm. At the table could be numerous guests. Simone Signoret would join us frequently. There were many other celebrities who just dropped in for a meal and others who stayed over. Some of those I still remember include Harry Belafonte, Bobby Short, Bill Cosby, Ray Charles, Quincy Jones, Sidney Poitier, Maya Angelou, or his great friend, Toni Morrison. After he participated in 1974 with Toni in an American TV debate, followed by lectures at Bennington College, Jimmy insisted on Toni coming for a vacation at his house. She came with her small son and stayed with us for about one week.

"Nina Simone always was in the house whenever she had any singing engagements in the region or just wanted a break. Jimmy used to tell her, 'This is the world you have made for yourself. Now you have to live in it.' She had become one of the greatest singers of her generation with her scorching renditions of jazz, blues, and folk, and was often compared to Billie Holiday and Edith Piaf. Jimmy convinced her to work for civil rights, and her song 'Young, Gifted, and Black' became the anthem for the Civil Rights Movement, thrusting her into the center of activism. Cecil Brown, who arrived regularly in the early '70s, became Jimmy's closest contact among the younger black male writers."

I asked Bébon for more about house activities. "We had chauffeurs since Jimmy couldn't drive. Jimmy had taken driving lessons, but one of his first lessons ended up in a frightening accident and a battered vehicle. There was Ray. Then a young man, Marcel, was hired. He was succeeded by a lovely German lady, Heidi Widenfelds, a statuesque, towering blonde German married to a Swede. I was still there when Heidi stopped and Yvan Nicoloss took her place at the wheel. After I left, I heard that one day Nicoloss and the big Mercedes had disappeared, never to be seen again. Maybe that's because he had not been paid for many months.

"When he was working at home," Bébon went on, "Jimmy wrote his texts with his left hand on long, white, unlined pads. After lunch, while we sat around the table, he would read the texts he had written during the night before to Bernard, David — if he was with us — and to me. He wanted us just to listen. He needed to say his texts out loud and then sought reactions, comments from us. Since I had some experience in publishing, as a reader at Denoël and then as a corrector at Universalis, sometimes I could be helpful with suggestions. When he was satisfied with what he had written, he typed them over himself and worked again after dinner, often through the night, aided by a bottle of whiskey or wine.

"I had worked for Jimmy for four years but I had to leave. I couldn't take it anymore. It was intense, tiring, twenty-four hours a day. I had no private life. His sister Gloria, who was his secretary before me, told me she left because her hair started falling out. He was always nice, amiable, but. . .his life pattern was so self-destructive that I couldn't bear to see him going on like that. I had to escape. I think I stayed the longest of any secretaries.

"After I left in November 1976, I traveled, did some theatre. I sent him birthday cards and came back every year until 1980 and stayed in his house — but that year I changed my life. I went to live in the mountains, returned to teaching, got married, and had children — two sons. We stayed in contact and he sent me a dedicated copy of his last book, *The Price of the Ticket*."

Following up Bébon's comment on Baldwin's affinity for Cecil Brown, I contacted Brown at his California home. Author, poet, playwright, screenwriter, and scholar, Cecil Brown is well known for his first novel, *The Life and Loves of Mr. Jiveass Nigger,* which became a best-seller among disenchanted blacks and was a cult classic on college campuses throughout the United States. That book, published in 1969 and reissued in 2008, dealt with a young black expatriate who fled to Copenhagen searching for invisibility in white society but returned disheartened to America.

We talked about why he went to Paris and how he became a

regular guest in the Baldwin household over the years, starting in 1973. His quest in the French capital was to meet older, established black writers like Richard Wright, Chester Himes, and others, but most of all, his great idol, James Baldwin. While I started taking notes, he told me he had written up his recollections and would mail them, after which we could talk again. The following are some texts edited from the material Cecil Brown sent me:

"About a week after arriving in Paris, I was sitting at the Café Flore when another African-American approached me and asked if I was not Cecil Brown the author. He said he was a friend of James Baldwin and that Mr. Baldwin would like to meet me. He flattered me, but I was naturally intrigued. I had come all the way to Paris with the hope that I would meet Mr. Baldwin and here was my chance.

"I realized that this would be a turning point for me. Baldwin meant so much to me. I had read everything he had published many times. I called him 'The Master.' And he was. I had read, for example, his essay, *The Discovery of What It Means To Be an American*, about what Paris was to him. Leaving America was as though [one] suddenly came out of a dark tunnel and found [oneself] beneath the open sky. And, in fact, in Paris, I began to see the sky for what seemed to be the first time. I could trace and retrace Jimmy's footprint in text and time.

"The next day I did meet him in the lobby of his hotel as Ray, who was Jimmy's chauffeur, had arranged.

"With a scarf waving from his neck and a cigarette in his fingers, Mr. Baldwin lived up to the reputation of a literary celebrity. He laughed a lot, and when he laughed, his entire face disappeared behind a picket fence of white teeth and a loud, raucous laughter.

"His favorite word was 'baby,' plucked from the argot of the Harlem slang and French speech. To hear him talk was like sitting down in front of a jazz drummer like Elvin Jones.

Brown recalled: "'You know,' he said, as he settled down with a Jack Daniels Black Label, 'I would think that you hated me.'

"'Why?'

"'All writers hate their elders.'

"He paused and stared for a moment into the back wall. 'I had such a difficult time with Richard [Wright]. I never could get through to him. It made our relationship terrible.'

"I did not know it then, but I do now, that Jimmy was serious about having a better relationship with the younger generation of writers.

"'If you want to be a writer,' he said, 'that's fine. But if you want to be a great writer, you're going to need a lot of help. I didn't get that from Richard, but I hope I can help you.'

"Bill Styron, one of Jimmy's pals in Paris, had tried to arrange for me to get a PEN fellowship but it didn't work out. Then I remembered Jimmy's earlier invitation. Why not? I called him and was delighted that the invitation was still on. One of the first things out of my mouth was how disappointed I was that I didn't get the PEN fellowship.

"'Well, baby, I ain't no fellowship for you,' Jimmy laughed. 'But you are welcome to come down here and eat a pork chop with me.'

"A few days later, when my train arrived in Nice, it was dark. Jimmy was waiting beside a big, black Mercedes. When I got in, the other guys in the car greeted me with smiles and laughter.

"'Welcome to the south of France,' Jimmy said. 'We are on our way to a party!'

"I felt as if I had entered the world of Jimmy's fiction. In that virtual world, you could be the ideal person you wanted to be."

Brown continued, "I told him the story of my mistake in first taking the wrong train. This was proof that he had been right, that you could take the black man out of the country, but you couldn't take the country out of a black man.

"We headed for the party, which was in a villa on a hill. I had read his description of the south of France in *Another Country* and felt as I entered the party with its beautiful people dancing under a strobe light that I had entered the pages of his novel with Jimmy Baldwin as my host.

"I remember the famous black faces at that party, like Josephine Baker and Bobby Short. I met them as if I were in a dream. At one point, I was standing on the patio looking out at the lights sparkling in the dark from the Provence hills. I turned and saw Jimmy. He was dancing and then he saw me and came over. Jimmy passed a joint to me and said, 'I can't wait to read about this in your next novel.'

"We must have gotten to bed around two or three. When Jimmy came home, instead of going to bed, he went to his typewriter, where he would write until about seven o'clock. After he fell asleep, he would get up at twelve. He lived the life of a jazz musician, working at night and sleeping the mornings."

The account went on. "The next day as I sat under the thatched roof of 'The Welcome Table,' Jimmy appeared, said 'Good morning,' and with a big smile on his face, said, 'I'm very proud of you.'

"'Thank you, but why?'

"'You have made the journey!'

"'From Paris to the south of France?'

"'No, from the American South to Paris and the south of France.'

"Then I started to reflect on the situation in the house. I quickly figured out Jimmy's life in this marvelous villa. I turned to marvel at the view. From where we sat, you could see the city of Saint-Paul up on the hill, shining like a diamond.

"That early afternoon, the topic was about Ray, who had been dismissed. He had been a good chauffeur for Jimmy, but he had to fire him because Ray was supposed to fly up to Paris and bring the manuscript of *If Beale Street Could Talk* but had arrived there without the manuscript. For a moment, Jimmy thought it had been lost. This was the last straw, apparently, and Jimmy was forced to let him go.

"It was, Jimmy corroborated, a horrible ending to a great friendship. The problem with Ray was that he had become distracted by some French actress that he met when she came to visit Jimmy. It didn't take me long to see what brought on Ray's problem. For reasons that I had not yet figured out, beautiful French women were attracted to Jimmy."

He related more about the trip. "As each day passed, I explored the surroundings, little by little. It didn't take me long to figure out the dream that I had fallen into. The little town of Saint-Paul de Vence had two principal parts. On the top of the hill was the business district, and below it at the bottom was the old city itself

surrounded by a medieval wall. A couple times a week, Jimmy had
to be driven to the little town to go to the bank. At other times, he
would stroll up by himself to meet friends at La Colombe d'Or.

"Since Ray had been fired, somebody had to drive Jimmy to the
bank and that chore fell to me. The first time I drove Jimmy up to
the bank was an early afternoon. With his scarf over his shoulder,
Jimmy went through his mail just as he got into the car. As I drove
along the highway, with the view of the hills stretched out lazily,
he said, 'There is a letter here. Somebody is suggesting that I
get a Nobel Prize for Literature!' He laughed at that suggestion.
'Evidently, they have read my books!' He regarded such things as
the Nobel Prize in a world of white values, which he found 'empty.'

"As I drove the twisting roads, Jimmy slipped into his private
reverie. He would talk about literature. His favorite writers were
Henry James and Fenimore Cooper. He liked James because he
knew how to 'load' a sentence and how to narrate a story. I told
Jimmy I was thinking of changing the narrator in my story from
first person to third. He said, 'Then you don't have the same story
anymore. Or you have a different story.' And Fenimore Cooper?
The Last of the Mohicans for Jimmy was the beginning of American
literature because it was about massacring Native Americans. He
said it was a terrible novel but he was always reading it."

He went on: "I drove us into the square, parked the car, and then
I waited at a café for him. I enjoyed watching the French people.
The colors, the gestures, their walks, the air, the sunshine — it was
like being in a dream or in the pages of one of Jimmy's novels.
His friends began to show up. Soon the whole table was full of his
friends, and drinks were ordered, consumed, and replaced.

"I recall that we went to another café and I remember noticing
that the entire table was full of young Frenchmen. I asked, '*Où
sont les jolies filles?*' [Where are the pretty girls?] They all looked at
each other and giggled. One of them said, 'We are all girls.' Jimmy
laughed, of course.

"I began to take the Mercedes all the way down to the Nice
Promenade. One day when I was strolling along the Promenade, I
saw a black man seated in the back of a chauffeur-driven Citroen.

'Who in the hell could that be?' I wondered. I didn't have to wonder long though, because as I got closer, I recognized Bill Cosby. He was seated beside a beautiful woman, his wife Camille.

"'What are you doing here?' he asked me.

"We had met before when he invited me to be on the Tonight Show while he was guest-hosting it for Johnny Carson.

"'What are you doing here?' I asked him.

"In the early seventies, if one black man saw another one in Europe, his question was: 'How did you get out of America?' The issue of status, fame, or wealth was not the question. The fact that a black American was not in America but in Europe and how he got out was the question."

Cecil carried on with his narrative. "I told him I was staying with James Baldwin. Would he like to come to dinner? I went back that night and told Jimmy that Cosby was staying at the Hotel du Cap Eden Roc in Antibes and would like to come to dinner.

"The next day, Cosby and Camille sat at 'The Welcome Table.' Cosby talked and entertained us with a scene from Miles Davis. 'Miles was really funny, you know,' he said. We cracked up. Jimmy commented, not actually replying to his story, that it was great to have black Americans at his table. He lived from the contact he made with blacks from America, he said, 'who come up for air.'

"Jimmy talked that evening about blacks abroad and how they always regarded each other with suspicion. While Jimmy talked like this, he also wrote like this. 'One Negro meeting another at an all-white cocktail party,' he wrote, 'cannot but wonder how the other one got there. The question is: Is he for real? Or is he kissing ass?'

"Black people, or Negroes, as Jimmy called us, know about each other what can here be called family secrets; and this means that one Negro, if he wishes, can 'knock' the other's 'hustle' — and give his game away. It is still not possible to overstate the price a Negro pays to climb out of obscurity, he wrote, for it is a particular price involved with being a Negro, and the great wounds, gouges, amputations, losses, scars, endured in such a journey cannot be calculated. This was said to us that evening as a sign that we had gone past that dangerous place."

He further recollected. "A few days later, Cosby reciprocated and invited us up to the Hotel du Cap, a luxury hotel that catered to the world's richest people and overlooked the Mediterranean. That trip, which was only about thirty minutes away, took us all morning. The black Mercedes was chauffeured by me and Philippe taking turns. With Jimmy and Bernard in the back, we meandered through the backstreets of Nice to find the highway to Antibes. Jimmy would lean his head out the window and read the street signs in French with a great deal of fun and joy.

"When we arrived at the Hotel du Cap, we were taken to a large table overlooking the sea, where Cosby extended his hands with a big smile. As we were being seated, Cosby nodded to his left. Quincy Jones and his wife Peggy Lipton were introduced. Quincy Jones! I flipped out.

"I began to understand why Jimmy invited black Americans to his villa. He wanted to stay in contact with the black culture and its language. He said, 'Wright had not been able to accept that all people, even white people, suffered. The past of the Negro is dripping with blood, not only generation upon generation of horror. But this is also the past, and the everlasting potential or temptation of the human race. If we do not accept this, we cannot relieve ourselves of our individual suffering. But to act this way is also to find a source of strength — source of all our power. But one must accept this paradox with joy.'"

I went back to Cecil Brown for some footnotes on his recurring French odyssey in the Baldwin household. He came up with a great variety of things remembered, such as the following:

"1973 was very propitious since it was my first year with Jimmy. I spent so much time there in the house — so much happened that year, as well as in all the other years I visited — but this was my inauguration to really getting to know Jimmy," he said.

"I was there in early August and it was very hot when his forty-ninth birthday rolled around. Jimmy refused to celebrate it even though the house was full of many friends waiting for him to appear. He had gone down to the basement after sadly proclaiming, 'One day I will not be here.' David went down to convince him he still had a good life ahead of him. He finally came up and became his usual jovial great host.

"Bill Cosby was there. He showed up with a bouquet of forty-nine roses. Maya Angelou appeared with her new husband, a Welsh writer. They were touring in a small car. She's a big woman and was exhausted from the traveling. They were staying at the hotel across the road from Jimmy's house for some days, and one night Maya called to ask Jimmy to come over for a drink. He told me to tell her, 'I'm under the gun—have no time.' But she insisted, so Jimmy told me, 'After one drink, pull on my coat and tell me I have to leave.' I followed his orders, only to be reprimanded with 'Why are you harassing me?' We stayed for hours before going home very late. Jimmy and Maya loved each other, and I know that she came back other times and stayed in his house."

Brown remembered his first impression of seeing black American expatriates in Europe in the early 1970s. "I found it strange that they could live in this foreign atmosphere so far from home and was reminded of my own expatriate character, Jiveass Nigger, who tried to blend into Danish society but had to come back to the US."

What did he think of Baldwin's situation? "Jimmy never considered himself an expatriate. He said he never felt like an expatriate and was confident, peaceful with no problem living in France. He was happy and insisted he did not miss America. When he came back on a visit, he often felt insecure. Once when I was with him in San Francisco, he was afraid to cross the street!"

Curious about Baldwin's fascination with Cecil Brown's upbringing in a small farming community in North Carolina, I sought Brown's explanation. "Jimmy liked me as a Southern boy, just like he respected Richard Wright who also came from the South. I had lived through the brutal history of racism, violence in our rural African-American life, which led to our marches and boycotts. In his eyes, I replaced his parents, who had fled that tyranny to go north. Don't forget that he was a grandson of a slave. Jimmy liked the Southern survival strategy that we blacks experienced."

Aware that Bill Cosby was a big Baldwin fan and always stopped by to see Jimmy at home whenever he was in the south of France,

I tried reaching him—but was told that he was not available for an interview. (Newspaper reports of women's' lawsuits concerning his use of drugs leading to sexual misconduct were rumbling in the background in 2015. He was criminally charged and faced trial in 2016.)

However, from another source, I did learn that Cosby sent a bouquet of roses, without fail, for every one of Jimmy's birthdays after his first visit with Cecil Brown. Over the next fourteen years, the number of roses increased by one each year corresponding to Jimmy's age.

Philippe Bébon, Jimmy's personal secretary, told me about an aspiring Turkish actor, Engin Cezzar, whom Baldwin chose for his sensuous looks as being just right to play Giovanni in the 1958 world *premiére* of *Giovanni's Room* at Manhattan's Actors Studio. They became friends over the years. Baldwin sought refuge from the United States in Istanbul on a number of occasions, staying with Cezzar and his wife, a well-known leading lady. *Tell Me How Long the Train's Been Gone*, published in 1968, was dedicated to David Baldwin, biographer and longtime friend David Leeming, and Engin Cezzar.

Engin Cezzar came to Saint-Paul several times during 1979 and 1980 to convince Baldwin to return to Turkey and write a screenplay for *The Swordfish*, a novel by a Turkish writer. Although unimpressed by the translation, Baldwin was lured into accepting due to his lifelong attraction to the magic of moviemaking. He arrived in Istanbul in early fall 1981 with his brother David. They spent several months at a farm rented by the Cezzars in southern Turkey, where Baldwin completed the script. After it was rejected by the interested producers, Cezzar attempted to revise it. Baldwin became furious and they never met again.

During my visit to Cezzar's Istanbul apartment, with its panoramic view over the rooftops as far as the Bosporous, he proudly gestured to a portrait painted by Beauford Delaney. Cezzar handed me a book of correspondence between Baldwin and him over the years. This collection of letters has an introduction by James Campbell, a close acquaintance of Baldwin. The compilation was translated into Turkish as *Dost Mektuplari [Letter from a Friend]*. Campbell writes a back-page column for the *Times Literary Supplement*. This weekly "NB" column appears under the pen-name J. C. He is an author of some ten books including the biography, *Talking at the Gates: A Life of James Baldwin*.

With a certain nostalgia for his lost friend, Cezzar recalled, "It was the same old Jimmy when at his house in Saint-Paul. Lots of parasites and others offering projects they wanted him to do. Though he had a big chauffeur, valet, all kinds of people serving him, he told me he didn't have any money to buy the house, even though Simone Signoret had come with a big bag full of dollars and threw it on the table, saying, 'I want you to buy this house. Here, take it.' Jimmy was a real part of Saint-Paul. No one regarded him as a nigger.

"Back in 1974, he had invited me to join him in Prague when he was going for a play opening and a meeting with producers interested in filming *Giovanni's Room*. He had written to me, 'Why don't you come and then we'll go back together to Saint-Paul? The house is huge and it's time that we see each other again. I'm still wearing your ring. Love brothers don't grow on trees.'

"I was always very aware of his exaggerated paranoia. He was convinced that the FBI could come at any time to arrest him. I tried to calm him by telling him that by this time the FBI must have eased off on him. Indeed, in those early years when Jimmy came to Turkey, he was watched by the FBI, and so were we and Yasar Kemal, the great author, who was always at our house with Jimmy. We were targeted all together. Kemal adored Jimmy. His English was perfect and he wanted to translate Jimmy's writing. Those were good days before he returned to Saint-Paul. After his disappointment and frustration when the play project fizzled out, we didn't communicate with each other ever again."

After learning about this saga in Turkey, I was anxious to hear more from Baldwin's friends who were very international in their activities. I then contacted George Wein, renowned for his launch of the Newport Jazz Festival in the 1950s. He followed with the Newport Folk Festival, the Grande Parade de Jazz in Nice, and nearly thirty other still-ongoing events in the United States, Europe, and Japan. His late wife, Joyce, an African-American biochemist, joined him as an advisor and partner in the global musical operations.

When I reached him at his New York apartment, Wein seemed delighted to recount his memories of time spent with Baldwin in the south of France. He told me, "I had met Jimmy many years ago at the house of Miles Davis. We became friends but didn't see each other that much since we were both busy traveling all over the place. Around 1974, while Joyce and I were in Saint-Paul, we went to a restaurant not far from Jimmy's house—and he was there. We were staying in a hotel, but he insisted that we move into his house. We met Beauford Delaney who was living there, but, unfortunately, he was becoming senile.

"Jimmy was one of the most unforgettable characters I've ever met—high up on my list, right up there with Duke Ellington. I can still hear him talking and I see his face. His image never goes away. He and Bernard lived on one of the most beautiful properties near the Côte d'Azur. It was idyllic, but Jimmy was drinking and smoking too much. Jimmy was a celebrity in Saint-Paul and the French love celebrities. Many tourists would eat on the terrace of La Colombe d'Or in the hope of sighting Jimmy, who dined there often.

"While we were staying at Jimmy's house, I got news that my great friend, the Duke, had died. I would have to go immediately to attend the funeral and would be away for a few weeks. Jimmy insisted that Joyce remain in his house. We had become family and he wouldn't consider her moving out. That house was a rallying place for many of his musician friends, like Ray Charles, for whom Jimmy composed several pieces of music; Julian "Cannonball" Adderley, Dizzy Gillespie, and, especially, Miles Davis, who was there very often. Whenever he went to southern France to play in the Nice or Juan-les-Pins jazz festivals, Miles blocked out a full week to relax and be with Jimmy in his house. Jimmy came every year to our jazz festival in Nice. He never missed a year. Everybody backstage knew him and loved him. We always had great dinners with Jimmy—clearly the centerpiece attracting everyone like bees to honey.

"I learned style from him. When I had to go to Bologna for a concert I was producing there, I drove in a small Chevy. At that time, Jimmy had just bought his big Mercedes and he was buying the great house he lived in room by room. He had no money, was always broke. He used up all his royalties and advances and owed all his publishers money. He was making a mess of his life, but he was always very generous to everyone who came calling, many often taking advantage of him. I didn't want to fall into his pattern, but it changed my way of thinking.

"Inspired by Jimmy, Joyce and I bought a decent car to keep in the south of France and found a wonderful house in Vence. We invited Jimmy and Simone Signoret over as the first to see it. Jimmy loved the house and expressed his enthusiasm in a touching, poetic manner. Simone, on the other hand, asked, 'How much did you pay?' I replied, 'You're the last person I'd expect that from. You're a little *yenta*.' [That's Yiddish for 'a gossip.'] Jimmy was hanging out all the time. He often came to our house for parties and dinners or just to listen to records of his favorite musician friends or records I brought over from the States."

Whenever his close friend, the author William Styron, attended the Nice Book Festival, he would move into the house to spend a few days with his old drinking buddy in order to catch up. Styron had offered his cottage, a guest-house on his Connecticut estate, to Baldwin in the early '60s so that he could escape New York and find a calm place to write. When he left, *Another Country* was unfinished. Styron told a Baldwin biographer, the late W. J. Weatherby, "There was a sense of a vacuum, a silence, in the house," and he appreciated that Baldwin had revealed to him "the core of his soul's savage distress."

One can only assume that Styron gave Baldwin an update on the New York publishing world and had "remember when" frolicking sessions and offered caustic remarks about Norman Mailer, their nemesis in common. These two longtime drinking companions had lots of political goings-on and literary gossip to keep them busy while they were imbibing into the wee hours in the comfort of the Baldwin residence in Saint-Paul de Vence.

Chapter 2

"The Welcome Table:"
Unending Hospitality

Curiously, though this would become his domicile and writing base for his generally autobiographical texts through seventeen years, Baldwin never used the property or village as a backdrop in any of his novels, essays or poems. There were no references to his life in southern France, nor even an allusion that he was abroad, not in the United States.

For an unknowing reader, Baldwin the American author was simply writing about American subjects and experiences from an unidentified location, presumably in America. The only exceptions at the end of his life were an article written about the house for *Architectural Digest* and an unfinished play, *The Welcome Table*, set in the house in Saint-Paul. The title of the work—as he also called his dining table in the garden under the olive vines and the one inside by the same name—was inspired by a verse from a Negro spiritual:

One of These Days

I'm going to sit at the Welcome Table
I'm going to feast on milk and honey
One of these days.

The many illustrious guests—as well as innumerable undistinguished and often unexpected freeloaders—were lavishly hosted by Baldwin preferably at the outdoor "Welcome Table," weather permitting. There was also a full retinue of intimates—friends from the village or those staying in the house during visits—who regularly joined Jimmy for meals since he always needed to be surrounded by people, some merely casual acquaintances encountered while walking in the village.

Among those regarded as a true friend was Dr. Roger Boizard, a general practitioner who had treated everyone living in the Baldwin open house for around a decade until he closed his office in 1980. He became one of Jimmy's most trusted cronies and they would eat and drink together three or four times a week.

Dr. Boizard remembered that "At the table there was always an amusing mix of homosexuals and heterosexuals. He welcomed young *dépenaillés,* ragged types who arrived with empty pockets and valises full of problems—unknown artists, poets, musicians. Jimmy brought home guys from bars with no money. His detractors insisted they were his new lovers. Sometimes that was the case. Valérie, his housekeeper, part of the family, reigned over the comings and goings. There were regularly around eight people living there. She yelled at all of them, like her own kids, and chased them out of her kitchen."

In reminiscing about the many very festive occasions Dr. Boizard was privy to, he found two most memorable. "Even though Jimmy included my wife and me in much of his entertaining, I was surprised when he called me on New Year's Eve 1977, casually saying, 'Come over, I'm having a few friends.' There were Robert Wagner, Natalie Wood, César, Simone Signoret, Yves Montand and us.

"On Jimmy's last birthday, August 2, 1987, there were more than one hundred people there. Poor Valérie. She had thirty chickens, many huge sacks of rice, all kinds of vegetables, delicious salads. Jimmy had given her a recipe he had gotten in the American South. Valérie asked him, 'But if the guests ask me the name of this recipe, what should I say?' Laughing, Jimmy replied, 'You tell them it's *poulet à la negre.' [chicken nigger-style].* When she protested, he added, 'It's an abominable word, but in your mouth it will be charming.' Jimmy loved Valérie and she merited it. When publishers sent him books, one of the first dedications was always for her. She always got the first piece of his birthday cakes.

"Jimmy was someone who charmed people, drew you to him," according to Dr. Boizard. "He looked like Gandhi with shining eyes and energy springing out and captured people's interest when he opened his mouth. You couldn't get away. He is the man who most attracted me in my life. He never spoke about his youth or his personal life. Jimmy was very interested in everything you had to tell. He was like a child who wanted to learn. Often he would agree but otherwise he would grow silent. I learned a lot from him."

A longtime friend, David Leeming—professor emeritus of English and comparative literature, religion and myth at the University of Connecticut—was always welcomed at the house like a brother coming home during college summer vacations. He was a favorite at the table. Their intense comradeship started when the writer fled to Istanbul in 1963 where he met Leeming, a young college lecturer, at a party celebrating publication of *Another Country*. They soon discovered a mutual interest in Henry James. Leeming had written his doctoral dissertation on James, who was clearly central to Baldwin's writing. They discussed at great length James's depiction of Americans and how his vision still applied today.

Leeming worked for a number of years as Baldwin's secretary/ assistant, first in Turkey and then later in New York. Their close bond was to continue for almost a quarter of century. David was at Jimmy's bedside in the last weeks of his life. He wrote the authorized *James Baldwin, A Biography*, as well as *Amazing Grace: A Life of Beauford Delaney*, plus numerous books on mythology.

During lunch in Manhattan, we discussed his frequent stays with Jimmy in Saint-Paul. As he was about to leave he turned to me and said, "Most of all I remember sitting at the outdoor 'Welcome Table.' We would be there for hours talking about politics, race, religion, a diversity of subjects with Jimmy presiding at the end of the table. I will always associate Jimmy with warm weather and the table.

"He never looked at me as a white man, he was completely race-blind. He saw me for me. It was not his thing to categorize. In his presence, I saw myself for myself, felt more myself than any other complex being. Jimmy was the only person I knew who could see through all those masks we wear."

Carole Weinstein added, "Often we would sit around 'The

Welcome Table' to read what he had written the night before.
Jimmy was always receptive to comments, never secure about the
way he wanted it. He was very fragile, not arrogant. Nothing he
wrote did he feel was ever good enough. He was humble, surprised
when people thought it was good.

Daniel Baldwin said, "When you grow up in that kind of
environment, all the famous people who came to dine with Uncle
Jimmy, they're just people. That's what 'The Welcome Table' was
all about. People sitting around talking. A house you go to for
that special environment. Jimmy spent so much time alone while
writing that he made up for it talking with all those people."

Dr. Henry Louis "Skip" Gates, Jr. was a young, eager black
American journalist based in London for *Time* magazine in 1973
when he was sent to France for a story on *"The Black Expatriate."*
Gates arranged to pick up the renowned singer Josephine Baker,
who was living in Monte Carlo, for an encounter with her longtime
friend, James Baldwin, at his home in Saint-Paul.

I reached Dr. Gates in his office at Harvard University where he
is the Alphonse Fletcher University professor and director of the
Hutchins Center for African and African-American Research. He
pointed out, "I put recollections of my initial meeting with Jimmy
and our extended relationship that followed in a book, *Thirteen
Ways to Look at a Black Man*. When I received that book from him,
the chapter titled, 'The Welcome Table,' was flagged with a yellow
Post-it.

"Baldwin had made his house, somehow, his own Greenwich
Village café," said Gates. "Always there were guests, a changing
entourage of friends and hangers-on. Always there was drinking
and conviviality. . . Cecil Brown, author of the campus cult classic,
The Life and Loves of Mister Jiveass Nigger, was also a guest. The grape
arbors sheltered tables, and it was under one such grape arbor, at
one of the long harvest tables, that we dined. The line from the old
gospel song, a line Baldwin had quoted toward the end of his then-
latest novel, inevitably suggested itself: 'I'm going to feast at the
Welcome Table.' And we did.

"I wondered why these famous expatriates had not communicated in so long, since Saint-Paul was not far from Monte Carlo. It was the first time Jo [Josephine Baker] and Jimmy had seen each other in years — it would prove to be the last.

"At that long 'Welcome Table' under the arbor, the wine flowed, food was served and taken away, and James Baldwin and Josephine Baker traded stories, gossiped about everyone they knew and many people they didn't, and remembered their lives. They had both been hurt and disillusioned by the United States and had chosen to live in France. They never forgot, or forgave.

"At the table that long, warm night, they recollected the events that led to their decisions to leave their country of birth, and the consequences of those decisions: the difficulty of living away from home and family, of always feeling apart in their chosen homes; the pleasure of choosing a new life, the possibilities of the untried. A sense of nostalgia pervaded the evening; for all their misgivings, they shared a sense, curiously, of being on the winning side of history.

"And with nostalgia, anticipation. Both were preparing for a comeback. Baker would return to the stage in a month or so; and it was onstage that she would die. Baldwin, whose career had begun so brilliantly, was now struggling to regain his voice.

"As an intellectual, Baldwin was at his best when exploring his own equivocal sympathies and clashing allegiances. . . A spokesman must have a firm grasp on his role, and an unambiguous message to articulate. Baldwin had neither, and when this was discovered a few short years later, he was relieved of his duties, shunted aside as an elder and, retired statesman. The irony is that he may never fully have recovered from this demotion from a status he had always disavowed.

"And if I had any doubts about that demotion, I was set straight by my editor at *Time* once I returned to London. They were not pleased by my choice of principal subjects. Josephine Baker, I was told, was a period piece, a quaint memory of the twenties and thirties. And as for Baldwin, well, wasn't he *passé* now? Hadn't he been for several years?

"Baldwin, *passé?* In fact, the editor, holding a wet finger to the wind, was absolutely correct, and on some level I knew it. If

Baldwin had once served as a shadow delegate for black America, the congress of culture, his term had expired."

[Note: Gates.'s incisive text, rejected by *Time*, was only published in 1985 as "*An Interview with Josephine Baker and James Baldwin*" in *Southern Review 21, no. 3*. While the conclusion has Baldwin predicting (in 1973) an "apocalypse" for America, the inimitable Josephine Baker, surprisingly enough, was more optimistic about the future of the land she had fled.]

"We stayed in touch, on and off, through the intervening years. Sometimes he would introduce me to his current lover, or speak of his upcoming projects. But I did not return to Saint-Paul de Vence until shortly after his death when my wife and I came to meet Jimmy's brother, David.

". . . There we had a reunion with Bernard Hassell, Jimmy's loving friend of so many decades, and met Lucien Happersberger. After a week of drinking and reminiscing, David Baldwin asked me just when I had met Jimmy for the first time. As I recounted the events of our visit in 1973, David's wide eyes grew wider. He rose from the table, went downstairs into Jimmy's study—where a wall of works by and about Henry James faces you as you enter—and emerged with a manuscript in hand. 'This is for you,' he said.

"He handed me a play, the last work Jimmy was completing as he suffered through his final illness, titled *The Welcome Table*. It was set on the Riviera, at a house much like his own, and among the principal characters were Edith, an actress-singer/star: Creole, from New Orleans; Daniel, ex-Black Panther, fledgling playwright, with more than a passing resemblance to Cecil Brown; and Peter Davis, black American journalist. Peter Davis—who has come to interview a famous star, and whose prodding questions lead to the play's revelations—was, I should say, a far better and more aggressive interviewer than I was, but of course Baldwin, being Baldwin, had transmuted the occasion into a searching drama of revelation and crisis."

Actually, when Dr. Gates returned, he was also accompanied by Wole Soyinka to investigate turning the house into the James Baldwin Foundation for upcoming writers.

I contacted the Nigerian playwright, essayist, lecturer, critic and educator—the first black African to be awarded the Nobel Prize in Literature—in Ile-Ife, Nigeria where he is professor emeritus at Obafemi Awolowo University. Professor Soyinka told me that he penned his recollections of that visit in a piece he called, "James Baldwin at the Welcome Table," which served as the foreword to Quincy Troupe's book, *James Baldwin: The Legacy*. Professor Soyinka agreed with my selecting excerpts:

". . . I did meet James Baldwin again!

"I heard him, watched his watchful eyes and listened with his intensely alert ears in the company in which he was so much at ease, so compassionately his own unique being. No, not in his second [and permanent place of exile but, paradoxically, in his first, Saint-Paul de Vence in the south of France.] It happened this way.

"'Skip' Gates had informed me earlier of the existence of a play, in manuscript only, which James Baldwin had written virtually on his deathbed. In April, 1988, visiting Saint-Paul with 'Skip,' I obtained the play script from him and read it. It was not the personal genesis of the work that made it, for me, such a poignant piece. It was the tangible personality of the work.

"James Baldwin's intense restive and febrile persona hovered, it seemed, over the pages, pulsated through the mannerisms, wiles and vulnerabilities of his manipulating and manipulated guests, a somewhat withdrawn ghostly host. I felt that I was listening, after all, to Baldwin's annotations to the dialogue which we never held, lightly touching on the paradoxes of human relationships, of emotions, of the treachery of memories, but consistent in its homage to that elusive quality which Baldwin had elevated to nearly the First Principle of the human existence—love.

"In the ambiguities of Baldwin's expression of social, sexual, even racial and political conflicts will be found that insisted modality of conduct, and even resolution, celebrated or lamented as a tragic omission—love. And herein lies the subjective unease which has been my portion from the bounty of Baldwin's creative ethic and its production.

". . . *The Welcome Table*, which, like *Giovanni's Room*, does not attempt to venture beyond the intricate loom of private relationships into the prejudicial terrain of race or politics, except as these intrude on the conversation.

". . . At 'The Welcome Table' in The Great Beyond, I have no doubt that we shall find Jimmy seated between some Grand Master of the KKK, Governor Wallace and the Scottsboro Boys, enjoying a wise laugh at the former's unease, applying to their self-inflicted wounds the soothing balm of his imperishable celestial prose."

——•——

Favorites of Jimmy's at his table were the well-known French-American sculptor, Arman, and his wife, Corice (Canton), who was born in St. Thomas in the Virgin Islands. I spoke with Corice, now a widow, first at her home in Vence and later again in Manhattan. "We often had lunch or dinner at Jimmy's home," said Corice. "Sometimes Bernard prepared the traditional lamb with green beans. Bernard was wonderful, jubilant, with a *joie de vivre*. I took care of him towards the end of his life, along with Pitou, who was there all the time." (Bernard died of AIDS in 1991.)

"Jimmy was funny and always soft spoken. I recall that when I was contemplating having surgery on my feet, I was asking everyone their advice but I remained undecided. I mentioned this to Jimmy and he remarked, 'Corice, I wouldn't do anything with my feet, because you never know when you will need them to leave town.'

"I remember the discussion of the Atlanta killings. We were all outraged and horrified at the same time. A serial killer and black? This, of course, led to Jimmy's book, *The Evidence of Things Not Seen*, about the killings. We also reminisced about the racism he experienced which led to his exodus to France where he felt liberated and appreciated. James and Arman had a definite connection and they saw eye-to-eye on many issues. They had long, deep conversations about Jimmy's lectures at American universities."

One of my local contacts advised me not to miss "the Dutch lady" who lived in a very narrow row house nearby. I was welcomed by a very friendly woman who immediately invited me in for a cup of coffee, a tradition she held over from her homeland. Wanda van Dijk had moved from the Netherlands to Saint-Paul in 1973 with her late husband, Dick, a professional soccer player with Ajax, the Amsterdam team, before he became the coach for OGC Nice.

They met Baldwin at the bar of La Colombe d'Or on the anniversary of Martin Luther King, Jr.'s assassination. They talked about the civil rights struggle and his essays about the confrontations they had read about in his books. Jimmy had fond memories of the liberal Amsterdam scene and his Dutch publisher, de Bezige Bij, which took on his works very early, often before they were considered publishable in the US. The contact clicked and Wanda and Dick became close friends and regulars at "The Welcome Table." Jimmy called Dick his 'Dutch brother.'

"Discussing his work became our first bond. Almost no one here in the village read his books which were published in French two or three years after the States. We didn't go into politics but very often he talked about racial problems. Jimmy was always Jimmy, fast to express his ideas. He made jokes about himself and about blacks and Jews. He believed in freedom and liberty everywhere, not just for the blacks. We were invited often to his house for meals. Once at a dinner a male guest told him they should send back all the 'boat people.' He was furious and lashed out at him for his blindness to this injustice — and told him he would never be invited back."

Wanda also recalled Jimmy's visits to their home. "Jimmy came often, whenever he wanted to just get away from too many people and noise at his place. He always felt he could relax here, sometimes not even talking. Often he would go into the garden and sing Negro spirituals."

Michael Raeburn says that Baldwin was lonely late in life. Raeburn was an English filmmaker who had worked with Baldwin for several years on a project to film *Giovanni's Room*. He said: "Jimmy was very lonely in his later years. I mean lonely in an intellectual sense. There were plenty of people around who could entertain him, or whom he found attractive in one way or another, but not many that he could talk to about books, or about a play, or about his current work."

It was not the literary scene he had known earlier in New York, Paris or even Istanbul. Fortunately, there were several writers in residence nearby over the years — and Jimmy avidly drew them close to his hearth.

A fellow author of some twenty-five fiction and nonfiction books, Nicholas Delbanco — born in London at the height of the German blitz and later naturalized American after his parents immigrated to the US — struck up a lasting friendship with Baldwin and was a welcome literary sparring partner in Saint-Paul. He lived nearby for some years and became a coveted guest.

I reached Nicholas at the University of Michigan where he is the Robert Frost Distinguished University Professor of English Language and Literature. I couldn't resist asking about the origins of his family name. He explained his ancestors were bankers in Padua, Italy in the sixteenth century and went to Venice where they were benefactors in the ghetto community.

In his book, *Running in Place: Scenes from the South of France,* he commented on how often he spent time at the table with Jimmy.

"More than half my life ago, I was a neighbor of James Baldwin. We'd met in the winter of 1970, briefly, in Istanbul. The next year, however, my wife and I moved to the south of France, and we ran into Baldwin in Cannes. Standing in line at the American Express office, I recognized Jimmy behind me. We shook hands. Then I said that maybe we could get together for a meal or drink.

"I was surprised, I think, at his alacrity; he invited us the next day. Elena's daybook for our final ten days in Provence lists five such occasions: dinner at his house, at ours, at a restaurant in Saint-Paul de Vence, and many talks and walks. He was completing *No Name in the Street*; he was planning to remain in France and would do so for years. His open-handed welcome, his insistence that we call as soon as we came back meant much, as did his cheerful certainty that we would return.

"I mattered to him, I suppose, as a practitioner of a shared trade," Delbanco said. "He told me he was starved for the chance to talk books, for a discussion, say, of Henry James with someone who had read him. We talked the way most writers do, in a kind of shorthand and sign language. We asked each other, always, how the work had gone that day, how this paragraph was doing, or that character and scene.

"In 1973, when we settled again in the house in Provence, Baldwin treated us like long-lost friends. He had established a work pattern and an entourage. He had a chauffeur large enough to double as a bodyguard, a cook, a companion named Philippe who acted as a kind of secretary-manager, and various others whose functions are less easy to describe.

"We were rarely fewer than six at a table, and more often ten. The cook and the *femme de ménage* [cleaning woman] came and went; the men stayed on. They treated their provider with a fond deference, as if his talent must be sheltered from invasive detail, the rude importunate matters of fact. They answered the phone and the door. They sorted mail. There was an intricate hierarchy of rank, a jockeying for position that evoked nothing as much as a Provençal court—who was in favor, who was out, who had known Jimmy longer or better or where, who would do the shopping or join him in Paris for the television interview or help with the book jacket photo. He was working, again, on a novel: *If Beale Street Could Talk.*

"Baldwin drank scotch. We drank wine. I have not yet described the quality of kindness in his manner, the affection he both expected and expressed. His face is widely known—that dark glare, broad nose, those large protruding eyes, the close-fitting cap of curls starting to go white. But photographs cannot convey the mobile play of features; the intensity of utterance, the sense he could contrive to give that attention matters and gesture can count. There was something theatrical in Jimmy's manner, and it grew automatic at times. He would embark on what seemed a tirade, a high-speed compilation of phrases that clearly had been phrased before, a kind of improvised lecture spun out of previous speech. He stared at you unblinkingly—you could not turn away. He wore expensive jewelry and fingered it, talking; he smoked. He had been holding center stage for years.

"You shifted in your seat. You said 'Yes, but. . . ' and he raised his imperious manicured hand. Dialogue, for Baldwin, was an interrupted monologue; he would yield the platform neither willingly nor long. He could speak incisively on a book he had not read. But again and again he impressed me with his canny ranging, his alert intelligence. 'Understand me,' he would say. 'It's important you understand.' And it *was important*, and in that mesmeric presence you thought you understood.

"My pleasure in our meeting is easily explained. Here was the spokesman of his generation and color, speaking directly to me. That he took my opinions seriously; that he read and respected my work, or appeared to; that he wanted us with him as often as possible—all this was flattering. When we parted late at night, Jimmy would say, 'See you two tomorrow.' If we came for lunch instead, he would urge us to stay on for dinner; when a friend passed through Saint-Paul, he would insist we meet.

"Why he wanted to spend time with us is, I think, less clear. Each friendship partakes of the reciprocal trade agreement, and I can only speculate as to Baldwin's motives in the exchange. He was the most sociable of solitaries; though constantly attended and attended to, he held himself apart."

"During the extended period that my wife, Elena, and I lived in Châteauneuf de Grasse, we were very frequent guests of Jimmy's, sometimes twice a day. When I wrote that book, I could not bring myself, however, to disguise James Baldwin; his was a lifelong insistence on the role of truthful witness. I was not in France when he died. His death in December of 1987 is therefore not part of this narrative. Yet it is an enduring loss. . . ."

Jeffrey Robinson—a native New Yorker, journalist and best-selling author of some twenty books—lived from 1970 to the early 1980s in St. Laurent du Var, not far from Saint-Paul. Since he was a regular at Jimmy's table, I called him at his Manhattan apartment to ask what he remembered from those encounters. He told me that "a young writer, who was a mutual friend, had introduced us. From the moment we met there was a warm contact. I recall Jimmy saying, 'A writer is only as good as his obsession.' For Robinson, books became his lifelong obsession that was real and motivating.

"Being invited to Jimmy's for a meal or party was always full of unexpected surprises among the interesting, usually well-known people who were there. There were always great conversations with a surprising mix of literati, musicians and show business personalities. What Jimmy liked the best was soul food and for dessert, bread and butter pudding, which his mother used to make when she bought stale bread. The French call it *pain perdu* [lost bread]."

Besides the many American jazz greats who came regularly to the house, there was the Englishman, Bill Wyman, who was the bass guitarist with the Rolling Stones for over 30 years and the first Stones member to have a worldwide hit solo single.

Contacted at his recording studio in London, Wyman is anything but retired, releasing over a dozen albums with his own two bands; gaining recognition as an accomplished photographer and writer/producer for film and television; appearing in several movies; and authoring seven books.

Wyman lived in Saint-Paul from 1971 until he moved back to Great Britain in 1982. Simone Signoret and César had introduced him to Baldwin at La Colombe d'Or in April 1975. He told me, "I recall that evening like it was yesterday. It clicked between us right away and we became friends. There were lots of dinners at his house or ours. We would hang out until 4 or 5 in the morning, talking and boozing. Jimmy loved his whiskey.

"We played records for each other of music we liked. He would put on a Ray Charles record for me. Ray was his great friend. I'd surprise him with music he didn't know, like Randy Newman's *Sailing Away* spoof on slavery and he would roar. Among many wonderful and memorable evenings was his 57th birthday party on August 2, 1981. It was great with all kinds of people. Suddenly, Jimmy started singing spirituals with a taste of the blues.

"He sang very well. He had a great voice. Sometime later I said to him, 'Jimmy we should do a record together.' He replied, 'Great idea. Let's do it.' Unfortunately, nothing came of it. I was gone from Saint-Paul a lot during the '70s and early '80s on tours with the Stones and he was often in the States for lectures and teaching at the universities. But whenever we were both in town, we got together.

"If I was anywhere nearby on the Fourteenth of July, commemorating the storming of the Bastille, symbol of the French Revolution, I would never miss watching the fireworks in the village from the terrace of his house. With lots of food and drink, it was a really fantastic happening. His hospitality was unforgettable!

"The last time I saw Jimmy was around 1982 but his memory remains vivid. I treasure the dedicated books he gave me," said Wyman.

Living close to Aix-en-Provence, I was aware that Baldwin had been invited there by Annie Terrier, founder and director of the prestigious *Ecritures Croisées in the Bibliothéque Méjanes*, [the municipal library complex]. Annie spotlighted the United States in a 1986 program titled, *Les Ecritures Trans-Atlantiques*, with James Baldwin featured in a discussion with a prominent French author, Annie Cohen-Solal.

Annie Terrier recalled, "Since he was scheduled first, I kept looking out the door at the rare snow storm that had turned the city white. A few months before, when we met in Paris, he had accepted the invitation with 'OK, OK, I'll come.' He had listened but did he really understand? Had he noted the date? Would he remember? All this was coming back to me especially since he hadn't confirmed his arrival during the weeks preceding the event nor returned any of my calls.

"I was afraid that he would be a no-show and I was already mulling over in my mind what excuses I would give in my opening remarks to the overcrowded hall when suddenly a taxi sloshed through the soft snow covering the ground near the entrance. Out stepped Jimmy with his unbelievable, almost comical, happy expression spread over his face and said, 'Baby, you got to believe me. You must trust my word, have confidence. If I said I was coming I would come — even in this snow storm.' Afterwards I felt badly that I had doubted him."

In Annie Terrier's miniscule office, cluttered with posters and piles of paper seemingly unfiled over the past quarter of a century, she launched into a vivid, unhesitating recollection of that evening's event which led to her going to Jimmy's house: "That night we also had a number of other well-known writers—along with filmed interviews, documentaries, recorded TV programs and jazz concerts—but the star and biggest attraction was clearly Jimmy Baldwin. I had invited the academic, writer, biographer, art critic and historian, Annie Cohen-Solal, to introduce and interview Jimmy."

Annie Cohen-Solal is best known for her biography of the French philosopher, Jean-Paul Sartre, titled, *Sartre: A Life,* an international best seller, which went from English into some twenty other languages. While serving as the French cultural counselor in the United States, she became interested in the contemporary art world after her encounter with America's most influential avant-garde gallery owner, Leo Castelli. This led to the biography, *Leo and His Circle: The Life of Leo Castelli,* with the American edition followed by numerous other language editions. Among her many books, there is also one on Rothko.

When I spoke to Annie Cohen-Solal in Manhattan, where she had been living in recent years, she was packing to move back to Paris, but she took the time to provide this account:

"I think that I was invited to interview Jimmy Baldwin because of my Sartre biography. It is well known that Sartre had been one of the first in France to introduce jazz music in his first novel, *La Nausée [Nausea],* and to fight racial discrimination in the US, notably in his play, *La Putain Respectueuse [The Respectful Prostitute].* He recognized the talent of many Afro-American artists and intellectuals to whom he devoted a lot of space in his magazine *Les Temps Modernes [Modern Times]* which he started as early as September 1945. For all those reasons, Sartre was and is still very highly considered by the Afro-American community.

"When I prepared my interview of Jimmy Baldwin for Aix-en-Provence, it was with all those elements in mind. Now a full audience was waiting, the time was 11 am but Baldwin was not there. We waited and waited and waited. Finally, we heard that he would be arriving around 2 pm. After the audience was notified, they came back even more numerous than earlier. And Baldwin arrived, escorted by a friend. I was introduced to him. He shook my hand, looked at me in the eyes, and simply said 'Sorry, we just had sex! I must say that I found that attitude altogether irreverent, arrogant and totally irresistible. The interview went wonderfully well."

I went back to Annie Terrier for her account of a follow-up:

"My good friend, Simone Jaworski, a professional photographer, was enthralled at meeting Jimmy at the session since she had read many of his books. She took a lot of great pictures during the evening. Simone asked if we could go to Saint-Paul to personally deliver the photos. Jimmy had no objection and we drove there a few weeks later. We were welcomed by Bernard [Hassell] who showed us in. Jimmy received both of us like childhood friends. Our conversation was about his books, of course, but we spent a lot of time talking about the house and grounds.

"I found this the most beautiful house I'd ever seen. It's more than beautiful, it's something from another time, very natural, enchanted with a personality uniquely its own, like Jimmy, resembling a character from one of his books. We spent the whole day together. I told him that we loved having him with us in Aix-en-Provence and felt that we had found a new friend. He laughed a lot and it was really an enjoyable experience.

"At one point during lunch, he got serious and started talking about his struggles during the Civil Rights Movement. As if looking to us for answers, he said, 'Integrate for what? The whites wanted us to become just like them while they keep their autonomy, their character, their supremacy. I didn't agree with that. We have our own culture, our own character, our own black language. We were fighting so we African-Americans could be on equal footing with them on our own terms, not as second class citizens.' But once he said that, his mood got light again.

"When Toni Morrison came to Aix in 2001 for our program, she was accompanied by her good friend, Gloria Baldwin. That evening at my house, I showed them the photos while we reminisced about Jimmy. Toni was very close to Jimmy and later edited all his essays into one book and his early novels and short stories in another book. Gloria asked me to help find someone interested in saving the house, which had fallen into ruin. She hoped it could become a center in honor of Jimmy for young writers and artists. I went down there with an architect friend. He drew up plans but nothing came of it since there were legal battles over ownership."

———•———

Among old friends who came regularly to visit Baldwin in his self-exile in Saint-Paul was the renowned Calypso singer, Harry Belafonte, born in Harlem of immigrant Caribbean parents. During a career spanning over sixty years, he always fulfilled his commitment to human rights, financed the Freedom Riders, supported black voter registration drives and in 1963 helped organize the March on Washington in which Baldwin participated. Belafonte bankrolled the Student Non-Violent Coordinating Committee during the 1964 Freedom Summer. In the 1950s, as one of Martin Luther King, Jr.'s . confidants and an early supporter of the Civil Rights Movement, he provided for King's family in view of the preacher's meager salary.

From his New York office, Belafonte recounted, "Jimmy and I go way back. I knew him as one of the black artists in New York and saw him frequently there. After he settled in Saint-Paul, I always made a point of stopping to visit him whenever I was on a concert tour anywhere in the region. I often joined Jimmy for lunch on the hotel terrace with Simone Signoret and Yves Montand. Many an evening I walked the mile down to Jimmy's house where we would dine on his outdoor table and talk into the wee hours of the morning, consuming numerous bottles of wine. Though Jimmy was a good singer, we never sang together.

"Jimmy had such a great philosophy, was so articulate. It was a joy to be with him and listen to his words. Our conversations covered a wide range of topics ranging from discrimination, America, his writing and his homosexuality. He often came up with an analysis of the relationship of race in politics and was clearly concerned about the African race beyond Africa. It disturbed him how badly the French treated immigrants from their former colonies after they received their independence. Or, where the world was going, expressing his particular concern for art and culture and the need for greater respect for writers, poets, intellectuals.

"He was not only romantic in his idealism but very involved with fundamental matters, existence, freer expression. Jimmy was frustrated by the number of things he wanted to accomplish and always referred to those as future projects. Jimmy talked passionately on a high intellectual level about the poor blacks and racial inequality in the United States."

I phoned Herb Gold, another of Jimmy's devoted cronies, in San Francisco. Herb is a prolific, distinguished author of some twenty novels, collections of poetry, nonfiction and a journalist with countless bylined magazine articles. He was extremely amiable and happy to tell me about his long comradeship with Baldwin, culminating in their intimate, frank conversations at the house while Jimmy was in the last period of his life.

Gold recalled, "Jimmy and I knew each other many, many years and we stayed in contact through all that time and saw each other in Paris, New York, San Francisco and Saint-Paul. We had a lot in common as writers. We were born in the same year and had similar attitudes about life.

"I was often on assignment for magazine reportages on the French Riviera or Paris and this gave me a very good excuse to see Jimmy in Saint-Paul. I remember one time when I was in his home that he had a young boyfriend he called 'Baby.' This guy started bragging that he had gone on a Greyhound bus from New York to San Francisco with his feet stretched out over a row of seats so that three or four white women had to travel standing up. 'Baby' was clearly an idiotic provocateur.

"He began praising Arafat for all he had done for his people, then launched into the iniquities Israel was imposing on the Arab world and how Jews were running the world. At that point, Jimmy, in a very paternal way, said, 'Baby, Herb is Jewish.' Jimmy was clearly uncomfortable because most of his supporters were Jewish.

"During the last time I saw Jimmy in his home, it was a terrible, terrible shock. He looked so haggard and weak, his skin tone grey.

We hugged and talked very honestly. I asked him, 'Jimmy, are you going to live?' He answered, 'The operation took six hours and the doctors said I need one month for every hour to recuperate.' I felt he knew he was not going to live but in his characteristic desire to make people happy, he didn't tell the truth. Jimmy asked me to come back the next day.

"When I got to the house the next day, I knocked on the door and called out. No one responded. Usually there were lots of people milling around. I walked in. There were no lights on. In the dark interior I saw a closed door and assumed Jimmy was asleep in that room. I left him a good-bye note. I would never see him again."

Sol Stein was one of the three schoolmates, who, along with Jimmy, at DeWitt Clinton High School in the north Bronx edited the school literary magazine, *The Magpie*. The other two were Richard Avedon and Emile Capouya.

Avedon, who became a world-famous photographer, co-authored with Baldwin a large book reflecting a cross-section of American society with, among other subjects, highlights of the Civil Rights Movement. Published in 1964, a year after John F. Kennedy's assassination, it was titled, *Nothing Personal*. Capouya became an essayist, critic, publisher and author. All three were white and Jewish. They remained important figures in Baldwin's life and literary pursuits through an extended friendship and collaboration which continued until his death.

Sol Stein — the only surviving member of the tight little group — often visited Jimmy at his home in Saint-Paul. He is a prize-winning playwright, an anthological poet and author of ten novels, including *The Magician*, which sold over one million copies.

As a young editor at Beacon Press, Stein had encouraged Baldwin to write his autobiographical *Notes of a Native Son*, coaxing him through the agonizing process while pulling it together for publication. "Laymen speak of a writer's style. Writers and editors speak of a writer's voice. As an editor, I was attracted to Baldwin's writing because of his voice and his literary intelligence, his use of visual particularity to make us see the places and people he was writing about."

Almost three decades after its initial publication, Baldwin had begun the preface to the 1984 reprint of *Notes of a Native Son* with: "It was Sol Stein, high school buddy, editor, novelist, playwright, who first suggested this book. My reaction was not enthusiastic, as I remember. I told him that I was too young to publish my memoirs. I had never thought of these essays as a possible book. Sol's suggestion had the startling and unkind effect of causing me to realize that time had passed. It was though he had dashed cold water in my face. Sol persisted however."

I had phoned Stein at his Manhattan office where he is still very active writing books, poetry and managing his multitude of literary properties. In his straightforward manner he said, "Everything you want to know about my long relationship with Jimmy is in *our* book, *Native Sons*. (This posthumous work by Baldwin, edited by Stein, appeared in 2004 with newly-discovered correspondence, photographs, a never-before published story, *Dark Runner*, and a play, *Equal in Paris*, which they had created together.)

In the acknowledgments, Stein wrote, "This is a book by and about two friends, one of whom has already been in Ferncliff Cemetery since 1987, but my conversations with him continued and were especially intense through the making of this book. When you read James Baldwin's letters, he will speak to you too."

Reflecting on their lifelong friendship, Stein recalled, "My wife and I went to Jimmy's house for drinks and then he invited us out for dinner. I think it was 1985 or 1986. He seemed to be very happy in France. Of course, we hashed over old times, going way back, and talked about many of the books he had published during the long period since we first worked together. When I next saw him, he was in a coffin during the funeral services in the cathedral."

A journalist/photographer, Alain Cinquini, had been among Jimmy's intimate circle of friends in town. Since he had moved away in 2005 to a village in the Vaud, near Epinal, we talked by phone and exchanged emails. Having arrived in Saint-Paul in 1975, and staying for three decades, Cinquini was the correspondent who served the media with news and pictures of the many stars, artists and other personalities who lived in and around the village or came to visit. He worked for *Paris Match, Nice Matin* and achieved international distribution through the Gamma photo agency.

For the book, *St.-Paul et sa Legende [Saint-Paul and Its Legend]*, written by André Verdet, also a Baldwin trusted crony, he supplied idyllic images of the old town. He provided the text and photos for a book, *Montand vu par Alain Cinquini [Montand Seen by Alain Cinquini]*. Everyone who was newsworthy was captured by his camera. The rare exception, and, only on special Baldwin request, was his good friend, Jimmy.

Cinquini explained his special contact with Baldwin in an interview. "I like friends who are *léger*, you know, easy-going, not burdensome, gentle. That's how Jimmy was—like me. I had never wanted to apply 'photographic pressure' on Jimmy and his well-known friends. I avoided that since I felt it was an intrusion on Jimmy's privacy. He knew enough to ask me for a photo if he wanted it. Jimmy was a writer, someone who is solitary.

"He didn't act or function in the same way as an actor, a rocker or other people. The gentleness in his relaxed rhythm of life was the basis of our relationship. Jimmy invited me often to his house and I came 'unarmed,' that is, to say, without my camera. We drank a glass or many more, talked about everything and nothing, we sang . . . nothing extraordinary!"

Cinquini laughed as he recalled an anecdote concerning an appointment they had at the bar of La Colombe d'Or before going to the house for dinner. "When Jimmy entered, I said to him, 'You don't look well, you seem to be very tired.' He answered, 'I'm exhausted. I've been working like a nigger.' I remarked, 'You shouldn't let that happen!' After a few seconds, he realized what he had said and broke out in an enormous burst of laughter."

I had heard that Sidney Poitier—a Bahamian-American actor, director, diplomat and author—had also been a frequent guest at Jimmy's home whenever he was in southern France to play golf.

Their friendship dated back to the March on Washington in 1963 when Poitier had been asked to read Baldwin's speech.

I phoned his production company in Beverley Hills, California. Getting to talk with Sidney Poitier turned out to be relatively easy. Sherry

Brooks, his assistant, passed on my query and came back with, "Mr. Poitier will be very happy to reminisce about his visits to Baldwin's home in Saint-Paul. He will phone you tomorrow." And he did.

Sidney Poitier was the first black to receive an Oscar as best actor for his role in *Lilies of the Field* in 1964. Three years later, he starred in a trio of films in which the characters he played were concerned with issues of race. Those films— *To Sir with Love, In the Heat of the Night* and *Guess Who's Coming to Dinner?* – made him the box office star of the year .

He had been the Bahamian ambassador to Japan since 1997, as well as ambassador of the Bahamas to UNESCO.

In 1992, the American Film Institute named Poitier "Among the Greatest Male Stars of All Times." Poitier was awarded the Presidential Medal of Freedom, the highest civil honor in the US, by President Barack Obama in 2009.

Baldwin had stood up for Poitier during critical as well as favorable periods.

In referring to him in *A Raisin in the Sun,* Jimmy wrote about the exceptionally large number of blacks attending the theatre performance: "It says a great deal about Sidney, and it also, negatively, says a great deal about the fact it certainly never would have been done if Sidney had not agreed to appear in it. The reaction of that audience to Sidney and the play says a great deal about the accumulating despair of black people in this country who find nowhere any faint reflection of the lives they actually lead. And it is for this reason that every Negro celebrity is regarded with some distrust by black people, who have every reason in the world to see themselves abandoned."

Jimmy defended Sidney when he was being demonized by blacks for having accepted the role in *Guess Who's Coming to Dinner?* "The unfavorable consensus was that Poitier had been made a fool of without his even recognizing it, exploited against his own people."

Jimmy stayed faithful to his good friend, defending him as a great actor who maintained the difficult balance with great dignity.

During our call, Sidney decided that it is Baldwin's legacy that should be remembered.

As requested, Sidney's appraisal follows: "James Baldwin was viewed in the literary world as a major talent. His work was highly respected in the country of his birth as well as all over the world. He has left an indelible imprint of how mankind of different ethnicities and cultures struggled to fashion a life within the many different ethos that today represents the seven billion human beings who constitute the family of man."

Chapter 3

Celebrity Haven:
La Colombe d'Or

Saint-Paul de Vence had a legendary and sometimes dramatic literary tradition in the early twentieth century. The area attracted George Bernard Shaw who signed the guest book in 1928, as well as Jean Giono, Jacques Prévert, H. G. Wells, F. Scott Fitzgerald, Maurice Maeterlinck and many other writers.

It was here on the outdoor dining terrace at La Colombe d'Or that F. Scott Fitzgerald spotted the beautiful celebrated dancer Isadora Duncan at a neighboring table and rushed over to be introduced while kneeling at her feet. Zelda, furious at her husband's behavior, leaped onto their table situated next to a retaining wall. She threw herself down a sheer ten-foot deep ravine. She survived with bleeding, bruises, and internal injuries.

It was also a refuge of artists, musicians, and actors. They would meet for drinks, meals, or overnighting at the modest inn, Chez Robinson, run by Paul Roux, son of peasants with a long Provençal ancestry, and his wife, Baptistine, who everyone called "Titine." This became a *guinguette*, a small restaurant with a mechanical piano for music and dancing on Saturdays and Sundays.

Roux welcomed these strange gentlemen, many wearing wide-brimmed hats, and became friends with them all, but especially with the artists, including Renoir, Dufy, Matisse, Signac, and others. He questioned them about their work, became obsessed with painting and bought their canvases or received works in exchange for meals and lodging. A sign was hung outside: "*Ici, on loge à cheval, à pied ou en peinture.*" [Roughly translated: "Here we lodge those on horseback, on foot or with paintings."] Those artists' works still hang, like in an intimate museum, in the dining rooms.

The inn expanded to become the iconic boutique hotel, La

Colombe d'Or [The Golden Dove] in 1932, its walls covered with modern masterpieces. The museum-worthy collection grew with later-day artists who came often for lunch, including Picasso, Miro, Braque, Giacometti, Dufy, Picabia, Utrillo, Derain, Signac, Matisse and Modigliani, among others.

Besides the indoor treasure house of invaluable canvasses, the terrace is enriched by oeuvres that renowned artists have created *in situ*. Immediately after pushing open the modest old wooden door, one encounters a sentry-like towering marble thumb created by César, an autoportrait of his own thumb soaring over six and a half feet into the blue Mediterranean sky.

Looking upward to a slanting tiled roof, you see perched a huge marble dove [*colombe*] sculpted by Ben Jakober surveying guests below. There is Fernand Léger's expansive ceramic mural of oversized womens' faces peering out from the fig trees. An Arman bronze deconstructed sculpture is on a stone base amidst the tables. At poolside there is an oversized green marble apple by Hans Hedberg, ceramic wall installations by Georges Braque and Sean Scully and, moving with the wind, a wonderful mobile by Alexander Calder.

On any given day, well-known figures could be seen seated around a special table on the hotel's expansive terrace hidden from the street by high walls, with resident doves fluttering overhead. This had become one of the most famous celebrity salons in the south of France.

When Jimmy was in Saint-Paul, he would often end up dining at the hotel with artists including Marc Chagall, Alexander Calder, Fernand Léger and Chaim Soutine as well as other celebrities like Simone Signoret, the actor Lino Ventura, as well as visiting luminaries such as Jean-Paul Sartre with Simone de Beauvoir, or the actor/author Dirk Bogarde. Pablo Picasso, poet/scenario writer Jacques Prévert and Yves Montand were particularly close to the Roux clan and often ate as part of the family.

Over the years, the who's who of Hollywood, literary stars, leading international political figures, socialites and other bold face names of the gossip columns found their way to this very discreet address to stay or have a meal. Guests have included Edward VIII (then Duke of Windsor) with Wallis Simpson, Orson Wells, Charlie Chaplin, Cary Grant, David Niven, Marlene Dietrich, Brigitte Bardot, Sophia Loren, Michael Caine, Bono, Madonna, Elton John, Roger Moore, Richard Attenborough, Kirk Douglas, and Tony Curtis.

It was not surprising that Baldwin had been brought to recuperate in this idyllic haven, since he had friends there from various visits in the late 1960s whenever he came to the Nice area. Most importantly, the Roux family had taken him as one of them, starting with Titine Roux, who ruled over the renowned kitchen. Later, her daughter, Yvonne, took over her chores and she, too, adored Jimmy, as did her children.

Jimmy was enchanted by the hotel's glamorous celebrity guests and the extremely personal embracement by the Roux clan. Once he settled in town, it would become his second home, a favored watering hole and a rendezvous for his own illustrious guests.

Michelle Roux, known as "Pitou" by everyone, is the effervescent eldest child of the late Yvonne. She has memories of Jimmy's visits that go back to the mid-1960s. She knew him longer and better than anyone else in town and remains dedicated to Baldwin with an almost mystical fervor. Jimmy was her protector and intimate counselor for over two decades. She now supervises the hotel's exquisite floral arrangements and serene gardens.

"Before he settled here," Pitou recalled, "Jimmy came a number of times to the region and always stopped by to visit my mother who he adored. I met him when I was eleven. I'll never forget that moment. My mother called me in my room here in the hotel to come down to meet someone. It was James Baldwin sitting under the Miro painting in the dining room. To me he looked just like the figure on the canvas. All I could say was 'Hello' and I ran away.

"I remember that he was here again in May 1968 during the student protests in Paris. Someone sent him to meet Simone Signoret who was living at the hotel. Jimmy was very interested in the events and discussed what they meant with Simone who was always pinned to the radio or watched TV all night, while phoning all over the world. She found Jimmy extraordinary from the moment they were introduced. Simone and Jimmy became almost inseparable after they met. He had found a soulmate and a good Scotch drinking partner.

"Later that year, when he was again at the hotel, he kept talking about the assassination of his friend, Martin Luther King, Jr. You could see how obsessed he was, how upset, and he kept repeating to me, with tears in his eyes, 'They killed Martin, they killed Martin.'

"Jimmy was charm, life, soul. You don't find anyone like that anymore. He functioned on different levels of understanding—and many people used that in their self-interest, but he loved them all. That was his great humanity. He had that special love for my mother and Simone because he knew they were sincere. Shortly before he died, Jimmy came to the hotel to say good-bye to my mother. He was very weak, leaning on his brother David for strength."

Hélène Roux remembers Jimmy well. I spoke to her in Saint-Paul on a visit from Geneva, where she teaches and coaches ballet dancers. As the youngest of the family, she was very close to her mother and, consequently, James Baldwin. She said, "Jimmy had received death threats in the US. Don't forget that his life was in danger after his run-in with Robert Kennedy who was the Attorney General. When Jimmy first started coming here, Saint-Paul was like a Band Aid on all his agony. He needed a resting place where he could feel safe. He couldn't function, had to get away, to find some place far away from home. His brother, David, came over to protect him while he was going back and forth to the United States after the assassinations. He couldn't trust anyone. He didn't know where the next bullet would come from.

"Jimmy had an extraordinary friendship with my mother. Their complicity was quite wonderful. He called my mother his 'sister,' part of the tribe. My mother, who had always wanted to become an English teacher, recognized that he was a great tutor. Along with Simone, she shared literature with Jimmy. They spent long evenings with him while he quizzed them about everything concerned with womanhood, including pregnancy, loyalty, sacrifice. This was a real true exchange, never a one-sided conversation. He used his findings in the novel, *If Beale Street Could Talk,* and the character Clementine ['Tish'] was based on my mother."

Describing her relationship with Baldwin, Hélène said, "It played off in two stages. As a child, it was obvious that my mother was anxious to have Jimmy be part of my life. Jimmy would come to the bar by around 6 or 6:30 pm, like a working man coming home, so he could say goodnight to me. As soon as my mother heard he was there, we dropped everything to go right down to see him. He was like a father asking me about my day and what we were doing in school. I remember when I told him that we were reading Alexander Dumas's *Three Musketeers,* he made the story come to life, acting out some of the parts he vividly recalled.

"He sold rights to his works and did everything to raise money so that he could buy the house on 71st Street in New York City for his mother and his whole family. Jimmy had always been more of a father to his eight step-siblings than their real father. He was supporting all of them. We had seen them for the first time when Jimmy told us his family was coming over. My mother set up a lovely table in the courtyard and five of his sisters arrived, dressed like Arab princesses, but they were lost. Not a word was uttered throughout the meal. During that period of my wonderful childhood with Jimmy as a key figure, I can still see him when he showed up wearing incredible African outfits with colorful tops, oversized African rings on his fingers and his fantastic smile that showed his wide-spaced teeth.

"When I was sixteen, I left Saint-Paul to go to New York to study ballet dancing. Jimmy told me, 'Here's my address on 71st Street. Here's my sister Gloria's telephone number. If you get in trouble with the law, don't mention that you know me.' I used to see him every year when he came over to visit his family. He was very different in the States, extremely tense, resenting the still-existent American racism. But when I saw him in Saint-Paul on my trips back home, he was the same old Jimmy I had grown up with. Whenever our ballet troupe performed in Nice, he was there.

"Even in Saint-Paul there were incidents involving Americans which became pretty ugly. Then the loving Jimmy could become very mean and his words came out like daggers. A hotel guest—a woman so naïve, so white—attacked him viciously but ended up leaving in tears. Afterwards her husband came back to apologize. The next day when I was putting stamps on postcards, I read what she had written: 'Guess who was in the bar last night? We had a lovely conversation. . . .' On another occasion, an American, who helped at night with flower arrangements at the hotel, became abusive in her stance on international politics. He finally silenced her by remarking that the UN was just a CIA tool. The conversation had sunk to that level. He was in pain again.

"Aside from those early hurtful intrusions in his expatriate existence, the sad thing was that while he was enjoying a great social life in Saint-Paul, he was the conductor on a big gravy train. The door was always wide open for all those freeloaders who took advantage of his kind nature and his inability to say no to any request. The situation was surreal. There was a string of lovers coming and going. I remember Fréderic, one of his young lovers with the most beautiful eyes imaginable, who was actually smitten with my mother. She found him 'the most boring human being I ever met.' That was part of Jimmy's problem. He surrounded himself with all kinds of people far below his own intellectual *niveau* [level]. And the alcohol flowed!

"At first the people in this village, all white Presbyterians, looked suspiciously at this little, ugly, black gay man who had come into their midst. But since he was a friend of La Colombe d'Or and Signoret, he was accepted."

François Roux, the middle sibling, directs the hotel. He was there when VIPs arrived looking for Jimmy. He was frequently up front near the unimposing reception window situated in the modest bar with low-cushioned seating. François recalled, "Walking into the bar area one day, I overheard a woman, who appeared unannounced, telling a waiter, 'I have an appointment with Mr. Baldwin.' Fortunately, I recognized the great writer, Marguerite Yourcenar, and could entertain her until Jimmy, who was always late, appeared. Jimmy often invited me and a group of friends for dinner at his home or here at the hotel and he always was a genial host."

Summing up his impression of Baldwin, François said, "He was too good to be on earth. He was very human, too human. He was *too nice.* I remember one time that an American was very abusive to Jimmy during a discussion in the bar. They couldn't have been further apart in their thinking. He was in extreme opposition to everything Jimmy believed in—but at the end Jimmy gave him a big hug. It's well known that Jimmy drank a lot but even when he was drunk, he never became nasty, only boring."

Rodolfe "Rudi" Ankaoua, a Baldwin disciple and financial advisor for many years, remembers the Hollywood parade. "Many well-known Americans came to Saint-Paul to see Jimmy. They usually stayed at La Colombe d'Or. After being introduced to Baldwin at the hotel by a mutual friend, a lawyer, I was with Jimmy on a number of occasions when celebrities like Peter O'Toole, Harry Belafonte, Curt Jurgens and Bill Cosby arrived. His writer friends included Cecil Brown, Carlos Fuentes, James Jones and William Styron. They usually waited for him at the hotel, had a drink and a meal there and then came back to his house. There was always a very animated ambiance at the VIP table set apart from the rest of the dining area in the courtyard.

"Even when there were no visiting stars, Jimmy, Simone Signoret and a few others would often settle there at that special table early in the evening, around 7 pm, well before the guests arrived for dinner at the other tables. They always took a theme and made up a play. Once, as a joke, they improvised on a black man's frustrating attempt to gain acceptance as a member of a Rotary Club, with Simone, acting like a very important member, pleading his cause. It was hilarious!"

Chapter 4

Black in a White Village:
Integration

How did James Baldwin fit in? I was curious to hear how Baldwin's settling in Saint-Paul was conceived by the inhabitants of this conservative bastion. I sought people who were witnesses on the scene of dazzle and discretion.

Bertrand Mazodier remarked in an interview, "When Jimmy came in 1970, there were unfriendly natives. People were initially not happy to have him move in. He was black, gay and left wing. He faced a color bar but it was not overt racism as vented by *Mlle*. Faure. Most of the villagers are simple people who talk only about their crops, vineyards, fruit trees, the weather and they like to drink. But Baldwin, with his openness, humor and disarming smile, quickly integrated into Saint-Paul life, admired and loved for the genuinely good person he was.

"We were always used to well-known people living here but most remained aloof and never sought any contact with the locals. Jimmy was the big exception. He actually went out of his way to talk to anyone he came across in town and often invited them to a bar for a drink. He soon knew many people who really were only drinking buddies, even if they considered themselves to be his real friends.

"Within six months, everyone liked him. There was no discussion of politics, nor anything literary. In the Café de la Place, one of his hangouts, where everyone was rightist, nobody bothered him. He was no longer black, he wasn't left—he was Jimmy! You can imagine the turmoil and insane shouting in the café during the drinking contests when the locals downed fifty glasses of *pastis*, sometimes seventy-five, of those mind-blinding aniseed drinks. There were lots of garrulous drunks but they never turned on

Jimmy. He was accepted as one of them. Jimmy was also a good drinker but preferred whiskey or wine."

By chance, on a day I was in Saint-Paul, Xavier Huvelin, who knew Baldwin well, happened to be there on a family visit, having come from Brazil, where he now lives. We met in Huvelin's daughter's house on the hill just behind the Hôtel le Hameau — which had been his residence until he emigrated. We looked out from an upper balcony at the now-desolate, crumbling residence and weed-infested garden of the once-glorious Faure estate where Jimmy lived.

He recalled, "One day, soon after Jimmy's arrival, when I saw him in the village I was shocked. There he was, a tiny, skinny guy dwarfed by two giant bodyguards at the Café de la Place bar. He had gotten threatening mail that he would be killed. Fortunately, the menacing situation passed and afterwards he would walk freely from the hotel to the village with nobody bothering him.

"I got to know Jimmy much better after he moved out of the hotel and went into Jeanne's house across the road. He and Bernard would come over to talk from time to time and occasionally Bernard would show up in the evening to borrow a bottle of whisky.

"At one of our early meetings, Jimmy reeled off a list of things he was against. On top, he told me, was politics in the United States. You forgot he was so ugly when you talked to him since he was so intelligent and made you think about his theories on politics, philosophy, and humanity.

"Of course, lots of well-known people came to see Jimmy. Sometimes he would book them into our hotel. Marguerite Yourcenar stayed twice. When she arrived, she told the reception that she 'was there for a personal meeting with Mr. Baldwin.' On one visit she had trouble with an ulcer and we served her a very light meal as ordered by Jimmy and his friend, Dr. [Roger] Boizard," who was a general practitioner in the village.

(In a later discussion, Dr. Boizard also referred to that visit when the renowned writer was ill. "Jimmy insisted that I first come to his house so that he could accompany me. He greatly admired Marguerite Yourcenar and wanted to express his concern. Showing respect to those he cared about was a very important part of his character. All the books he dedicated to my wife and me are signed, 'with love and respect, Jimmy.'")

The ex-hotelier continued, "But besides those 'stars,' there were always young, unknown, aspiring black artists and writers who he sent to us and paid for. There were always parties and we heard the jazz wafting across the road. Those crowds of people really took him for a ride, cost him a fortune and often kept him from working.

"Money was an ongoing problem for Jimmy. Bernard handled whatever he had or could get his hands on to keep up their grandiose lifestyle without a cent! Once they rented out rooms for an antique dealer from Paris to show his collection. They disposed of Jeanne's family heirloom furniture. Bernard sold off two parcels of Faure land adjoining the main estate even though this valuable property was not legally theirs. Jimmy was obliged to travel extensively for lectures and teaching assignments in American universities since there was too little income being generated from his books."

Despite Baldwin's unceasing financial problems, the façade he maintained always included having a big car and a driver. Acting on ex-secretary Philippe Bébon's mention of Heidi Widenfels, the German chauffeur, I went to the art gallery bearing her name a few doors down on the main street from Mazodier's boutique. Heidi was stacking contemporary paintings when I walked in. She was justifiably surprised at my queries about her long-ago position as Baldwin's chauffeur. Then she said, "I remember when Jimmy came over to me in the Café de la Place to ask if I could drive a big car. I was taken aback and flattered at the same time.

"Actually, I had never done so before but I said, 'sure.' For me it would be a good job. He was a nice guy who I knew through people at the café. I had first read his books in German, then later in English. You can't be friends if you don't know his books. I worked for him for three or four years. Life was easy with him, no stress. From time to time, we had lunch or dinner together. I drove him to conferences all over France.

"Many of his friends were dark. I was the only blonde. I think he liked having a big car driven by a big blonde. Wherever we went, people were curious at the sight. Sometimes we heard foreigners say things like, 'How can a nigger have a big car like this?' When we were alone, his insecurity often came out when he would lament: 'I'm the ugliest one in the family–small and ugly—not the son of my father.' He had a hang-up about being illegitimate.

"If there were ever any problems, Jimmy always extended a hand. For me and everyone, he was a small, big person. We stayed in contact after I stopped driving him and he often invited me to parties and open house receptions. He never forgot friends."

Heidi suggested I contact Marc Bosco, a taxi driver, who loyally served Baldwin throughout the last decade of his life after the big auto and Nicoloss, the last chauffeur, were gone. At his home in neighboring Vence, Bosco said, "With his easy laugh, friendliness, openness to everyone, Jimmy had no trouble with people accepting him in Saint-Paul. But he was over-sensitive to anything he might interpret as racism in everyday things, like if he got bumped or pushed in a crowd, or if waiters were slow in serving. He would often see these things in the wrong way and mutter to me, 'I'm black, it's normal.'

"Jimmy was extremely generous, always loaning people money, even if he himself was broke. He was cultivated, sang really well, spoke good French. He was very close to the intelligentsia *gauche* [leftist intellectuals] and a great friend of the culture minister, Jack Lang; the film star, Donald Pleasence, who lived here; and the pianist, Bobby Short, who had a house nearby in Mougins, where I often drove Jimmy for long evenings of their singing Negro gospel songs together. Jimmy was very much at home in the village and the surroundings."

Looking further than the village I sought contact with Caryl Phillips who I knew from his articles in *The Guardian*, published in London. He had visited James Baldwin at Saint-Paul on numerous occasions. Phillips is a British journalist, born in St. Kitts in the Caribbean, author and professor of English at Yale University. Thanks to a *Guardian* book editor, I was able to reach Phillips in New Haven. We made a date to meet on a weekend at his apartment in New York overlooking Manhattan's Central Park.

We talked about Jimmy choosing to settle in Saint-Paul after so many years of rootless journeys seeking a place where he would feel at home. Caryl said, "Jimmy was the odd person in Saint-Paul—and not only because he was black. He became an attraction. People came into the village asking where he lived. Saint-Paul was the perfect place for him, rather than an anonymous, rustic village hidden away somewhere, since it gave him the two things most important to him. It enabled him to hide in the sense of a retreat and, secondly, it enabled him to be flamboyant. He could be reluctant, hermitic, while exhibiting his other side as an extravagant showman—both traits residing in his personality.

"That's the reason he stayed in Saint-Paul for seventeen years. It was the place where he could live so long at that pace. It lengthened his life. Paris had extended his working life. How long could he have survived in New York? Saint-Paul is a unique place offering both privacy and glamor. It's the most glamorous village around. Jimmy wanted to see and be seen. He didn't want to be left alone. *La Colombe d'Or* provides perfect dazzle and discretion."

Caryl gave me a book, *The European Tribe*, pointing out that the essay, *Dinner at Jimmy's*, was about a visit in 1984, in which he wrote, "Whenever I arrive at the tall iron gates separating James Baldwin from the outside world, my mind begins to wander. The gates remind me of prison bars. I wonder if Baldwin has been in prison, or whether this exile, his homosexuality, or his very spacious home are the different forms of imprisonment. My mind becomes supple, it feels strong and daring, and although the questions and thoughts Baldwin provokes are not always logical, I have always found that there is something positive and uplifting about his presence. Baldwin, unlike anybody else I have ever met, has this ability to kindle the imagination.

"That evening we stayed at home, ate dinner, drank an excessive amount of Johnnie Walker Black Label, and watched a bad disaster movie called *Airport 77*. The film had been dubbed into French. I laughed at the physical humor, Jimmy at the verbal. After thirty years on and off, though mostly on, as a resident, Baldwin's French is perfect. When the movie was over, Jimmy switched off the television and began to talk about integrity, and the greatest crime an artist can commit, which is to abandon that gift in order to pursue money—or honors—or both.

"The following evening Jimmy pressed me to dine with him and his guest, Miles Davis, who was playing at the Nice Jazz Festival. My head was swimming with questions to field to him, but I decided not to attend the dinner. I made some lame excuse, walked up the hill to the walled village and felt miserable."

Caryl also related, "I had left Jimmy's before Miles Davis arrived. The reasons for my departure may seem a trifle feeble now, but I felt them intensely at the time. Part of me desired, however naïvely, access to whatever conversations they might have on more equitable terms than my age and status would allow, but the more important reason lay in the heart of Jimmy's talk the previous evening.

"I had never before noticed how lonely Jimmy was. His garrulity could always overwhelm any occasion, company, or atmosphere; he is a larger-than-life character. But that night his quiet conversation was so saturated with references to his past, to what other writers should have done, and to people that he knew I had never heard of, but whom he still felt compelled to talk about, that I realized that he needed to be alone with someone who could relate fully to all the nuances of his predicament, past, present, and future. 'When Sidney Poitier goes to the Cannes Film Festival he always comes by. When Miles Davis comes to Nice, he stops by, too.' A spiritual fix is a serious business, especially when they come as irregularly for Jimmy as they do these days. I would only have been in the way."

Baldwin claimed FBI surveillance over so many years and police cars parked near the house. Caryl remembered: "August 15 is Assumption Day, an important Catholic holiday in France. As I began to stagger back down the hill, I passed hordes of people walking up it to witness the midnight fireworks display. It was a warm, clear summer night, and I stopped outside the huge iron gates. The lights were on, and in the distance I heard a laugh.

"Across the road four blue-suited gendarmes eyed me suspiciously. Two stood attentively, while the other two were perched on a Citroen hood. They all had guns on their hips, and all but one had a Gauloises cigarette in his mouth. They scowled in my direction—French policemen seldom smile. I heard another laugh from inside the house, then one of the perched policemen turned to the others and passed a comment. He twisted back round and stared again at me. *'Les nègres, ils sont très jolie, n'est-ce-pas?'* [The Negroes are very beautiful, aren't they?] Perhaps he did not say that, and I simply imagined he did."

Wanda van Dijk, Jimmy's Dutch widowed friend, recalled, "He didn't want to admit that he felt threatened. He said he accepted always being followed as a fact of life, and being watched as if he was a 'danger for America,' very Kafkaesque. One time we were having drinks with him at the café when an American woman imposed herself in our conversation. She started questioning him about the Bayreuth Festival, wanting to know where it was, had he been there, was he going? All three of us were astonished as she went on with all kinds of weird questions. When she finally left us, Jimmy's face broke out in his characteristic toothy smile and said, 'Probably from the FBI. It's so obvious from her insistence and dumb questions.'"

Among others who remarked on Baldwin's suspicions of surveillance was his former secretary, Philippe Bébon. "There were no longer direct threats or menacing letters like he had experienced earlier in the United States when he feared being killed because of his civil rights work. But he still was very, very paranoid, convinced that the American intelligence agencies were trailing him. Jimmy and Bernard often told me that, besides the US following him, our phone was bugged and that a police car kept passing to check. I never saw any car nor did I witness any other surveillance. He became nervous even when he had to go to the American Consulate in Nice for routine confirmation of his signature on documents. He told me that a young black girl had been placed there to spy on him because Washington knew where he had fled."

I heard numerous comments confirming or denying an ongoing vigil of Baldwin by the FBI, or possibly by their French colleagues, while he lived in Saint-Paul. I ventured to find proof that he was targeted by the intelligence agency during his last decade in New

York before he fled to France. The evidence might substantiate—
or discount—Baldwin's professed valid concern or paranoia
about being shadowed—truth or fiction—and the specter of "big
brothers" watching from cars parked near his house.

Records show that FBI Director J. Edgar Hoover had already
focused surveillance on Baldwin in 1960 when he was a member of
the Fair Play for Cuba Committee, along with Jean-Paul Sartre, I. F.
Stone and Norman Mailer.

Surveillance intensified in 1963 after Baldwin's outspoken
defiance of Attorney General Robert Kennedy. It was about
Kennedy's position on civil rights during a meeting he attended
with leading black and white personalities, along with a young
black man, Jerome Smith, who had been brutally beaten, jailed, and
then beaten again, while on a Freedom Ride in Mississippi. Smith,
with his scarred face and body, limped into the meeting room as a
testimony to the failure of governmental support of non-violence
efforts.

Baldwin was designated in COINTELPRO, a counter intelligence
program against dissidents, in 1964 and received an anonymous
threatening letter. He became a focus in Hoover's attack on Black
America called "Racial Matters," which referred to him as "that
well-known pervert" and, incorrectly, as a "Communist."

FBI shadowing, phone-tapping, organizing neighborly "spies,"
mail checking and many other devious undercover tactics were
employed until 1974, two years after Hoover's death.

Though Baldwin was living in Saint-Paul from 1970, every
time he returned to the United States, red lights went off at FBI
headquarters—and the hunt continued.

I found more evidence in James Campbell's *Afterword to the 2002
Edition* reprint to his biography, *Talking at the Gates: A Life of James
Baldwin*. It's a report of his lengthy legal struggle, James Campbell,
plaintiff versus US Department of Justice, defendant, to secure
definitive confirmation of FBI surveillance of Baldwin.

Campbell wrote, ". . . A large box thumped on my doorstep. It
contained 1,000 pages, including many duplications and useless
copies of index cards, from the records that FBI HQ in Washington,

and field offices in New York, Los Angeles and San Francisco, had compiled on Baldwin. Smaller batches of records came from the CIA and from Army and Air Force intelligence services.

"The huge black squares of 'exemptions' were everywhere; in places a form had been interleaved, stating that a number of pages had been withheld. The almost decade-long legal battle revealed paltry, altered evidence of the obsessed spying on Baldwin executed by the US government over so many years."

Campbell had also written that "Baldwin often referred to his 'friendly file,' sometimes in my presence, and was certain that, on more than one occasion, his telephone had been bugged."

Baldwin and other writers, including Ernest Hemingway, were justifiably convinced about being shadowed and harassed as was later proven. Hemingway's depression and purported suicide have been linked to the government surveillance fingered by the malicious FBI chief J. Edgar Hoover.

Chapter 5

Taking Distance from America:
Love/Hate Relationship

James Baldwin exploded when he saw Angela Davis in chains on a November, 1970 cover of *Newsweek*. His earlier crusading fire burst out in an open letter that he wanted the world to read in defense of his dear friend and collaborator in the Civil Rights Movement. He could not remain detached from the racial scene in America.

Davis was a scholar, educator, author, lecturer, feminist, pacifist and political activist. Starting in the 1960s, she had been in the headlines as a prominent militant associated with the Black Panther Party for Self-Defense, the Student Non-Violent Coordinating Committee, the Civil Rights Movement and as a leader of the Communist Party USA. She had been implicated in an unsuccessful escape of African-American inmates from Soledad Prison on trial in the Marin County Hall of Justice in California and an attempted hostage-taking which resulted in the killing of the trial judge and three other people.

Supposedly the guns were registered in her name. Angela Davis was charged with aggravated kidnapping and first degree murder in the judge's death. This led FBI Director J. Edgar Hoover to catapult her into the national spotlight as the third woman ever to appear on the FBI's Ten Most Wanted Fugitives list. She disappeared underground and eluded arrest for several months, hiding in friends' houses, moving every night, until she was discovered in a New York City motel.

She was jailed for sixteen months awaiting trial. President Richard Nixon congratulated the FBI on its "capture of this dangerous terrorist, Angela Davis."

Thousands of people across the nation rallied to her defense. More than 200 committees in the US and nearly seventy in foreign countries called for her release. This outcry had its effect. An all-white jury acquitted her of all charges, freeing her as not guilty.

In his impassioned reaction, *An Open Letter to My Sister, Angela Davis*, dated November 19, 1970, Baldwin expressed his long-felt, bitter disappointment: "One might have hoped that, by this hour, the very sight of chains on black flesh, or the very sight of chains, would be so intolerable a sight for the American people, and so unbearable a memory, that they would themselves spontaneously rise up and strike off the manacles. But, no, they appear to glory in their chains; now, more than ever, they appear to measure their safety in chains and corpses. . .You look exceedingly alone—as alone, say, as the Jewish housewife in the boxcar headed for Dachau, or any of our ancestors, chained together in the name of Jesus, headed for a Christian land.

Baldwin described vividly black self-hatred. "The American triumph—in which the American tragedy has always been implicit—was to make black people despise themselves. When I was little I despised myself, I did not know any better. And this meant, albeit unconsciously, or against my will, or in great pain, that I also despised my father. And my mother. And my brothers. And my sisters. Black people were killing each other every Saturday night out on Lenox Avenue, when I was growing up; and no one explained to them, or to me, that it was intended that they should; that they were penned where they were, like animals, in order that they should consider themselves no better than animals.

In his concluding paragraphs, he wrote, "We know that we, the blacks, and not only we, the blacks, have been, and are, the victims of a system whose only fuel is greed, whose only god is profit. We know that the fruits of this system have been ignorance, despair, and death, and we know that the system is doomed because the world can no longer afford it—if, indeed, it ever could have. And we know that the perpetuation of this system, we have all been mercilessly brutalized, and have been told nothing but lies, about ourselves and our kinsmen and our past, and about love, life, and death, so that soul and body have been bound in hell."

His text revealed the change in him and his questioning of an earlier optimism: "The enormous revolution in black consciousness which has occurred in your generation, my dear sister, means the beginning or the end of America. Some of us, white and black, know how great a price has already been paid to bring into existence a new consciousness, a new people, an unprecedented nation. If we know, and do nothing, we are worse than the murderers hired in our name."

The letter reignited FBI surveillance and alertness to any renewed "subversive" intentions.

"If we know, then we must fight for your life as though it were our own—which it is—and render impassable with our bodies the corridor to the gas chamber. For if they take you in the morning, they will be coming for us that night. Therefore: peace.—Brother James."

The agent supervising the Baldwin file at the Federal Bureau of Investigation headquarters in Washington, DC highlighted Baldwin's advice to "fight for your. . . life" as being extremely threatening and inflammatory.

Baldwin went to the United States in spring, 1972 on a fundraising tour for Angela Davis, who was still in desperate need of legal counsel. On his way back to France, he stopped in Manhattan where he was interviewed by George Goodman of *The New York Times* (June 15).

Baldwin told the journalist he realized black destinies were in black hands and only black hands. Baldwin said he had gotten over the emotional malaise following the murder of his friends but he would never again believe in the promise of America as he had done before.

He also told Goodman there was no point in appealing to the moral conscience of the country since it had none.

Baldwin described his visit to Angela Davis as marked by laughter, lots of drinking and talking about their mutual responsibilities. He told her he had begun as a dancing dog without even being aware of it.

In the interview, Baldwin indicated he would return to France because he could work there unencumbered by black-white issues.

But what Baldwin did not tell that journalist was about his earlier role as a main speaker on an evening organized by Davis and the so-called Soledad Brothers—George Jackson, Fleeta Drumgoole and John Clutchette—in the Radical Actions Projects Group on behalf of Angela. (George Jackson would soon get killed by guards in a prison shootout.) Following Baldwin's other speaking engagements for Davis and the Soledad Brothers in Germany and Great Britain, French authorities were visibly angered by Baldwin's supporting role. There were veiled mumblings about revoking his residency permit. One can only question why there was any French objection to his crusading for American black causes in other European countries. Could there have been some pressure from across the Atlantic by the long-armed FBI?

———•———

I wondered what Angela Davis recalled from her relationship with Baldwin during this difficult chapter of her life. Her manager, Cassandra Shaylor, at the office in Oakland, California would schedule telephone conversation with Angela at her home when she returned from a lecture series.

She is now fully engaged in speaking commitments since her retirement from the History of Consciousness and Feminist Studies Department as distinguished professor emeritus at UCSC, the University of California, Santa Cruz.

When I had Angela on the phone, it was immediately clear in her recollections that her fondness for Baldwin had not dimmed with the years. "I had Jimmy's support from the first hour. When I asked him in 1969 to participate in the fundraising organization for the Radical Actions Projects Group, his immediate response was 'Of course, I'll do it.' Later when I went underground and was arrested, he was in touch with people working for my freedom. Since he couldn't call me in prison, he frequently wrote wonderful, supportive letters of encouragement. His message in *Open Letter to My Sister* was so powerful that when I wrote my first book, I took the title, *If They Come in the Morning: Voices of Resistance,* from it.

"The FBI intimidation and threatening surveillance never stopped him from continuing in his position to help. What he did was typical of him. For Jimmy to participate in this struggle in the causes of racism and civil rights was not exceptional for him.

"He invited me on a number of occasions when I got out of prison to come stay with him in Saint-Paul but I was caught up with lecturing everywhere. I couldn't take time off but we did meet a few times in Paris and had some really good talks. Since Jimmy also supported the Black Panther Party, when he came to the San Francisco Bay area, he and I visited the home of Huey Newton, who was the co-founder of that party."

———•———

Baldwin was inextricably concerned with the ongoing racial injustice prevalent in America. He wrote to President Jimmy Carter, dated January 23, 1977. In *An Open Letter to Mr. Carter*, his message started with: "I have a thing to tell you, but with a heavy heart, for it is not a new thing." Some excerpts from his lengthy, fiery missive:

> In North Carolina, as I write, nine black men and one white woman are under sentences of a total of 282 years in various prisons on various charges, including arson. The Rev. Ben Chavis, who was 29 years old yesterday, is the best known of the Wilmington 10.
>
> In Charlotte, three black men are on bail and facing sentences, equally savage, on charges equally preposterous.
>
> It must be relatively rare to find ten people [who have never before committed any offense] who merit 282 years in prison. As for Ben Chavis, the courts have totally failed to indicate what he has done to merit 34.
>
> If I know, you must certainly know of the silent pact between the North and the South, after the Reconstruction, the purpose of which was — and is — to keep the nigger in his place.
>
> If I know, then you must certainly know, that keeping the nigger in his place was the most extraordinarily effective way of keeping the poor white in his place, and also, keeping him poor.
>
> The situation of the Wilmington 10 and of the Charlotte 3 is a matter of federal collusion, and would not be possible without that collusion.
>
> When those black children and white children and black men

and white men and black women and white women were marching behind Martin up and down those dusty roads, trespassing, trespassing wherever they were in the wrong waiting room, at the wrong coffee counter, in the wrong department store, in the wrong toilet, and were carried off to jail, they found themselves before federally-appointed judges, who gave them the maximum sentence. Some people died beneath that sentence, some went mad, some girls will never become pregnant again.

Well, I dared to write you this letter out of the concrete necessity of bringing to your attention the situations of the Wilmington 10 and the Charlotte 3. I repeat, their situation is but a very small indication of the wretched in this country: the non-white, the Indian, the Puerto Rican, the Mexican, the Oriental. Consider that we may all have learned, by now, all that we can learn from you and may not want to become like you. At this hour of the world's history it may be that you, now, have something to learn from us.

I must add, in honor, that I write to you because I love our country: And you, in my lifetime, are the only president to whom I would have written.

During Baldwin's stop-over on a trip to the United States, he was interviewed by Robert Coles for *The New York Times* (July 31, 1977). Baldwin affirmed that the situation for blacks in America had changed in a positive way, although hardly a paradise for blacks in Alabama or Mississippi. He felt that personally the black man and the white man could get along. Baldwin was hopeful and thought the races were less obsessed with each other on the campuses than when he lectured in the 1960s. But he wasn't sure that when black students said they paid no attention to whites if this was not actually to conceal their feelings.

Baldwin had been working on a novel about the life and death of a gospel singer which would take up where *Go Tell It on the Mountain* left off. He told Coles he still had some months to work on it but was leaving for France in a few days since that was where he could best complete it. Baldwin also reflected on how many people were asking him when he was coming home. He always replied that he had to finish something first.

Baldwin explained that when he first arrived in France, since he could not speak French, he was still an outsider—not as a black man but as an English speaking writer. Away from America, he felt he could breathe with no one's hand on his throat. He said he was like so many other Americans who needed to get away to find themselves, and France was the beginning of his writing life. It was there that he wrote *Go Tell It on the Mountain.*

———•———

Through the intervening years, while Baldwin continued to vent his revulsion of the racial situation in the US, he remained a target of sharp criticism primarily from American black authors and the black press.

One such case was the interview by Robert Chrisman, poet and co-founder of *The Black Scholar,* for the December 1973 issue. Chrisman asked: "Brother Baldwin, how do you see yourself as a black man here in the 'sunny hills of southern France' and your relationship to black people who are struggling all over the world against racism and exploitation?"

Baldwin replied: "The south of France is not as sunny as people think it is. I know why I am here but I could say, you know, that I found a haven although I know very well that's not true. You have to remember, first of all, that the world is very small, and it is no longer possible for an American, and certainly not an American black man, or an American black writer, and certainly not James Baldwin, to leave America. You have to remember that France and America are friendly nations and it may cost me more to live here than I am willing to tell.

"In any case, the most difficult thing for me to accept in my life was that I am a writer and that there are no excuses. I must get my work done. It is not up to the world to tell me how to do it—it is up to me. The important thing is the work. The world's judgment is something I have to live with. I learned how to do that a long time ago. In the meantime, I'm working. I can't do more than that and I am not in exile and I am not in paradise. It rains down here too."

———•———

Baldwin used author advances in many ways. He received a substantial advance for a proposed account of his Algerian gardener's expulsion from France, *No Papers for Mohammed*—which was never written. He was able to buy other parts of the big house with the intention of eventually owning all of it.

Almost in defiance of *The Black Scholar* criticism, he also engaged in a luxurious folly. He went to Nice to purchase a six-door Mercedes Benz. When the salesman proposed one finished in the tone, *tête de nègre* [literally, a Negro's head], Baldwin replied, "I think that color would be perfect." The salesman turned beet red as he completed the bill of sale. (He could hardly rationalize the embarrassing designation by explaining that a French pastry has the same name).

———•———

"Much of what I knew of the plight of the black American I learned from reading him," the writer Nicholas Delbanco conceded in his book, *Running in Place: Scenes from the South of France.*"And what sometimes seemed like paranoia could be argued as flat fact. The deaths of Malcolm X, Medgar Evers, Martin Luther King, Jr., Bobby Kennedy, George Jackson, the named and nameless legion in what he called 'the royal fellowship death,' his own impending fiftieth birthday; the sickness of a beloved friend and mentor, the painter Beauford Delaney—all weighed heavily that winter. 'This face,' he'd say, and frame it with his slender glinting fingers. 'Look at this crazy face.'

"In the early 1970s, while Richard Nixon reigned unchallenged, the Watergate scandal was building, but the hearings had not yet begun. We discussed America with the fervor of the unrequited lover, curdling into scorn. We went for walks; we dawdled over drinks; we visited each other often during those months. 'Hey, baby, what's up?' 'Hey, darlin, where've you been?' he would ask."

Baldwin never renounced his American citizenship. Though

disenchanted with American society, he had spent much of his adult life in France. In the late 1970s to the mid-1980s, he regularly flew to the US for numerous teaching and lecturing invitations. He preferred to think of himself as a "commuter" between countries.

In a radio interview, he had explained to Studs Terkel: "I am an American writer, this country is my subject." On another occasion, Baldwin said, "I love America more than any other country in the world, and for that reason I insist on the right to criticize her perpetually."

As the French historian Michel Fabre noted in his book, *From Harlem to Paris: Black American Writers in France, 1840-1980*, "France may have served as a place of shelter from what Baldwin called 'the American madness.'"

Baldwin launched a caustic commentary about his fellow Americans during a 1986 interview: "It is astonishing that in a country so devoted to the individual, so many people are afraid to speak."

Baldwin was asked by journalist Jere Real (*The Advocate*, May 27, 1986) what he defined as expatriate.

"Well, it's a term that isn't used in other languages as we use it. Expatriate is strictly an American usage. A Frenchman might say someone is in exile, or the British might refer to someone as living abroad, but the specific way in which the word expatriate is used in America carries with it an accusation. There is a sense of betrayal about the way the word is used that is unlike other countries."

"Like the bumper sticker slogan–*America: Love It or Leave It?*"

"Exactly. If you exit the Land of the Free and the Home of the Brave, then maybe you don't love it."

In other words, an American writer living abroad, such as Baldwin, is viewed as having no right to comment on American political affairs since he no longer lives here, since he has abandoned America.

Even though Baldwin had a love/hate relationship with the United States, he looked for opportunities to go back on a temporary basis, preferably not to New York, the city of his early and extended misery. Frankly, he desperately needed income and realized that teaching could be a rewarding source, especially since he had always wanted to connect with the young.

After guest professorships at various institutions for several years, Baldwin came back to America in 1983 as the visiting five college professor in the W. E. B. Du Bois Department of Afro-American Studies of the University of Massachusetts in Amherst. He would return for a semester each year through 1986.

Baldwin's classes, usually limited to small groups of about twenty aspiring writers, focused on literature and the history of civil rights, as well as seminars in creative writing. Among those he strongly influenced there was Suzan-Lori Parks who would later be honored with the Pulitzer Prize for drama. Baldwin stirred up student excitement as a celebrity, as well as faculty envy, with his laid-back, stimulating and provocative approach.

Baldwin was worshipped at the university by the faculty and the students, as well as across the city, for the extremely fine human being that he was and his genius for friendship. He was respectful to students with a lack of arrogance, a beloved figure. When his classes finished at 5 pm, long lines of students waited to talk to him. He never got away before 9 pm. He listened to their problems and was never perfunctory.

However, some students were disenchanted with his disjointed style, likening him more to a preacher or jazz musician. Baldwin became known for his late arrival in class and twice he never showed up at all. It was clear that as a night person he would have been more comfortable at 10 pm with a cigarette and whiskey talking informally.

———•———

Julius Lester—a black Jewish professor at the University of Massachusetts—interviewed Baldwin a few months before his sixtieth birthday (August 2, 1984) in a piece headlined, "*James Baldwin: Reflections of a Maverick,*" in *The New York Times Book Review* (May 27, 1984). There was no mention nor questions concerning the Lester-sparked controversy at the university about Baldwin being anti-Semitic several months earlier that year.

Virtually from the day Jimmy set foot in Saint-Paul until his passing, his schizophrenic bond with America was a frequent point of discussion among friends visiting his household.

The writer Maya Angelou confirmed that "The ambiance and climate of Saint-Paul gave Jimmy the opportunity to be more of an American than the climate offered in the United States."

Harry Belafonte said, "As Americans we often discussed America. We each had our wounds from the past but Jimmy was particularly hurt, before and after he moved, by the criticism aimed at him both left and right. He talked like an expatriate living in France as contrasted to his living in the US and how agonized he had been there, frustrated, angry, preoccupied by race problems and violence.

"Jimmy sensed the threatening mood in America as an impediment to his writing. Once in France, he felt he could deal with life, celebrate his freedom, the newly-found ease of his existence, a capacity to handle problems without someone breathing down your neck. Yet, he missed being away from the country he was writing about. France was far more accommodating. He was emotionally and physically freer by being far away but this absence turned out to be an impediment to his writing. He was not as prolific in his production as before. He was out of his American element, yearning to come back home."

Echoing Baldwin's fear of American government representation was Peter Murphy, who was the consul general of the United States in Nice from September 1975 through August 1977. Murphy said, "I remember that whenever Baldwin came to our office for notarial services two or three times during the period I was posted there, he would always first ask for Sharon Hunt, vice consul, who is black. She was extremely nice and welcoming and I'm sure she put him at ease in our office—his only contact with the United States government abroad. They always chatted for a long time before he came to see me for the legalization of his signature on various papers.

"Of course I knew who he was. I had read some of his books and recognized him as an important writer. I also knew his background in the United States, problems during the McCarthy era, the FBI surveillance under J. Edgar Hoover and personal attacks during his civil rights activities which finally led to his coming to France and settling not far from here.

"He always seemed uptight, jumpy, nervous at first but then we got into long conversations, mostly about music, and he relaxed. Since we were both jazz fans, it was easy to discuss the American groups playing at the jazz festivals in Nice and Juan-les-Pins. I told him about Harold Robbins, who spent his summers in Nice and gave large sums of money from his royalties to support orphanages since he, himself, was an orphan. Baldwin was clearly not impressed by Robbins's writing—nor his generosity."

His taxi chauffeur, Marc Bosco, confirmed Baldwin's ongoing uneasiness. "Jimmy always talked about politics. He was afraid of [President Ronald] Reagan controls and feared going to the United States Consulate in Nice to get documents signed or to pick up papers. Jimmy was sure about the house being watched all the time, convinced he was always being followed and his phone bugged.

"He couldn't get what was happening in America off his mind. Jimmy often recalled the Atlanta massacre insisting 'it only occurred because they were black.' Then, suddenly, as if he wanted to relieve his pent-up aggravation, Jimmy would break into a broad smile and say something like, 'I am black, leftist and homosexual. What could be worse? It's everything to be burned for.'

"Jimmy was very tolerant, never aggressive. When he met Malcolm X, he found him too violent. He was constantly upset by the hysteria of racism in the United States and told me a number of times how frightened he had been going back to America because of the assassinations," Bosco concluded.

Near the end of his life, Baldwin defined *Notes of a Native Son* as being of crucial importance in his struggle to define himself in relation to his society. "I was trying to decipher my own situation, to spring my trap, and it seemed to me the only way I could address it was not to take the tone of the victim. As long as I saw myself as a victim, complaining about my wretched state as a black man in a white man's country, it was hopeless. Everybody knows who the victim is as long as he's howling. So I shifted the point of view to *we*. Who is the *we*? I'm talking about *we*, the American people."

Likewise, in the spring of 1984, just a few short years before the author's death, he recalled his ambivalence about America and his pressing need to leave the States for his first exile during an interview. Baldwin explained, "I was broke. I got to Paris with $40 in my pocket, but I had to get out of New York. My reflexes were tormented by the plight of other people." Why did he choose France? "It wasn't so much a matter of choosing France—it was a matter of getting out of America. I didn't know what was going to happen to me in France but I knew what was going to happen to me in New York."

In *Re-Viewing James Baldwin: Things Not Seen,* edited by Daniel Quentin Miller in 2000, this Baldwin comment appeared; "I love America more than any other country in the world and, exactly for this reason, I insist on the right to criticize her perpetually."

Actually, Baldwin had already expressed the motivation for his earlier escape in *The New Lost Generation Collected Essays,* (1961). "I think exile saved my life, for it inexorably confirmed something which Americans appear to have great difficulty accepting. Which, simply, is this: a man is not a man until he is able and willing to accept his own vision of the world, no matter how radically that vision departs from that of others. . . What Europe gives an American . . . is the sanction to become oneself."

Chapter 6

A Displaced American Author: *Anxiety*

James Baldwin's last publications had been in 1968 when the printed version of a play, *The Amen Corner*, dating from 1965, came out, as did a novel, *Tell Me How Long the Train's Been Gone*.

The publishing world, critics and his wide international coterie of readers, distressed over the lengthy fallow period, were speculating on whether he had dried up. Trade gossip wrote him off as "being finished."

Baldwin had become ill, unsure of himself and unable to complete the manuscript he was working on. With his move to Provence in 1970, Baldwin's overwhelming insecurity and anxiety concerning any remaining interest from his American publishers and readers intensified. He was still suffering from his last confrontation with a violent, hateful American South and the assassinations of his friends and fellow activists.

When his brother David became aware of the "block," he hastened to fly over in 1971 to pick up the incomplete text for a reading by an editor. The book was eventually finished and published a year later as a collection of essays, *No Name in the Street*. Also in 1972 Baldwin published *One Day When I Was Lost: A Scenario Based on Alex Haley's The Autobiography of Malcolm X*.

No Name in the Street

The novel was based on personal recollections of his early life in the poverty of Harlem, followed by the stormy sixties and early seventies. Although Baldwin poured out his deep disillusionment and anger at America, he sounded an optimistic note in *No Name in the Street*. "We are responsible for the world in which we find ourselves if only because we are the only sentient force which can change it."

Critics were generally enthusiastic, though some remarked that his position had changed concerning African-Americans seeking independence since earlier he had prescribed violence as possibly the only route. However, he indicated that the African-American could never be a racist since he is powerless.

Comment in *The Nation (1972)* typified the general press criticism: "Characteristically beautiful. He has not himself lost access to the sources of his being — which is what makes him awaited by perhaps a wider range of people than any other major American writer."

During Baldwin's drought preceding *No Name in the Street*, there was the publication of two non-books, actually taped dialogues in 1970 with Baldwin — at that time the world's most celebrated black author. One was with the globally acclaimed American anthropologist, Margaret Mead. The other was with Nikki Giovanni, an African-American author of some thirty books for adults and children. The 7½ hour long confrontation with Mead was published as *A Rap on Race* by Margaret Mead and James Baldwin in 1971. Baldwin's exchange in November 1970 with Giovanni on the PBS television program, *Soul!*, was likewise recorded and subsequently published in 1973 as *A Dialogue*.

A Rap on Race, with the older, better-known Mead, was in sharp contrast to *A Dialogue* with Giovanni but both showed Baldwin as one of the rare authors who worked well in collaboration. These exceptionally accomplished women were challenging intellectual sparring partners in the discussions which sometimes reached sizzling heights amidst frequent interruptions.

A Rap on Race

Mead called on her wisdom about racism in remote societies while Baldwin spoke from his own firsthand experience with the legacy of black American history. Press reviews of *A Rap on Race* were generally critical, bordering on hostility.

Richard Elman used a scythe coated with sarcastic humor to undercut the seriousness of the recorded talks and the resulting book (*The New York Times*, June 27, 1971.)

He mocked both Mead as a world-famous anthropologist and

Baldwin as a brilliant black writer for ideas neither here nor there, with interest for no one except friends — or discussions for people in bars and taverns and labeled it baloney. Bland, chewy stuff like in a Hebrew National salami.

Baldwin said to Mead, poignantly enough, at one point, "because we are still each other's only hope." But, eventually, they got so angry and muddled that he was being accused of mouthing anti-Semitic nonsense and, as a final *quid pro quo*, he lumped her among his potential enemies and victimizers. Rather smugly, the anthropologist said that she could not possibly be a racist because of her impeccable upbringing and because she once or twice coddled babies in Africa, Samoa, and West Irian, a former English name for Papua. Baldwin countered by asking how could he be an anti-Semite since one of his best friends was Jewish.

One wonders how these two intelligent people could stoop to such banality.

A Dialogue

Nikki Giovanni — one of the most widely read American poets, an educator, commentator and activist who was among the most celebrated figures of the Black Arts Movement of the 1960s — is a Virginia Tech University distinguished professor teaching English and Black Studies. Nikki phoned back from her university base in Blacksburg, Virginia during a break in a national book-signing tour to explain how her collaboration with Baldwin had been effected.

"I had been asked by Ellis Haizlip, a producer at PBS, to be featured on a program and I immediately indicated that I wanted to talk with such a prominent international figure, the premier black writer of our time, James Baldwin. I loved the prospect of one generation talking to another. Since Jimmy was living in Saint-Paul, we settled on London which was the half-way point. He didn't want to come to the United States, and I can't say I blame him. This would be our spontaneous conversation, sent out live.

"I heard later from Jimmy that he enjoyed talking generationally, finding it to be an awakening. It helped him understand in greater depth our younger generation's attitudes about race and gender.

He told me that our friendship, and the book, enabled him to build up a respected relationship with the upcoming young black writers, almost in defiance of the earlier devastating dismissal by Cleaver and others."

When the two authors launched into their encounters, a confrontation quickly became clear — light-hearted but piercing. Blame it on their age difference, background experiences and individual takes on life as blacks in the United States and, in Jimmy's case, various periods of self-exile.

Though Baldwin had been hardened with the years, he remained his jovial self, while Giovanni, always respectful, did not pull any punches in their discussions that ranged over many subjects while seeking agreement often on painful truths, especially the problems confronting black and white Americans.

Excerpts follow:

Baldwin: It takes a long time before you accept what has been given to you from your past. What we call black literature is really summed up for me by the whole career, let's say, of Bessie Smith, Ray Charles, Aretha Franklin, because that's how it's been handed down, since we couldn't read if you were black. It was punishable by law. We had to smuggle information, and we did it through our music and we did it in the church. You were talking before about the church you went to visit. I thought about the Apollo Theater. That last time I saw Aretha, what did she do at the Apollo Theater but turn it into a gospel church service!

Giovanni: Everybody testified.

Baldwin: And that's true religion. A black writer comes out of that; I don't mean he has to be limited to that. But he comes out of that because the standards which come from Greece and Rome, from the Judeo-Christian ethic, are very dubious when you try to apply them to your own life.

Giovanni: Why do we, as black writers, seem to be so hung up on the truth?

Baldwin: Because the responsibility of a writer is to excavate the experience of the people who produced him. The act of writing is the intention of it; the root of it is liberation. Look, this is why no tyrant in history was able to read but every single one of them burned the books. That is why no one yet really believes there is such a thing as a black writer. A black writer is still a freak, a dancing doll. We don't yet exist in the imagination of this century, and we cannot afford to play games; there's too much at stake.

Giovanni: That "he's-not-black hype," I don't need it because it doesn't make me any better.

Baldwin: People invent categories in order to feel safe. White people invented black people to give white people identity.

Giovanni: It's insane.

Baldwin: Straight cats invent faggots so they can sleep with them without becoming faggots themselves.

Besides the collaborations with Mead and Giovanni and his *No Name* essays, no novel was forthcoming until 1974 when *If Beale Street Could Talk* came out—six years after *Tell Me How Long the Train's Been Gone*. Before *Beale Street* was published, Baldwin wrote to a friend defending himself against all the criticism and tongue-wagging about his absence from the literary scene for so long. "This devil" could still "find work," Baldwin said.

If Beale Street Could Talk

With a strong accent on the importance of black families, the novel portrayed with humor and sensitivity the intense problems facing a ghetto family in which the younger generation is striving to build a life for itself. In effect, it is a touching love story of a pregnant girl and her young sculptor friend, who, though innocent, is being accused of rape.

There was exalted commentary, such as *the New Republic*: "A major work of black American fiction. . .His best novel yet, even Baldwin's most devoted readers are due to be stunned by it."

The Library Journal talked about "Emotional dynamite. . .a powerful assault upon the cynicism that seems today to drain our determination to confront deep social problems."

While weathering some severe criticism, it nevertheless became a Book of the Month Club selection and a best seller. Though the press had insisted that Baldwin had become bitter, losing the passionate tone of earlier writing, he maintained that his message was his unrelenting call for universal love.

The well-known author, Joyce Carol Oates, analyzed Baldwin's checkered career of criticism and praise in *The New York Times* (May 19, 1974).

She described how hard it is for a black writer to strike the balance of not being patronized for being black and being attacked for not being black enough. Oates wrote the assumption that the black author represents his race, that his vision of race is collective, is a forced one. Unfortunately he risks being praised by people who have never read the book — a terrible fate for a serious writer. Oates goes on to say he will be resented by others for speaking of them or for them, intentionally or not.

———•———

In the summer of 1976, Baldwin's concentration hit a low ebb and hampered his writing. He was extremely distressed by Beauford Delaney's mounting delusions leading to the onset of insanity. Delaney, in his mid-seventies, drifted into senility and did not recover from his last mental breakdown. He died in a Paris hospital.

Apropos of Delaney, during my talk with François Roux on the Colombe d'Or terrace, he opened his Baldwin file bulging with clippings of landmark events in the author's career saved over the years. "Look at these," he said, with his face muscles tightening, as he pulled out two yellowing newspaper clippings dating from mid-July 1976. "After all these years I still get angry at the vitriolic, unjustified attack on Jimmy in *Le Canard enchaîné*. They wrote a long column saying that Beauford Delaney was chased out of his atelier by property developers and bulldozers, ended up on the streets as a vagabond, wandered in a daze, picked up weak and thin by the police, brought to that place for crazy people and chained to a chair so he couldn't escape. *Le Canard* reported that the staff doctors concluded he would never again produce anything, thus an *artiste fini*, worthless, waiting to be put in the garbage pail.

"On went the story," Roux said, "the judge had appointed many guardians of his property, including James Baldwin, who they said was a black writer who splits his time between New York and his villa in Saint-Paul, apparently not concerned if Beauford recovers his liberty or not and doesn't want his friends to visit him. What little game is he playing? Beauford is becoming a real *nègre cinglé* *[crazy Negro]* being stuffed with couscous in the hospital. Is the New Orleans orchestra getting ready for a second class burial? It'll be folkloric.

"I remember very clearly when he had to put Beauford Delaney in a Parisian mental hospital for professional treatment. I knew firsthand how lovingly Jimmy always took care of Beauford in his home in Saint-Paul until the old man's condition had deteriorated so much that it was impossible to keep him here. This kind of sensational journalism infuriated me and I was so upset by their article that I never bought the paper again, not once in all the intervening time.

"Jimmy wrote a letter to the editor objecting to the unjust criticism. Here, read it:

"'Apparently you believe that I am not interested in Beauford securing his liberty. I had requested a number of times, through the person of Bernard Hassell, the other guardian, for his release from the asylum, and even rented an apartment where he could live, but the doctors insisted his condition required permanent surveillance within a hospital. You said that I didn't want his friends to come which is a slanderous assertion with no proof. Visits are free in hospitals and I don't see how I could block anyone from visiting him.'

Roux continued, "Jimmy pointed out that 'a Parisian doctor had examined Beauford when he was allowed to go out for a day recently among the living and established with a certificate that the hospital was not favorable for his physical balance and cannot but accentuate his dilapidation.'"

Biographer friend David Leeming—who stayed in the house in summer 1976, as he did during most vacations from his university teaching post—added a footnote to the saga. "The pain of Beauford's slipping away was alleviated in part by a long visit in the summer 1976 by Jimmy's nephew Daniel, David Baldwin's three-year-old son. Daniel was accompanied by his mother, Carole Weinstein, and he succeeded in turning what, with Beauford's deterioration and the problems with a new novel, could have been a depressing summer, into something original and revitalizing. Jimmy wrote to David saying he wished he could 'keep the laughing Daniel. . . but honor is a tyrant.'

"Jimmy loved doing avuncular things, taking the boy to the aquarium in Monte Carlo, showing him off at the bar of La Colombe d'Or, where, according to a letter to David from his brother, entitled *Intercepted Memo: Classified*, Daniel talked happily with the parrots, the owners, and the guests. He was even spotted teaching an English couple how to play dice and watching television with Simone Signoret. Much of the time was spent 'with his uncle's Arab gardener' and speaking 'a kind of Creole' with Valérie. After Daniel left, Baldwin told his Saint-Paul friends that the child had made him feel alive again."

Little Man, Little Man: A Story of Childhood

Beauford Delaney's decline had impeded Baldwin's work for two years on his long novel, *Just Above My Head*. He sought solace in producing a short children's book, *Little Man, Little Man: A Story of Childhood*, which was illustrated by an old artist friend, Yoran Cazac, who he had met years earlier through Delaney. Based on Baldwin's own love for children, it was written from the perspective of his seven-year-old nephew, T. J., one of his sister Gloria's sons, on New York and the world, and those "who are black, poor and less than four feet high." Jimmy dedicated it to Josephine Baker, the world's most famous protector of "the children," who had died a year earlier.

The language Baldwin used was "Black English."

This work was dismissed by the critics as being extremely insignificant.

Julius Lester—a leading black voice of the new generation—expressed his regret in *The New York Times* (September 4, 1977) at not being enthusiastic about the book. He found it a minor work from a major author he greatly respected.

The Devil Finds Work

Baldwin made it known in 1976 that his next book, entitled *The Devil Finds Work,* was a novel portraying black people in American films from *Birth of a Nation* to *Lady Sings the Blues.*

David Leeming, in his biography, provided insight to his friend's motivation in undertaking this subject. "In *The Devil Finds Work,* Baldwin uses movies as a catalyst for an extensive discussion of the American psyche, his own life, and the socio-political climate in America. The book is in one sense a fifty-year-old's evaluative reminiscence. It touches on several important themes and subjects that had been treated less fully elsewhere. Baldwin pays extensive tribute to Orilla "Bill" Miller, the white, elementary school teacher who introduced him to serious theatre, cinema and politics.

"He revisits his Harlem childhood and his early reading. *Uncle Tom's Cabin* and *A Tale of Two Cities,* and the 1936 film version of the Dickens work clearly had 'something to tell me. It was this particular child's way of circling around the question of what it meant to be a nigger.' Sylvia Sidney and Henry Fonda in *You Only Live Once* was "Bill" Miller's compensation for the fact that no one resembling the Scottsboro Boys, 'nor anyone resembling my father' had 'yet made an appearance on the American cinema scene.'"

Orde Coombs, a longtime James Baldwin devotee, reviewed the book in *The New York Times* (May 2, 1976). He praises Baldwin's early works but was disillusioned by *The Devil Finds Work.*

He wrote how much Baldwin's books had influenced him and his fellow undergraduates a decade earlier. For black students searching for their own identities, Baldwin's cutting words and his certainty in the American vision were consoling. Coombs remarked as well that because Baldwin existed we felt that the poison of racial prejudice would not destroy us. He saved our lives by preparing us to face a hostile world.

Yet Coombs concluded that the book is a disappointment since everything Baldwin now says was said before and better. Coombs clearly states that Baldwin's writing had suffered by leaving America.

I phoned Orilla Miller's niece, Dr. Lynn Orilla Scott, at Michigan

State University, where she is a visiting assistant professor of English, after learning that she could give me more family insight to her aunt's preoccupation with Jimmy, as well as her own literary activities centered on him. Dr. Scott has authored *James Baldwin's Later Fiction: Witness to the Journey;* co-edited with Lovalerie King, *James Baldwin and Toni Morrison, Comparative Critical and Theoretical Essays;* contributed to the collection, *A Historical Guide to James Baldwin,* published by Oxford Press (2009), and wrote numerous essays on African-American literature which included allusions to Baldwin.

When we talked about the family link and her scholarly research and writing, she revealed that her lifelong interest had begun "when my Aunt Orilla sent me a copy of *The Fire Next Time* in 1963 for my thirteenth birthday. Since she was such a strong advocate for racial justice and an avid reader, I wasn't surprised to receive that book. I remember when reading it that got my first glimpse of yet another world, one that was also American, but a long way from the America I knew.

"Only later did I learn that Orilla was the white school teacher Baldwin talks about in *Notes of a Native Son* who had become so close and supportive to him as a pre-teen, probably 10 to 12 years old. My aunt, only twelve years older than him, was hired by the WPA Theatre Project's Educational Division to stage plays. She had requested Harlem since it was walking distance from her apartment and she wanted to work in that segregated school with virtually all black children who were all hungry and were fed there. It was the worst poverty I ever saw, she told me.

"Jimmy's homeroom teacher allowed Orilla to take Jimmy out of class because he was way ahead of everything they were studying. My aunt was impressed by his brilliance and made him a 'special assistant.' They read *A Tale of Two Cities* together. She recalled 'those long conversations in the school attic about Dickens which she enjoyed more than conversations about the book with adults.'

"Since Jimmy was writing plays, Orilla felt he should see theatre and more of the world. She went to the Baldwin apartment to ask permission for Jimmy to go with her. His mother, Berdis, was very supportive and appreciative of the teacher's interest in her son, but his stepfather was extremely disapproving, though she only found this out much later. While they went to all kinds of productions, a performance by Orson Wells made an indelible impression on the young boy. Orilla and her husband used to take Jimmy on outings, treating him 'like a little brother.' My aunt described him as a 'very sweet child . . . always a pleasure to have around.' Their intimate friendship lasted around two years, ending when he became a preacher."

In her book, Scott recalled, "It was not until 1976 when *The Devil Finds Work* was published that I started to appreciate the significance of that relationship, not only for Baldwin and my aunt, but the legacy it left me and my family, a legacy of hope that we can cross barriers of race, class and culture, that we can share a vision of the way things should be, that we can be friends, comrades and lovers."

Baldwin's passage in the *Devil* concerning her aunt reads: "It is certainly partly because of her, who arrived in my terrifying life so soon, that I never really managed to hate white people—though, God knows, I have often wished to murder more than one or two. But Bill Miller, her name was Orilla, we called her Bill—was not white for me in the way, for example, that Joan Crawford—was white, in the way that the landlords and the storekeepers and the cops and most of my teachers were white. She didn't baffle me that way and she never frightened me and she never lied to me. I never felt her pity, either, in spite of the fact that she sometimes brought us old clothes (because she worried about our winters) and cod-liver oil, especially for me, because I seemed destined, to be carried away by whooping cough."

Scott also recalled another incident involving her aunt's determination as a political activist which Baldwin also described in the *Devil*: "Bill took us on a picnic downtown once, and there was supposed to be ice cream waiting for us at a police station. The cops didn't like Bill, didn't like the fact that we were colored kids, and didn't want to give us the ice cream. I don't remember anything Bill said. I just remember her face as she stared at the cop, clearly intending to stand there until the ice cream all over the world melted — or until the earth's surface froze. And she got us our ice cream, saying, 'Thank you,' I remember as we left."

Baldwin also paid tribute to Orilla in *The Price of the Ticket* (1985), acknowledging that she could teach him about poverty — but not about blackness. He had written, "From Miller, therefore, I began to suspect that white people did not act as they did because they were white but for some other reason, and began to try to locate and understand that reason."

Just Above My Head

The first novel in the five years since *If Beale Street Could Talk* would become his sixth and final one, *Just Above My Head* in 1979. Baldwin referred to this work in *The New York Times* interview during his summer 1977 stop-off in Manhattan.

The longest and perhaps most ambitious in his writing career, it dealt with the intertwined lives from childhood to adulthood of a homosexual gospel singer from Harlem, his brother and a young girl who is a child preacher.

The story reflected Baldwin's struggle against intolerance and his ambivalence about his own homosexuality, as well as the place of gospel music in black culture. Upon publication, the writer remarked that he "had come 'full circle,' that *from Go Tell It on the Mountain* to *Just Above My Head* sums up something of my experience . . . that sets me free to go elsewhere."

Dial Press, his publisher since 1955, had passed on the book. Several years after Baldwin completed the book, Dial agreed to risk publishing it.

In an interview, Daniel Baldwin remembered being at the house when *Just Above My Head* came out. "There was a lot of excitement. We were there, I was six then, and went to read it immediately. I can't remember if I understood much of it but I was so excited when I had his new novel in my hands. It was that same summer when I discovered a book in Chinese in his book shelves. I was fascinated and said something like, 'Look, Uncle Jimmy, your name is on this book. I want to learn that language so I can read it.' He took it off the shelf and gave it to me with a wonderful dedication. Much later I found out that this was *The Devil Finds Work*."

The reviews were predictably mixed for *Just Above My Head*. He was criticized for spending too much time in Turkey and France. Some focused on his celebrity status rather than his latest literary oeuvre. John Romano in *The New York Times* (September 23, 1979) was among those who were somewhat disappointed. He found the book narrow and tame, further criticizing Baldwin for doing his favorite scenes—ambivalent sex, reunions, quick accesses of love rather than focusing on political, economic or social issues.

Romano went on to say that the book was absorbing, entertaining and insightful in some parts but forced and repetitious in others. He was reluctant to lay the blame for the unevenness of the book on Baldwin's shifting inspiration nor would he say it was a work of passion rather than a work of art. Romano was harsh, calling it formless and unrealized.

Notwithstanding the generally cool press reception, Darryl Pinckney, writing in the influential *New York Review of Books* (December 1979), praised Baldwin. He called him the best essayist in America.

The book had been chosen as an alternate selection of the Book of the Month Club. Dell paid $305,000, after fierce competition, for the paperback rights. It stayed on *The Washington Post* best-seller list for thirty seven weeks.

In spring 1981, *Playboy* magazine invited Baldwin to go to Atlanta, Georgia—a city that claimed to be "too busy to hate"—for a personal investigation of the unsolved serial murders of twenty-eight black children over a period of twenty-two months in 1979 and 1980. Baldwin was exhilarated by the call which would assure him prominent attention in a period when all his writing attempts were floundering. He rejoiced, saying, "I am just beginning as a writer."

Beyond being pleased, he could thumb his nose at the younger generation of black writers who were writing him off as a relic of the older generation whose time had passed. He was fifty-seven, not yet with the distinction of being a "grand old man," extremely sensitive and hurt by the callous youthful criticism. Having attended the court trials, he lampooned the farcical proceedings which underscored his pointed, skeptical, condemning appraisal of American racial justice.

Jimmy's Blues: Selected Poems

It was only in 1983—four years after *Just Above My Head*—that Baldwin brought out a slim book, *Jimmy's Blues: Selected Poems*.

Library Journal was laudatory. "To his achievement as a novelist, essayist, and playwright, Baldwin adds this collection of nineteen lyrics that merge intense feeling about racism and oppression with a street-wise yet visionary voice. In the powerful and earthy cadences of the blues tradition, the black's tragic voice, he confronts the destructive uses of power and asks us to reassess what constitutes a just society. In place of bitterness he offers compassion, and he looks beyond the rhetoric of protest, of personal and national failure to the palace of wisdom. His upbeat conclusion is 'Our children are/ the morning star.'"

Chapter 7

Baldwin's Home: *Author's Only Written Description*

The only written reference and description of his residence published during his lifetime was the article, "Architectural Digest Visits: James Baldwin, Text by James Baldwin," which appeared in that magazine's August 1987 issue — four months before he died. Excerpted from his text:

> A house is not a home: we have all heard the proverb. Yet, if the house is not a home (home!) it can become only, I suppose, a space to be manipulated — manipulation demanding rather more skill than grace. I have lived in many places, have been precipitated here and there. The beginning of my life rather recalls a shipwreck, and the shipwrecked can find it difficult to trust daylight or dry land. . . .
>
> Martin Luther King, Jr. was assassinated on April 4, 1968, while I was living in California. That devastated my universe and was ultimately to lead me to this house.
>
> I wandered around after Martin's death — directed a play in Istanbul, for example, visited London, visited Italy. For some reason, I don't know why, I seem to have avoided France. I collapsed physically several times and when I came back to Paris I collapsed again. Friends then shipped me, almost literally, out of the American Hospital to Saint-Paul de Vence.
>
> It was grief I had been avoiding, which was why I had collapsed. A friend of mine came down from Paris to look after me, and was so outraged at my hotel bills that he packed my bags and moved me here, to what was then a rooming house. Part of my family came to see me. Eventually, I looked around me and realized that I had rented virtually every room in the house. Then, I thought, Why not stay here?
>
> I was forty-six years old then, which means that I have been here for sixteen years. It is far from certain that I will live another sixteen years, and so I consider that the house found me just in time.
>
> It's a fine stone house, about twelve rooms, overlooking the valley

139

and at the foot of the village. My studio is on the first floor, next to a
terrace; it was once the studio of Georges Braque. Visitors need not
find themselves on top of each other, and there are several acres of
land.

It is, also, a very *old* house, which means that there is always
something in need of repair or renewal or burial. But this
exasperating rigor is good for the soul, for it means that one can
never suppose one's work is done. And perhaps I have reached the
age at which silence becomes a tremendous gift, and the vineyard in
which one labours a rigorous joy.

The "*old* house" attracted young authors like Nicholas Delbanco
and Jeffrey Robinson, who were regular visitors, as well others
living nearby who had chosen to reside abroad. They sought
out Baldwin for an exchange reflecting their mutual self-chosen
situation and his position as a writer.

Delbanco noted in his book:

Those authors who sustain careers as continual expatriates are few
and far between. True exile is technically involuntary; many writers
leave their native land because they cannot live there, or return.
Early on, for instance, I asked Jimmy Baldwin what the title of his
novel *Another Country* derived from, what was its original source.
I thought perhaps he was making ironic reference to Hemingway's
short story or to *The Jew of Malta* and Marlowe's famous phrase, 'but
that was in another country, and besides the wench is dead.' It was,
he told me, a Miltonic reference to a nettle that grows wild at home
but that in another country would prove a valued flower. Voluntary
exile is a subtle, sapping thing; if Paris had been *de rigueur* for writers
in the twenties, it had come to seem a bit beside the point. The point
was, Jimmy said, to decide your subject and to see it steadily and
whole.

Jimmy's acolytes believed the process sacramental; as if behind
his study door strange rituals took place. He would shut himself
away at midnight and somehow produce an object to which accrued
money and fame. They had little sense, I think, of how much it was
costing him to keep them all in style, of the anxious wrangling in the
watches of the night.

His acclaim had diminished of late, and he knew I knew it. The
alchemy of which his friends were confident was less mysterious to
me and therefore more compelling; he worked at continual risk. And

I was moved by his intensity, his struggle with a form that had come to seem elusive. *Beale Street* is not as finely honed as *Go Tell It on the Mountain* or *Giovanni's Room*. Yet writers must begin anew each time they start to write. That Baldwin had been consequential to a multitude of readers made all of this more poignant; he had made himself the benchmark to be passed.

Robinson's analysis of the situation in my interview with him: "Baldwin understood his place and responsibility now as a senior writer. He was no longer an angry black man as in his New York period when he had good reason while struggling to achieve equality. Never dangerous or radical, he had made a difference. But the fires had diminished, his youthful anger was lost when he moved to France. Jimmy had become another person, more peaceful in his adopted new surroundings which were very welcoming. In southern France there was no problem with blacks, only with North Africans.

"Jimmy relished celebrity. Had he stayed in the States he would have been toasted as a literary lion in New York. His reputation preceded him to France where his fame brought in its wake a mélange of strange, often opportunistic, people showing up all the time. Bernard was protective in keeping them, as much as possible, from disturbing Jimmy. Though he wrote every day, he had doubts about his work and sensed he no longer had the voice and power he possessed in the '60s and '70s among whites and felt he was being forgotten.

"We had great conversations. We talked about civil rights, the Black Panthers — everything except his boyfriends. I was particularly taken by his first-person narrative about Leo Proudhammer in *Tell Me How Long The Train's Been Gone* and told him I'd love to see him go back, revisit him in another novel — but he never did. Middle-aged black men grew up reading him. There were a few others but the young took over. Jimmy had paved the way for them. We discussed a short story idea and we both had the same title, *Strangers in the Village*, which gave Jimmy a kick."

George Wein recalled: "Jimmy often went to the States to teach at universities and to stay in touch with America though he had chosen not to live there. When he was asked to go to Atlanta to write an investigative article on the serial child murders, he took the assignment since he wanted to find out firsthand about the still-prevalent US failure regarding civil rights. People had been saying that he had given up the fight when he moved to France but this wasn't true. He was continuing his crusade through his writing.

"We did not discuss his writing. There was only one time he told me that when a black writer writes it always has to be quasi-autobiographical. When he does, he frees himself and can write anything without restraint about his life, not holding anything back, without shame, honest like an honest writer. He reminded me that one must consider the whole human situation in the skin of an African-American. And it was evident that once Jimmy got into writing, he did not stop and wouldn't come out of his office for hours or even during the whole night."

Rodolphe "Rudi" Ankaoua, who advised Baldwin in financial matters, was clearly as busy as ever in his Paris office when I contacted him. He added this account of the exiled writer's money juggling: "It was in 1973 or 1974 that I was introduced to Baldwin at La Colombe d'Or and it clicked immediately. After that, I came often to his home to see him. We had become very good friends and I started handling much of his business affairs from soon after we met until he died. I provided all my services without any fees and traveled on his behalf at my own expense because he was a dear friend. I gave advice on his author's rights and other financial aspects of his writing. Material things did not interest him but he always needed money.

"I handled his New York business correspondence, recorded receipts of money received from royalties and honorariums and prepared his returns for US and French taxes. He was hopeless with money and everything related to finances. A big problem was that he gave money to everyone. I tried to guide him, help him like a friend but it wasn't always easy since he had that extremely good nature. Sometimes he even gave away his rights without realizing it.

"There were always people coming up with propositions to make his books into films but they never worked out. I remember one casting director was going to line up Robert De Niro and Jane Fonda to play in *Another Country*. Jimmy was excited and then disappointed when once again it was pie in the sky.

"In 1974 I went to see his New York publisher, Doubleday, to ask for a large sum of money which he desperately needed for taxes and to pay Jeanne Faure for some more rooms he had bought in the house. The editor, who was very reluctant to give me anything, said, 'Jimmy still owes me two books. I can't give you any money.' I argued that he couldn't work if he didn't have peace of mind in that house. She gave in a little and offered a small sum. I refused it. She then doubled it. It was still not enough to cover Jimmy's obligations, debts and necessities of his daily life pattern. I then told her I'm not going to *marchander* [bargain]. If she can't meet our demand, I would go to Toni Morrison's publisher, Simon & Schuster, at 8 am the next morning before leaving on the Concorde to return to Paris.

"At 7 am his editor called me at my hotel, agreeing to the large sum we had asked for. Jimmy was delighted when I handed over the check for a really substantial sum. He could pay Jeanne some of the money he owed her. They had a strange relationship, arguing all the time, but he truly loved her. Excited with this windfall, Jimmy phoned his friend, Georges Garin, a retired Michelin two-star chef, to invite him and his American wife, Mary, to a renowned restaurant not far from where they lived in Hyères. When we arrived in Jimmy's big car driven by Heidi, the elegant chauffeur, Garin insisted on cooking a celebration meal at home.

"When Jimmy left Saint-Paul for visits to the United States to see family, lecture or promote his books. I was often asked to go with him. Once on a trip to New York for a Ray Charles concert, he appeared on stage praising his friend as a musical genius. Whenever he was in America he would usually take time to visit prisons and talk to the black inmates. When I was on his German tour organized by Revolt, his publisher in Hamburg, I saw how the Germans were crazy about him. I never forgot a question during a press conference and how impressed I was with his response. An African radio reporter asked, 'Are you pessimistic, Mr. Baldwin?'

'No, I'm not pessimistic,' replied Jimmy. 'Why not?' insisted the journalist. Jimmy replied, 'Because I am a man.'"

———————•———————

"Jimmy had a problem writing," Philippe Bébon, Baldwin's private secretary, told me. "Working on his novels was always difficult for him, often taking three or four years to complete a work, while the essays flowed more easily. When I came in 1972, he was just finishing *If Beale Street Could Talk,* Dial Press in New York paid him $100,000 in 1973 for that book and an advance on *No Papers for Mohammed* about Malcolm X, in which he uses Valérie as his model for Angelika—but he never completed that work. He put that money down as the first payment toward his purchasing part of the house, while he continued to rent more and more space. But soon afterwards he again had financial difficulty. He spent more than he earned, gave money to everyone and was generous to a fault.

"While I was there, I was privileged to witness the process as he extended a *Playboy* article into the book of essays, *The Devil Finds Work,* published in 1976. He had a contract to do a book with Tony Maynard, his one-time chauffeur and 'man Friday,' who ended up in prison for alleged murder in a trumped-up case with racial overtones. Jimmy intervened and he was later released—but the book was never written."

Chapter 8

James Baldwin & Henry James:
Writers in Exile

Henry James was Baldwin's role model and literary mentor, inspiring him to go into self-exile in order to write. Jimmy's bookcase in his bedroom office was bulging with books by and about James. The American author's philosophy was frequently quoted and influenced Baldwin's own writing.

A friend of Jimmy's, presumably being witty or possibly wanting to sound an alert, sent him a quotation from William James, cautioning his brother, Henry, about the ill effects of exile on a writer: "Keep watch and ward, lest in your style you become too Parisian and lose your hold on the pulse of the great American public."

As if to underscore this danger, that friend also quoted from Henry James Henry James's *Daisy Miller*, in which a woman admonishes her nephew: "You have lived too long out of the country. You will be sure to make some great mistake."

Baldwin was offended by the insinuation that he had erred in choosing to settle abroad. He sent the friend a copy of his *A Dialogue* with Nikki Giovanni with this text underlined: "It's very valuable to be forced to move from one place to another and deal with another set of situations and to accept that this is going to be — in fact it is — your life. And to use it means that you, in a sense, become neither white nor black. And you learn a great deal about — you're forced to learn a great deal about — the history out of which all these words and conceptions and flags and morals come."

On an earlier occasion, Michael James, grandson of William James, had sent Baldwin a photo of John Singer Sargent's renowned portrait of Henry James painted on the writer's 70th birthday. The prized photo, signed by both Sargent and James, was accompanied by a note praising Baldwin for a civil rights speech in Chicago and an article he wrote for *Ebony* magazine called, "The White Man's Guilt." Baldwin hung the photo over his writing desk where it would remain throughout his lifetime as an important source of inspiration. David Leeming indicated that "the picture became a kind of direct link between him and a writer who, as far as Baldwin was concerned, came closer to sharing his concerns than any other."

Baldwin gave the impression that 'his relationship with Henry James was of a very special sort, perhaps of the sort that existed between James and Balzac,' when James as a novice was worshipping at the feet of a literary god. James was Baldwin's criterion for what he strived to achieve as a novelist. Though *Another Country* bore no relation to James's writing, the Jamesian influence on Baldwin and his work was undeniably evident.

Baldwin, in fact, had cited James in *Another Country*: "They strike one, above all, as giving no account of themselves in any terms already consecrated by human use; to this inarticulate state they probably form, collectively, the most unprecedented of monuments; abysmal the mystery of what they think, what they feel, what they want, what they suppose themselves to be saying." David Leeming had written that "*Another Country* was very different from James on the surface—the shocking, sensational, emotional, sexual, biracial, thoroughly contemporary surface—but Baldwin's intention in using that James quotation was to stress that his Americans were much like James's in the dilemma they faced in their lives."

During a New York visit in 1972, shortly after *No Name in the Street* was published, Jimmy had run into an old friend on Broadway close to his mother's home on West 71st Street. The friend, was accompanied by a young black man recently released from prison. He invited them both to the downstairs apartment which he used in the house. The ex-con gave him a copy of Henry James essays, *The American Scene*, a work Jimmy had not yet read.

With almost childish glee, Baldwin instructed his young French companion to pack the book in the luggage for their return to Saint-Paul. In the meantime, the ex-inmate, who had been checking Jimmy out with astonishment, whispered indignantly to his friend, "Is that the writer of *The Fire Next Time* I read in prison—that queen?" The friend, clearly perturbed, snapped back, "He's more of a man than most you know, I bet." Baldwin had gotten accustomed to these kinds of insulting remarks since Eldridge Cleaver had published his condemning attack on his sexuality in *Soul on Ice* in 1967.

Baldwin had made it known that the nearest thing he could find "for the means to order and describe something that had happened to me in the distance—America—was James." He had acknowledged that to finish a novel about his family, he had found that "James was my key." Baldwin often quoted from James's writing in prefaces to his books. His start on an essay based on *The Ambassadors* was initially titled, *The Self as Journey*, and later, *The Self as a Voyage*. Baldwin worked on it some years but it was never completed.

In the manuscript of the *Ambassadors* essay, Baldwin was explicit about his relationship with America. "In principle I could stay here and never go back to Harlem and New York City again. I think that's what I'd like to do, in a way. But I can't do it. I can't do it because if I were to avoid the journey back to America I'd be avoiding everything—the people who have produced me, both black and white, the central reality of my life. And once you do that I don't know what you can write about or what you can write out of. To avoid the journey back is to avoid the self, to avoid 'life'. . .I've always felt that I had no real choice about the journey. In a way I learned about it in the streets. If you're frightened of something in the streets you walk towards it. Turn your back and they've got you."

David Leeming, in an interview for the *Henry James Review* (1986), asked Baldwin to elaborate on his fascination with James and to talk about the *Ambassadors* essay in particular. "He spoke first about the importance to him of James's style and technique. It was something about point of view, something about discipline, that had originally attracted him, he said. But later what drew him most to 'the Master' was the realization that they shared a central theme, that of 'the failure of Americans to see through to the reality of others.' It was this failure that lay at the base of the 'white man's guilt' in the current racial struggles in America, and it was this failure that was implicit in the 'innocence' from which Lambert Strether—like all Americans—had to free himself if he was to achieve the voyage to selfhood.

"The essay on *The Ambassadors* was, he said, to have been an exploration of this theme. James was 'the only American writer. . . who seemed to have some sense of what was later to be called *The American Dilemma*. . . some sense of the American. . . personality.' Americans 'have a tremendous sincerity. . . they are certainly sincere about what they call the 'Negro problem' and about the Indians; they're sincere, in fact, about everything. And they understand nothing.'

"As a writer I needed a box to put thoughts in—a model. I couldn't use D. H. Lawrence, for example. (I was far too much like him.) I had to find someone else, and James became, in a sense, my master. It was something about point of view, something about discipline. And something about the silence in which I myself was living began to help me because I was able to go back to something in myself in that silence."

Colm Toibin—an Irish journalist, critic, poet, short story writer, essayist, playwright and author of ten works of fiction, including most recently, *Nora Webster* and *Brooklyn* and fourteen nonfiction works—is currently professor of humanities at Columbia University. He succeeded Martin Amis as professor of creative writing at the University of Manchester. He wrote *The Master*, a fictional account of five years of Henry James's life and the introduction to a reprint of Baldwin's *Another Country*.

Speaking with him in Brooklyn, where he now resides, Toibin cited from his tribute titled, *The Henry James of Harlem: James Baldwin's Struggle* (*The Guardian*, September 14, 2001. Reprinted with permission.)

"He was, for some of his life, a pure artist, using Jamesian techniques and cadences. . . . From Henry James, he also learned a great deal about character and consciousness in fiction, the use of the single point of view, and of nuance and shade. Early in his career, he had what Eliot said of James, 'a mind so fine that it could not be penetrated by an idea;' but later on public events, and indeed private ones, pressed in on his imagination, and forbade him the sort of freedom he naturally sought. His own heritage both freed and cornered him, freed him from being a dandy and freed him into finding a subject, and then cornered him into being a spokesman or an exile, cornered him into anger."

Baldwin lectured at several universities in the US and abroad on such James's novels that had mystified him as a youth. The aims of James and Baldwin as writers were much the same: "to examine the problem of learning to live in a 'civilized' society whose manners, conventions, prejudices often threaten individual integrity; of coming to terms with that society's demands; and of managing to make the necessary compromises—but without giving up one's essential self."

As his lifelong creed, Baldwin heeded advice from Henry James's *The Ambassadors*: "Live all you can; it's a mistake not to."

Chapter 9

Artistic Soulmates: *Creative Companionship*

Soon after he was settled in Saint-Paul, James Baldwin sought the companionship of local artists. Most of them were struggling for recognition and were hardly known beyond the village. That didn't matter to him. He liked their free spirit and determination to break through. Perhaps he was influenced by his overwhelming esteem and admiration of Beauford Delaney. Jimmy bought drinks in town and welcomed artists home for meals and parties. In no time he became the artists' best friend, worshipped like a patron saint. Many insisted on painting his portrait and offering it to him.

The late André Verdet was a preferred guest and confidant. He was a Holocaust survivor of the Auschwitz and Buchenwald death camps in World War II. He would later write a book of poetry as an homage to Jimmy on the occasion of an UNESCO tribute to him in Saint-Paul in 1998. It was a part of the International Slave Route Project.

Since I wanted to meet some of the artists in Jimmy's circle, I went to Henri Baviera's studio built up against the town's old walls. Henri began to reminisce about his contacts with the writer. "Often we would meet in the Chat Noir, the café/restaurant on the rue Grande. He came many times to see my work and was always good-humored and extremely friendly. Our conversations dealt with the way artists create in times of changing society and norms. Despite his personal struggle as an American black, to which I was very sensitive, he exemplified a very generous and positive attitude that was encouraging for us painters.

"We dined at his house on some occasions with André Verdet, Jimmy's companion, Bernard Hassell, and several other friends. The subjects of conversation were mostly about literature, movies and, of course, life in Saint-Paul which was the source of many stories and gossip.

"He was loved by all the artists who lived in Saint-Paul. He was interested in their work, looking at it at the same time receptively and philosophically. One sensed that he carried the weight of his revolt but with the detachment of an intellectual. Like many of my fellow artists, I have kept him in high esteem. He was a personality who left his mark on everyone he ever met.

"André arranged that he would sit for me for a portrait commissioned by a magazine. That image is still embedded in my head.

"I have one of Jimmy's citations on my wall which I think we should always keep in mind:

"'What societies really, ideally, want is a citizenry which will simply obey the rules of society. If a society succeeds in this, that society is about to perish. The obligation of anyone who thinks of himself as responsible is to examine society and try to change it and to fight it — at no matter what risk. This is the only hope society has. This is the only way societies change.'"

Michole Cohen had been among the many artists in Jimmy's intimate circle of friends in Saint-Paul, although her atelier and home is now in Saint Tropez. She told me, "If Jimmy didn't love men, I would have really gone for him. He wasn't handsome, not like Bernard, but I really loved him very much for who he was and what he did for me. He calmed me when I was depressed. His understanding, his words, brought clarity to problems. He was very soothing. I could talk to him about everything. I gave him portraits and sketches since I wanted him to have something from me. We had wonderful evenings together at my house and we often went to jazz concerts together. I miss Jimmy. He was a very important man in my life."

Gilles Quenaou, a ceramicist, has a pottery boutique, *le Tournesol*, in Tourrettes-sur-Loup, a village close to Saint-Paul de Vence. "I was often in the gatehouse with Bernard as one of his lovers—it seemed he had many—that's the way it was during most of the 1980s. I got to know Baldwin through lunches and dinners in the garden and at the house. We became friends and I was his chauffeur for some time when neither Jimmy nor Bernard had a car. Jimmy adored being driven everywhere, even to places very close by.

"I hadn't read Jimmy's books before I got to know him, but after I did we discussed them. Not the books actually, but the message in them. Obviously I'm not a racist but he explained to me *'racisme ordinaire'* [everyday racism], a reflex of the whites which has existed since forever, nothing recent. His clarity and intelligence greatly influenced how I would think about the color problem from then on.

"He was close to the painter, Gérard Morot-Sir, Michole's partner. After Gérard had a serious car accident, Jimmy took him into his house to recuperate. It was always open house for his artist friends from Saint-Paul and I met a lot of them I knew there. Jimmy was always in a good humor, laughing easily, making everyone feel welcome in his home. But I was never invited when Jimmy had a lunch or dinner with his VIP guests. Then he always insisted on being alone so he could give his full personal attention to those famous visitors without distractions."

Early on Jimmy had also became friendly with two internationally-known artists residing in the region, César and Arman, who were sculptors with burgeoning reputations as pioneers in the French New Realism movement. Arman, a French-born, naturalized American, was known for turning everyday objects into sculpture as "accumulations"—a re-composition of those objects, or destruction of them. A violin in his hands burst open into the hallucinating, self-reproductive multi-image. Humor was always evident in his works, such as *L'Heure de Tous, [Everyone's Time]* which soars skyward with a collection of oversized railroad station clocks facing the Gare Saint Lazare in Paris or "Rostopovitch's Tower" composed of cut-up bronzed cellos in New York City.

César used a hydraulic press to form radical compressions of compacted automobiles, discarded metal and rubbish, expansions in polyurethane foam sculptures and fantastic representations of animals and insects. Occasionally, he worked with a welding torch or a sledgehammer. Whenever Jimmy dined on the terrace of La Colombe d'Or, he always insisted on being seated facing the towering sculpture, *la Puce*, a representation of César's thumb.

Intrigued by these artists' creative processes, it was not surprising that Baldwin readily accepted an invitation from César to attend a *démystification de la machine* [demystification of a machine]. A brand new Honda motorcycle was fed to a *presse à paqueter*, [a compressing machine]. Jimmy likened this performance to a *pendaison publique*, [a public hanging], and retreated to a café for a drink.

I spoke with Philippe Durand-Ruel at his home in Rueil-Malmaison. He remembered that transformation of his motorcycle forty-five years ago like it was yesterday. He invited this writer to "come see the sculpture which still has a place of honor in our living room. It measures around 70 centimeters high and is 50 by 50 wide and deep (27.5 by 19.6 by 19.6 inches). When I look at it almost every day, I see César in front of me with a lot of friends and James Baldwin, who we met on that occasion."

Unquestionably, Durand-Ruel has art in his genes. He's known as a pioneering collector starting with the fledgling French *Nouveau Réalisme* movement. His great-grandfather, Paul Durand-Ruel had opened a gallery in New York and established French artists' reputations there before they were recognized in France. He was foremost in recognizing and promoting Monet, Renoir, Degas and other Impressionists, as well as the floundering *Provençal* painter, Cézanne.

Philippe's wife maintains the Archives Denyse Durand-Ruel, concentrating on French artists, including César and Arman. She had her husband's handwritten notes in her archive from the happening which she passed on to me.

A yellowed paper containing recollections written four decades ago at the time recounted: "We went to a motorcycle dealer in Nice to buy a Honda 125. No sooner said than done, I mounted the vehicle, with César on the back seat, and we were off—with the whole group following Indian-style through the streets. We went directly to the place where they had a machine to crush cars. After the oil and gasoline had been drained out, my purchase was transformed straight away in several minutes from something utilitarian right off the production line to a crumpled compression by César. Baldwin, horrified at the 'assassination,' as he called it, left early."

Lionne Sacramone, the curator of a major César retrospective at the Fondation Cartier in Paris, brought me in touch with Stéphanie Busuttil, César's last partner, who currently regulates the César Administration. She provided me with the preface Baldwin wrote for a book on César's compressed jewelry, titled *Compressions d'Or*, which Yvonne Roux had translated into French from Jimmy's English text:

"The ceremony in question began, democratically messy as usual, in front of the shop of the Honda dealer. Democratically standing in rows were the lookers-on, the photographers, the mechanics, the journalists, the passers-by and the kids who would have given whatever they had — if ever they did have anything of their own — to buy a new Honda. They stared at the machine, they stared at César, they stared at us. One could read in their eyes both expectation and incredulity, as if they wished the Honda to be destroyed and, at the same time, as though they were scared at that very idea. As they were staring at the scene, it was not clear in their eyes whether what they felt was hatred, envy, or simply some kind of sacred anarchy, a need for liberation resulting in an urge to destroy as well as create. . . ."

Baldwin admitted to a certain fear and recounted: "I began to be afraid, without knowing exactly why, so I withdrew to a neighboring local *bistrot* to have a drink. Later on, a man who looked very sober finally purchased the Honda and off we went to the dumping ground in which the ephemeral life of the Honda was to come to its close. There was something about that event which recalled the atmosphere of a public hanging. The Honda was brought along. The tank was emptied as solemnly as if it were extreme unction administered to a dying person, with the same kind of compulsory mental complicity. Now César was about to set to compressing a machine made of steel, iron, aluminum, rubber, leather and glass."

Baldwin goes on to describe the violent death of the Honda. "The device he was going to use is a 'crushing machine' provided by a firm called Cosmos. The first engine to be put into the press was a smaller, more miserable victim, which underwent an unspeakable, indescribable transformation. I could not help thinking of heads being chopped off and shown to the crowd. Now came the turn of the Honda, but it withstood its doom in quite an unexpected way. It was new, it was heavy, it was huge. Six men, including César, lifted it and dumped it into the press which looked just a little too small for it. But after giving rise to a good many doubts in our minds, it eventually got into the press. I sat somewhere, on something, in some corner so as to watch from above what was going on.

"The dying motorcycle filled the place with an abominable noise, but when the press was opened, the beast was not dead, though it was horribly mangled. The lid of the press was lowered once more. The noise was heard again. I began to sweat. I felt somewhat uneasy; I came down from the place where I sat and took a few steps. The Honda had grown into a square object in an utterly unaccountable shape. The only thing I could say for sure was that nobody would ever ride it again. Never again? The poor thing had gone straight from the factory to the junk heap."

Another of Baldwin's prominent art world friends—Jean-Louis Prat, the innovative director of the Fondation Maeght from 1965 to 2005—was a pivotal force in achieving global recognition of this family collection. We knew Jean-Louis from our attendance at many of the noteworthy exhibitions of celebrated twentieth century artists he organized and were aware that, earlier on, he had often welcomed Jimmy to this museum and to his home.

Prat, currently living far from Saint-Paul in Auvergne at Pont-du-Château, now organizes museum shows worldwide. He remembers Baldwin as an enthusiastic visitor to the Foundation and a very dear friend. "We first met at the bar of La Colombe d'Or. Of course I knew him as an author and we would often discuss his writing. He even brought me books as gifts.

"When Jimmy and Bernard came together to an exhibition, Jimmy focused immediately on what interested him. He loved the Giacometti court and was enchanted by the Miro labyrinth. He strived to uncover these artists' personalities almost as if he were searching to create characters for his books. The mosaics of Chagall and Tal-Coat interested him more than classical painting. His preference was for sculpture. He also came for concerts and shows and loved especially *la caca*, an almost primitive musical folkloric troupe who performed in costumes designed by Miro.

"Jimmy came regularly to my house to dine. I would pick him up and bring him back since he didn't drive. When Bernard would join us, he would use their car. Since my work often took me to the United States, I would discuss with Jimmy what I perceived as the changing, improving situation there. I felt more progress was being made with integration than here in France where many immigrants still remain outside our society. Jimmy disagreed with me but expressed the hope that liberty and equality would arrive in the States one day. To me, he himself was an icon of liberty, tranquil and confident in what he sought to recount to the world. His work, like that of all great artists, could touch the most humble of persons.

"While there were always artists and well-known personalities, French and foreign, at Jimmy's many dinners and parties, he was equally attentive to everyone from his housekeeper to the most important guest. Jimmy never played the role of a celebrated writer but was more modest, an *artisan au travail* [craftsman at work]. He epitomized the universal man."

One of Jimmy's favorite artistic jaunts was a chauffer-driven ride to the house of his immediate next door neighbor, Theo Tobiasse, an Israeli-born, French artist. It was so close, perhaps some 30 meters away, that the expansive *Mlle.* Faure property where he lived actually touched Tobiasse's back garden. A close relationship evolved in 1982 after Baldwin invited Tobiasse to a big party he organized at the Café de la Place with his inner circle art crowd. César, Arman and numerous other local sculptors and painters were there, along with André Verdet who read Baldwin's texts along with his own poems. From that evening on, Baldwin and Tobiasse frequently exchanged home visits and became good friends.

Catherine Faust-Tobiasse remembered her late father telling her that Jimmy's visits to the house increased when Chaim Potok— an American rabbi and author of many books including the best known, *The Chosen* – started coming in 1983. "Baldwin never missed an opportunity to stop by when he knew Potok was visiting. Potok often stayed for extended periods, sometimes as long as six months, in order to write in the calm of Saint-Paul.

"The Potok/Baldwin relationship was centered on their discussions about writing, problems of racism, immigration policies and youth. Both were very concerned about young people and their future and had university teaching posts to assure regular contact with the next generation.

"The two of them often insisted on cooking together and ended up squabbling about the preparations. Sometimes, as a light note after a long evening of eating and drinking, Jimmy would saunter into the garden to sing some jazz."

In an early interview with Studs Terkel, later published in *Conversations with James Baldwin* (1989), Jimmy said, "Art has to be a kind of confession. I don't mean a confession in the sense of that dreary magazine. The effort it seems to me is: if you can examine and face your life, you can discover the terms with which you are connected to other lives, and they can discover them, too—the terms with which they are connected to other people."

On another occasion, he commented, "Now it is true that the nature of society is to create, among its citizens, an illusion of safety; but it is absolutely true that the safety is always necessarily an illusion. Artists are here to disturb the peace." And further, "Art is important. Art would not be important if life were not important and life is important."

In *The Price of the Ticket*, he included an early essay which signalled, "All art is a kind of confession, more or less oblique. All artists, if they are to survive, are forced, at last, to tell the whole story, to vomit the anguish up."

With over a thousand-year heritage, Saint-Paul de Vence rises upward from medieval bastioned walls encircling the hillside village to the bell tower and 14th century Collegiate Church, with the blue Mediterranean Sea nearby. © Saint-Paul de Vence Tourist Information Office Photo: Elisabeth Rossolin.

Military architecture, exemplified by the Machicoulis Tower, a vestige of the destroyed 14th century walls, has machicolations — floor openings to drop stones on attackers — and other defense means. The pedestrian level leads one through the tower, also known as the Gate of Vence. © Saint-Paul de Vence Tourist Information Office Photo: Elisabeth Rossolin.

Left: Square of the Great Fountain on the rue Grande, the cobble-stoned main street, which runs through nearly the entire town from north to south, has always been the busiest spot in town. The fountain and wash basin are classified national monuments. © Saint-Paul de Vence Tourist Information Office Photo: Elisabeth Rossolin.

Below: James Baldwin often went through the Vence Gate for a peaceful stroll through the stone-walled, arcaded, narrow winding streets in this idyllic village center — a far cry from Harlem and the havoc that engulfed him in America. © Saint-Paul de Vence Tourist Information Office Photo: Elisabeth Rossolin.

Simone Signoret and her husband Yves Montand stayed in separate rooms in the iconic hotel La Colombe d'Or for many months every year. It was Signoret, who, after convincing Baldwin to settle in Saint-Paul, negotiated living quarters for him in the house of an elderly spinster, Mlle. Jeanne Faure, an outspoken racist who disliked people of color. © Saint-Paul de Vence Tourist Information Office Photo: Jacques Gomot.

Gate house, on the Route de la Colle sur Loup leading up to the village center some 900 meters away, assured total privacy for Baldwin in his home. © Photo: Christophe Messineo.

The propriété Faure, as it was known, boasted an impressive bastide, a country house set amidst the ten-acre property with almond and peach orchards, vineyards, and centuries-old pine, banana, lemon, and pear trees. The interior had frescoed walls painted by Italian artisans who decorated the big houses in Saint-Paul in earlier times. © Photo: Christophe Messineo.

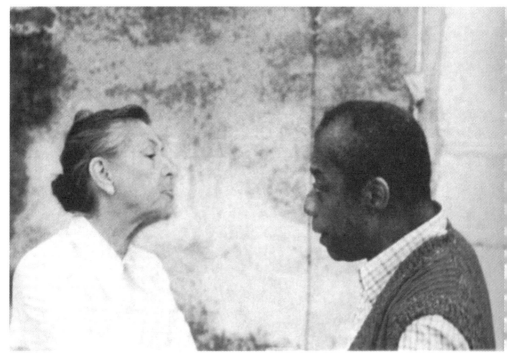

Jeanne Faure with James Baldwin in the early 1970s. Initially, the racist landlady constructed a wall separating her quarters from his, but with the years apartheid turned into friendship – and the old maiden came to love him. She wanted "her Jimmy" to have the house after her death.

Above: James Baldwin in his office, a space that had earlier served as a studio for the renowned French artist, Georges Braque. A youthful portrait of Jimmy, painted by his lifelong muse, the African-American artist Beauford Delaney, hung behind his desk. © Saint-Paul de Vence Tourist Information Office Photo: Jacques Gomot.

Jeanne FAURE, historienne passionnée de son village et James BALDWYN, le romancier noir américain, vivent en parfaite amitié dans une vieille ferme de St-Paul-de-Vence

Dans une vieille demeure, au pied des remparts de Saint-Paul-de-Vence, une authentique Provençale, passionnée par l'histoire de son village, Jeanne Faure, et l'un des plus célèbres romanciers noirs américains du moment, James Baldwin, vivent en parfait voisinage, liés par une solide amitié... Lui reçoit, dans l'aile qu'il habite, des artistes et amis du monde entier. Elle, paisible et active, compulse des archives, dans la seule compagnie de son frère et de son chat.

Le 20 Messidor de l'an III de la République (1795) un homme a été décapité sur la place des Ormeaux à Saint-Paul-de-Vence. Sur cette charmante place où des célébrités du monde entier viennent jouer à la pétanque avec les gars du pays. La guillotine y a été dressée pour un voleur accusé de vol à main armée sur la voie publique et... d'assassinat non consommé ». On ne plaisantait pas à cette époque.

Cet épisode sanglant de la Terreur blanche vient d'être découvert grâce à une monnaie demoiselle presque octogénaire, Jeanne Faure. Depuis de nombreuses années, elle passe le plus clair de son temps à dépouiller les archives départementales pour reconstituer l'histoire du village où elle a passé toute sa vie.

Depuis 54 ans, elle demeure dans une merveilleuse ferme construite au XVIe siècle, entourée de trois hectares de vignes et d'oliviers. Elle vit là avec son frère Louis, de 18 mois son cadet. Et avec un énorme chat qui répond au nom de Sébastien.

Il y a quatre ans, elle a vendu une partie de la propriété au célèbre romancier noir américain, James Baldwin. Elle l'appelle Jimmy et le tutoie. « C'est un peu comme un parent pour moi. Il est hypersensible et s'il n'avait pas senti de l'amitié de ma part, jamais il n'aurait accepté que nous vivions si près l'un de l'autre. »

De la petite pièce qui lui sert de bureau et dont les murs comme la plupart des autres pièces de la maison sont recouvertes de fresques polychromes de l'époque d'Henri IV, on aperçoit l'aile de la ferme occupée par « Jimmy ». « Il écrit dans la grande pièce du bas, de plain-pied avec le jardin. C'est une ancienne étable où je trayais les vaches autrefois. »

Jeanne Faure, l'érudite, la fine et spirituelle Provençale, n'a pas fini de nous surprendre. Après avoir fait des études convenables à Nice et « appris le destin dans l'atelier de Mlle Trachel », elle a dû se plier à la rude vie de cultivatrice et fermière tout de suite après la guerre de 14-18. « Mon frère avait été gazé et avait besoin de plein air. Mes parents ont acheté cette ferme où je venais déjà jouer au diabolo quand j'avais 12 ans. Et puis, mon frère, la ferme et moi, nous ne nous quittons plus jamais. »

Dans la paisible retraite de Saint-Paul, Jimmy Baldwyn, le chat Sébastien et Jeanne Faure.
(Photo: Ralph Gatti)

« Je sens qu'il y a encore des tas de choses à découvrir. Il n'y a pas une minute à perdre... » C'est beau quand on approche des 80 ans d'avoir tant de projets en tête.

UNE SOLIDE AMITIÉ

Son grand ami James Baldwyn a beaucoup d'admiration pour elle. Il est heureux de travailler dans cette ambiance feutrée qui fleure bon la lavande et le serpolet.

« Jimmy » que nous avons aperçu en coup de vent — il débarquait tout juste de Paris — « a envoyé à New York, il y a quelques jours, le manuscrit de son dernier roman « Si Beale Street pouvait parler ». Un livre qui retrace la vie d'un pauvre Noir en prison pour un vol qu'il n'a pas commis. »

Dans ce paysage provençal où il a choisi de passer sa vie désormais, il oublie chaque jour davantage l'enfant malheureux de Harlem qui avait si peur des grands hommes blancs en uniforme.

« Je lui demandais un soir comment il arrivait à veiller si tard dans la nuit, parfois jusqu'au petit matin, pour écrire ses livres, nous confie Jeanne Faure. Il m'a répondu : « J'ai un entraînement qui vient de loin. L'aîné d'une nombreuse famille, je veillais toute la nuit sur les plus petits pour éviter qu'ils soient dévorés par les rats... »

HUNE PUISCHARD

Left: The leading regional newspaper featured an article about the surprising landlady/tenant relationship which had slowly developed. The double interview was headlined, "Jeanne Faure, passionate historian of her village, and James Baldwin, black American novelist, live in perfect friendship in an old farm in Saint-Paul de Vence." Jimmy explained his all-night writing habit having developed after years of protecting his younger siblings from being devoured by rats at night in the Harlem apartment. © Photo: Nice Matin.

The sculptor known as César, Yves Montand, Pitou Roux, (seated), her mother, Yvonne Roux (standing), granddaughter and daughter respectively of Baptistine "Titine" Roux on the right, wife of Paul Roux, the hotel founder. It was Titine who initially drew Baldwin into the family soon after his arrival in Saint-Paul. © Photo: Roux family, La Colombe d'Or.

Yvonne Roux with César and Baldwin. Yvonne carried on the traditional warmth for Jimmy as part of the Roux clan, as did her children — François, Pitou and Hélène. They grew up with the writer who they saw at the hotel on an almost-daily basis. © Photo: Roux family, La Colombe d'Or.

Bernard Hassell, a dancer in the Folies Bergère, was invited by Jimmy to come live in his Saint-Paul house. Hassell was a faithful confidant, "man Friday," and friend who was included in everything Baldwin did. His office and bedroom were in the gate house. © Saint-Paul de Vence Tourist Information Office Photo: Jacques Gomot.

Jimmy's brother, David Baldwin. He was the writer's favorite among his eight stepsisters and brothers.

*Carole Weinstein, who insisted that Baldwin refer to her as his "sister-**out**-of-law," was David's partner. Jimmy adored his nephew, Daniel Baldwin.* © Photo: Carole Weinstein.

Daniel Baldwin and Jimmy. He taught his nephew to play chess, took him on sightseeing trips and proudly strolled with him, hand in hand, through the village. © Photo: Carole Weinstein.

Left: Maya Angelou, the celebrated poet and novelist, giggled while recounting her various visits to Jimmy's house. "When we were together in Saint-Paul, it must have been a hilarious sight since I'm six feet tall—but he was always my big brother." © Photo: Caged Bird Legacy LLC. www.MayaAngelou. com.

Below: Jimmy with Carole Weinstein (center) and his sister Gloria Baldwin in the early 1970s. © Photo: Carol Weinstein

Jimmy with Wanda van Dijk. Jimmy often spent evenings at the Saint-Paul home of Dick van Dijk who he called his "Dutch brother," and his wife, Wanda. After dinner Baldwin would wander alone into the garden to sing Negro spirituals. © Photo: Dick van Dijk.

Baldwin witnessing his sculptor friend César crushing a brand new Honda motorcycle. Calling it "like a public hanging," Baldwin retreated to a bistrot for a drink. © Photo: Jean Ferrero.

Nina Simone – the great jazz, blues and folk singer – often stayed at Jimmy's house. Photo: Photographs and Prints Division, Schomburg Center for Research in Black Culture, The New York Public Library, Astor, Lennox and Tilden Foundations.

Jimmy and Toni Morrison. She and her young son were guests for a week in Jimmy's house in 1974. © Photo: Jay Acton.

Bill Wyman lived in Saint-Paul from 1971 to 1982. When not touring the world as the Rolling Stones bass guitarist, he was very often with Baldwin. Here, a quiet moment together at La Colombe d'Or (1976). © Photographer Bill Wyman. © 2016 Bill Wyman Archive.

From his youngest days, Jimmy loved the movies. He beamed at his VIP treatment as a literary star at the Cannes Film Festival in 1975. © Photo: Agence France-Presse.

Left: Beauford Delaney — artist and mentor for James Baldwin — in St. Anne's Hospital, Paris in 1978 shortly before his death. Their friendship and Delaney's encouragement dated back to Baldwin's early days in Greenwich Village. © Photo: Max Petrus.

Below: At a César exhibition opening in Nice at the Galerie Sapone in 1977, (from left) Bill Wyman, César, Antonio Sapone, Astrid Wyman, James Baldwin and artist/poet André Verdet, a Holocaust survivor, who was a close Baldwin friend. © Photo: André Villers, ADAGP.

Left: At the Picasso Museum in Antibes, Jimmy with friends, Louiguy (Louis Gugliemi), left, composer of many hit songs, including "La Vie en Rose," and sculptor Arman. © Photo: Cinquini.

Below: Harry Belafonte and Baldwin at La Colombe d'Or. Belafonte always made a stop in Saint-Paul while on a concert tour anywhere nearby. He recalled, "As Americans we each had our wounds from the past but Jimmy was particularly hurt, before and after he moved, by the criticism aimed at him from both left and right." © Saint-Paul de Vence Tourist Information Office Photo: Jacques Gomot.

Left: David Linx, a young Belgian singer and composer, moved into the house in 1983 at Jimmy's invitation. He stayed until the writer's death in 1987. © Photo: Akiva Potok.

Below: Chaim Potok, (from left), Theo Tobiasse, Baldwin. Potok, author of many books of which The Chosen *is the best known, regularly visited his French artist friend, Tobiasse, whose house was just behind Jimmy's. The two writers often met there in the 1980s, discussed many subjects from racial strife to their great common interest in young people and sometimes they cooked together.* © Photo: Akiva Potok.

Standing in the garden, Baldwin, with the village of Saint-Paul high on the hill behind him in August 1985. © Photo: Cinquini.

Annie Terrier—founder and director of the prestigious Ecritures Croisées in the Aix-en-Provence municipal library complex—invited Baldwin for a 1986 program focusing on American literature. Ms. Terrier in Saint-Paul, seen here between Baldwin and Bernard Hassell. © Photo: Simone Jaworski.

President François Mitterrand bestowing the distinction as Commander in the French Legion of Honor, the highest recognition of service to the country, on Baldwin at the Elysée Palace in 1986. © Photo: Pascal George/Agence France-Presse.

Leonard Bernstein, the renowned American composer, conductor, author, music lecturer and pianist, was also named Commander in the French Legion of Honor. © Photo: Pascal George/Agence France-Presse.

Traditionally, over many years, Jimmy and his devoted photographer friend, Alain Cinquini, celebrated Baldwin's first arrival in France on November 11 with drinks at the La Colombe d'Or bar. In 1987 David Baldwin had to help his brother arrive for the last toast several weeks before the author's death on December 1. © Photo: Jacques Gomot.

Last picture taken a few nights before the writer died by his American biographer and devoted friend, David Leeming, who stayed in the house to be with Jimmy in the final period. © Photo: David Leeming.

S^T-PAUL : ADIEU « JIMMY » BALDWIN...

L'écrivain noir américain James Baldwin est mort au cours de l'avant-dernière nuit, à son domicile de Saint-Paul, des suites d'une cruelle maladie. Agé de 63 ans, celui que les Saint-Paulois appelaient familièrement « Jimmy », depuis son installation au village, en 1972, était unaniment reconnu comme un apôtre de la cause des Noirs et de toutes les minorités, et comme un des représentants les plus éminents de la littérature américaine contemporaine.
(Photo Cinquini)

Front page news in Nice Matin, *headlined, "Jimmy Baldwin: Death of a righteous man." It praised his courage, optimistic outlook and remarked on his being considered by American literary critics as one of the rare indispensable authors. There was also a Saint-Paul goodbye to Jimmy praising him as an apostle for black and minority causes. (December 2, 1987).* © Photo: Cinquini/Nice Matin.

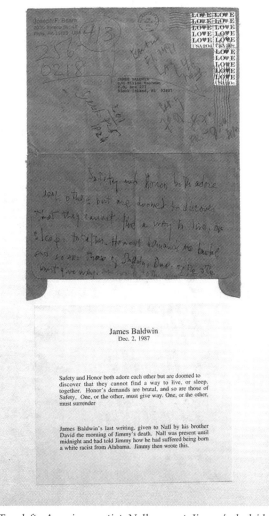

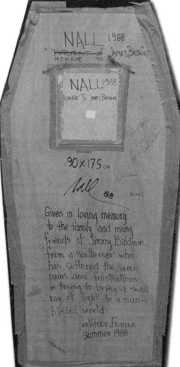

Top left: American artist Nall was at Jimmy's bedside during the evening hours before he died. He completed two sets of coffin paintings: one donated to the Civil Rights Museum in Birmingham, the other for his own memorial to his friend. Front view. © Photo: Nall.

Below, left: Rear view of the Baldwin coffin painting by Nall. © Photo: Nall.

Above: When Nall returned during the night of Jimmy's death, David Baldwin handed him a red envelope with a message written on it intended for him. It was Jimmy's last poem. © Photo: Nall.

Casket of James Baldwin being carried out of the Cathedral of St. John the Divine on December 8, 1987 with family and friends as pallbearers. Left: David, brother; Tejan (T J) Karefa-Smart, nephew; George, brother. Right: Wearing a hat, Wilmer (Lover), brother; Jerome Smith, old friend of the deceased as a fellow civil rights activist. The monumental Gothic Revival structure, started in 1892 but never completed, overflowed with crowds onto the sidewalks. Guinness rates this as the world's largest cathedral since St. Peter's and Notre-Dame are classified as basilicas. © Photo: Ted Pontiflet.

Fellow writer friends (from left) Amiri Baraka, Maya Angelou and Toni Morrison were among the many prominent personalities who attended the funeral service. Diagonally above Amiri's right shoulder is David Dinkins, a former New York City mayor, who was the first African-American elected to this position. © Photo: Ted Pontiflet.

UNESCO rendered a tribute to James Baldwin in November 1988 during a ceremony in Saint-Paul marking the 150ᵗʰ anniversary of the abolition of slavery. His well-known "Open Letter to Angela Davis" was included in the exhibition. Photo: UNESCO invitation.

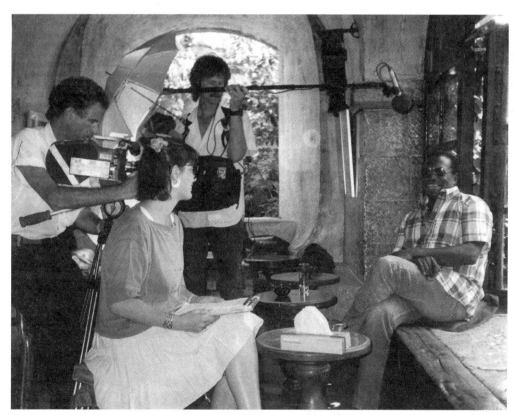

In summer 1988, Nobody Knows Productions filmed David Baldwin's account of his brother's life in Saint-Paul as part of a one-hour documentary for international distribution called simply "Jimmy." The setting was the writer's favorite seat in the bar of La Colombe d'Or. © Photo: Cinquini/Nice Matin.

Left: Following Baldwin's death, a legal battle for ownership of his home ensued until 2007. During the two decades of abandonment, the once elegant country house fell into ruin from rain leakage and stolen doors and windows, leaving it open to the elements. The Italian artisans' frescoed walls were scarred mementoes of earlier days. © Photo: Christophe Messineo.

Below: A commemorative stamp as the 20ᵗʰ in the USPS Literary Series honoring Baldwin was issued in July 2004 just before what would have been his 80ᵗʰ birthday on August 2. The back sheet affixed to the stamp reads: ". . . Whose works explore race relations, as well as the arts and human relationships." © Photo: United States Postal Service.

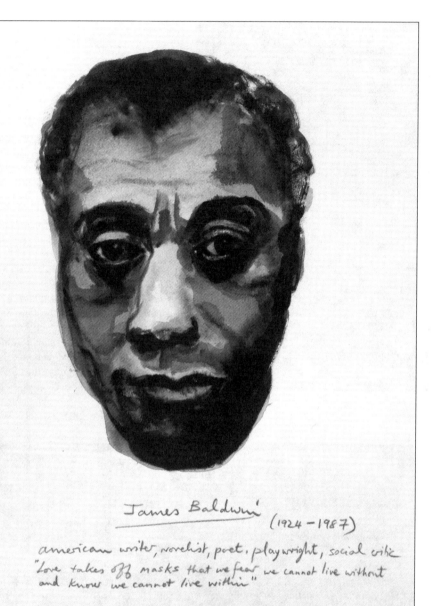

James Baldwin (1924-1987)

american writer, novelist, poet, playwright, social critic
"Love takes off masks that we fear we cannot live without
and know we cannot live within"

Internationally-renowned South African artist Marlene Dumas, now residing in Amsterdam, created in 2014 a compelling, beautifully drawn ink and pencil on paper single series, "Great (Gay) Men," which included a portrait of James Baldwin. © Photo: Marlene Dumas.

The James Baldwin Place on 128th Street, between Fifth and Madison Avenues, facing the high school which Jimmy attended, was inaugurated in celebration of what would have been the writer's 90th birthday on August 2, 2014. On the left, Baldwin's nephew Trevor Baldwin; sister Paula Whaley; on the right (with hat) sister Elizabeth Dingle; Sade Lythcott, CEO of the National Black Theatre. A provisional sign was used owing to a city councilwoman's late introduction of the resolution. © Photo: Herb Boyd.

The James Baldwin Place became official with the placement of a municipal street sign in April 2015. Jimmy's boyhood school is now known as the Harlem Renaissance High School. A plaque in the hallway honors him, as does one in the Walk of Fame on 135th Street in Harlem. A third plaque commemoration in New York City, unveiled in 2015 at 81 Horatio Street in Greenwich Village, recalls Baldwin's residence in the late 1950s, early 1960s. Much of "Another Country" was written here. © Photo: Trevor Baldwin.

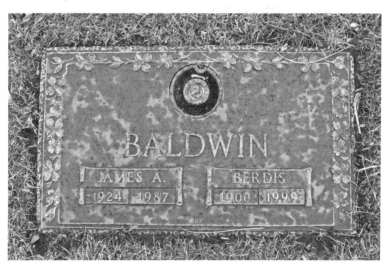

James Arthur Baldwin was buried in Ferncliff Cemetery in Hartsdale, close to New York City in Westchester County, in December 1987. As the discreet flat bronze marker at Hillcrest A, number 1203 shows, the other half of the double plot had been held open for his mother, Emma Berdis Baldwin, until her death in 1999. She was known familiarly as Berdis.

Chapter 10

Sex:
Tranquility

James Baldwin's proclivity for male partners continued throughout the various stages of his career. Yet, he was continually searching for a permanent relationship. He cherished the memory of Lucien as his "great love," but the status had changed to "devoted friend," which he remained until the end.

There was no need for explanations nor embarrassment during the last seventeen years of his life with Saint-Paul as a tranquil setting for his sexual expression.

Partners came, stayed, left or were chased out of what seemed to be a revolving door. Doctors on a sick call at Jimmy's bedside were nonplussed when the bed was filled with another male body. The visitor of the night simply rolled over. Nothing was said.

In *The Price of the Ticket, Collected Non-Fiction, 1948 – 1985*, which bundled almost forty years' writing, Baldwin included as his final essay, "*Here Be Dragons*," deflating the illusion of masculinity. This had originated as an autobiographical article, "*Freaks and the American Ideal of Manhood*," in *Playboy* (1985). Though he wrote this late in life, it concerned his sexual experiences as a young man in Greenwich Village in the 1940s.

It referred to an unnamed woman he almost married and how he had thrown the engagement rings into the Hudson River. He did this at the spot near the George Washington Bridge where a male friend — who had hinted at a possible relationship — had jumped to his death. Baldwin wrote, "We are all androgynous, born of a woman impregnated by a man, each of us, helplessly and forever, contains the other — male in female, female in male, white in black, black in white. . . Love between a man and a woman, or between any two human beings, would not be

possible did we not have available to us the spiritual resources of
both sexes. . . ."

At one point he expressed his theory, "You cannot learn how
to touch a woman until you know how to touch a man." He was
suspicious of "macho men—truck drivers, cops, football players."
He commented, "I know from my own experience that the macho
men . . . are far more complex than they want to realize. That's why
I call them infantile. They have needs which, for them, are literally
inexpressible. . . I think it's very important for the male homosexual
to recognize that he is a sexual target for other men, and that is why
he is despised, and why he is called a faggot. He is called a faggot
because other males need him."

Suffering from scoliosis, a latent curvature of the spine, Baldwin's
way of walking, a slight stagger that was seen as effeminate,
contributed to his being targeted for name-calling.

As a young man experiencing the Bohemian lifestyle in Greenwich
Village, he was attracted to women as well as men while he was
trying to determine for himself which inclination to follow.

His sexual trysts with men were usually one-time encounters.
He did not want to be known as a "black stud," just as in later years
he did not want to be recognized as a "black writer."

As one of the relatively few blacks living in the Village, he stood
out. He drew discriminating remarks which were often coupled
with derogatory sexual comments by supposedly "straight" men
cruising the streets and men's rooms.

With women, he had other problems, while continuing to have
relationships with them. Some, especially the white women, seemed
determined to "cure" his homosexuality, while they relished
their erotic "Negro experience," fantasizing the myth about black
sexuality.

When he was eighteen, Jimmy fell in love with Jessie, a twenty-
four-year-old Jewish divorcee. He also had a relationship with
another white woman. During the period of late 1946 to early 1948,
he lived with Grace, a black girl, who, presumably, was the unnamed
woman to whom he became engaged and planned to marry. He was
twenty-two when their relationship started. He finally understood

when they broke up that he had been self-questioning and doubtful about his actual sexual affinity. He concluded for himself that the best way to love women was not to make love with them.

Never a closet homosexual, he was open about his attraction to men. When he came in contact with new friends, he quickly cleared the deck by pronouncing "I am a homosexual." This gave them the opportunity to stay — or leave. He had even underscored this declaration in his diary. It remained a very personal acceptance for him with no intention of exploiting this stance to gain attention during the still-prudish years of public scorn of "deviates."

He had cancelled his wedding plans before fleeing to France the first time in 1948. When he got to Paris he again slept with women, though in decreasing numbers as his male partners grew in frequency. He came to realize that his desires were exclusively for men.

Women were among his closest friends and at various stages he expressed regret that otherwise he would have happily married one or the other — if his sexuality had followed another path.

Baldwin conceived *Giovanni's Room* as a torrid account of two white male lovers and a woman based on people he knew and probably slept with in Greenwich Village. In this work, he came out publicly about homosexual love in one of the first American novels not treating a traditional heterosexual relationship. His agent, as well as his New York publisher, Alfred A. Knopf, were disappointed that it was not another awaited novel based on black experience in Harlem. They were shocked upon reading the manuscript. They urged him to burn it.

They relished publishing a black writer — but publishing a black homosexual writer was unthinkable, besides the absence of black characters in the work or handling the "Negro problem." Knopf also feared facing a possible legal suit for propagating this unacceptable homosexual behavior.

Baldwin rejected completely suggestions that he should tone it down or no one else would touch it. Any compromises, he felt, would destroy the work.

"When I turned the book in," Baldwin later recalled, "I was told

I shouldn't have written it. I was told to keep in mind that I was a young Negro writer with a certain audience and I wasn't supposed to alienate that audience. And if I published the book, it would wreck my career. They wouldn't publish the book, they said, as a favor to me."

Furious at the prudish, conservative American stand, Baldwin went to London in late 1955 where Michael Joseph, a British publisher, readily agreed to produce it. He agreed despite risks of a public outcry and advice to the contrary from his lawyers. Likewise, he offered to publish everything Baldwin would subsequently write—and he kept his promise. Meanwhile, Baldwin's agent found a small American publishing house, Dial Press, that would take the risk. *Giovanni's Room* was published in Britain and the United States to wide acclaim and ranks among his most important pioneering oeuvres. Baldwin was now being called a homosexual writer rather than a black writer, while he wanted to be recognized simply as a writer.

Much later, at the beginning of the 1980s, while he was teaching at Bowling Green, he was upset by an aggressive partner he was trying to get rid of. The partner meddled in his affairs, interrupted his classes and announced to the press that he was Baldwin's lover. David Leeming recounted, "Baldwin had always avoided publicity in his relationships, and he began to suspect that this 'Joe' was attempting somehow to lock him into a situation that was not necessarily healthy for either of them. He had generally avoided taking a stance on issues governing the 'gay movement.' Sexuality was a private matter, and he resisted the idea of being called 'gay.' To be 'gay' was to be defined—imprisoned—in still another way. Besides, he felt, words like 'gay' and 'queer' belittled the reality of love. He was not a 'queer' or a 'gay' man; he simply loved individuals, many of whom were men."

Jimmy was determined to keep his private life to himself. When people gossiped about his living and traveling with a "muscular, good-looking New Yorker in his late twenties," his agitated rebuttal was, "I love a few people; some are women and some are men." Though he had had a series of affairs with both men and women, he had eventually concluded that his desires were exclusively for men — but he preferred positioning himself as androgynous.

In his play, *The Welcome Table,* Baldwin's last uncompleted work, a character reflected once again the author's own preference for being called *androgynous* rather than *gay* when he said, "The last time you had a drink, whether you were alone or with another, you were having a drink with an androgynous human being; and this is true for the last time you broke bread. . . or made love."

Many years before, he had written, "I was, in a particular truth, a very lucky boy. . . all of the American categories of male and female, straight or not, black or white, were shattered, thank heaven, very early in my life. Not without anguish, certainly; but once you have discerned the meaning of a label, it may seem to define you for others, but it does not have the power to define you to yourself . . ."

During Baldwin's visit to New York in 1984, Richard Goldstein, an editor at the *Village Voice,* said at that time, "Since I belong to the generation of gay men for whom Baldwin's fiction was an early vector of self-discovery, I decided to broach the subject for myself." He interviewed Baldwin about his sexuality for a piece called, "Go the Way Your Blood Beats" (June 26, 1984). Some excerpts reprinted with permission:

Goldstein: Do you feel like a stranger in gay America?
Baldwin: Well, first of all I feel like a stranger in America from almost every conceivable angle except, oddly enough, as a black person. The word 'gay' has always rubbed me the wrong way. I never understood exactly what is meant by it. I don't want to sound distant or patronizing because I don't really feel that. I simply feel it's a world that has very little to do with me, with where I did my growing up. I was never at home in it. Even in my early years in the Village, what I saw of that world absolutely frightened me, bewildered me. I didn't understand the necessity of all that role playing. And in a way I still don't.
Goldstein: You never thought of yourself as being gay?
Baldwin: No. I didn't have a word for it. The only one I had was 'homosexual' and that didn't quite cover whatever it was I was beginning to feel. Even when I began to realize things about myself, began to suspect who I was and what I was likely to become, it

was still very personal, absolutely personal. It was really a matter between me and God. . . .

Goldstein: So when we talk about gay life, which is so group-oriented, so tribal. . . .

Baldwin: And I am not that kind of person at all.

Goldstein: . . .Do you feel baffled by it?

Baldwin: I feel remote from it. It's a phenomenon that came along much after I was formed. In some sense, I couldn't have afforded it. You see, I am not a member of anything. I joined the church when I was very, very young, and haven't joined anything since, except for a brief stint in the Socialist party. I'm a maverick, you know. But that doesn't mean I don't feel strongly for my brothers and sisters.

Goldstein: Do you have a special feeling of responsibility toward gay people?

Baldwin: Toward that phenomenon we call gay, yeah. I feel special responsibility because I would have to be a kind of witness to it, you know.

Goldstein: You're one of the architects of it by the act of writing about it publicly and elevating it into the realm of literature.

Baldwin: I made a public announcement that we're private, if you see what I mean.

Goldstein: When I consider what a risk it must have been to write about homosexuality when you did. . . .

Baldwin: You're talking about *Giovanni's Room*. Yeah, that was rough. But I had to do it to clarify something for myself.

Goldstein: What was that?

Baldwin: Where I was in the world. I mean, what I'm made of. Anyway, *Giovanni's Room* is not really about homosexuality. It's the vehicle through which the book moves. *Go Tell It on the Mountain*, for example, is not about a church and *Giovanni* is not really about homosexuality. It's about what happens to you if you're afraid to love anybody. Which is more interesting than the question of homosexuality.

Goldstein: Is there a particularly American component of homophobia?

Baldwin: I think Americans are terrified of feeling anything. And homophobia is simply an extreme example of the American terror that's concerned with growing up. I never met a people more infantile in my life.

Goldstein: Do you think about having children?

Baldwin: Not any more. It's the one thing I really regret, maybe the only regret I have. But I couldn't have managed it then. Now it's too late.

Goldstein: But you're not disturbed by the idea of gay men being parents.

Baldwin: Look, men have been sleeping with men for thousands of years — and raising tribes. This is a Western sickness, it really is. It's an artificial division. Men will be sleeping with each other when the trumpet sounds. It's only this infantile culture which has made such a big deal of it.

Goldstein: So you think of homosexuality as universal?

Baldwin: Of course. There's nothing in me that is not in everybody else, and nothing in everybody that is not in me. We're trapped in language, of course. But homosexual is not a noun. At least not in my book.

Goldstein: Perhaps a verb. You see, I can only talk about my own life. I loved a few people and they loved me. It had nothing to do with these labels. Of course, the world has all kinds of words for us. But that's the world's problem. Is it problematic for you, the idea of having sex only with other people who are identified as gay?

Baldwin: Well, you see, my life has not been like that at all. The people who were my lovers were never, well, the word gay wouldn't mean anything to them.

Goldstein: That means that they moved in the straight world.

Baldwin: They moved in the world.

Eugene B. Redmond, professor emeritus of English, African-American Literature and Creative Writing at Southern Illinois University, was the founding editor of *Drum Voices Revue* and authored or edited dozens of collections of poetry and diverse writing. He described an evening with Baldwin in his book, *The Way Love Never Dies.* "'I love men but I'm not a homosexual,' Baldwin told *Black Scholar* editor-publisher, Robert Chrisman, and me during a dinner at Maya Angelou's home in Sonoma, California in the mid-1970s. 'Bullshit,' came a retort from a third listener, who clearly was out of Jimmy's earshot by that time. I think I knew what he meant. I, too, love men, especially my big brother, John Henry Redmond, Jr., and, I am, it goes without saying, not homosexual. But I think Jimmy meant something else, something to do with labels and dismissals and categories and what he once referred to as a wrongful familiarity, i.e., 'tampering with the insides of a stranger.' But there was poetry in that enigma."

In *Advertisements for Myself*, Norman Mailer was clearly anguished and bewitched by Baldwin's sexuality and black sexuality in general. Baldwin's essay on their relationship, "A Black Boy Looks at a White Boy," written for *Esquire* (1961), later incorporated in *The Price of the Ticket*, exposes the erotic undercurrent between them, acknowledging that this was a "love letter" to Mailer. In *Nobody Knows My Name*, Baldwin, in his non-aggressive manner, wrote, "I could not, with the best will in the world, make any sense of *The White Negro*."

Mailer had written that essay in Paris in the late 1950s around the time that he and Baldwin had embarked on their tortuous alliance. Mailer spawned his theories on the complicated subject of race relations, blackness and "hip." Baldwin—insecure, frail, sensitive, gay—was immediately attracted to the brash Mailer, depicting him tenderly in his *Black Boy* text as "confident, boastful, exuberant and loving, striding through the soft Paris nights like a gladiator."

David Leeming wrote, "Mailer was perhaps curious about Baldwin's homosexuality and by the myths associated with his race. He also enjoyed sparring with him verbally. Baldwin was attracted by Mailer's 'macho' characteristics even as he disapproved of and was suspicious of them. He was even 'a little in love' with Mailer, rather in the way he was a little in love with Marlon Brando. Like Brando, Mailer exuded an aura of confidence that Baldwin envied**.**"

In *Myth, Literature and the African World*, a collection of essays (1976), Professor Wole Soyinka referred disparagingly to homoerotic intimacy as "misanthropic" and "pathetic," while describing homoeroticism as a product of Western decadence. More pointedly, he linked the Mali author Yambo Ouleguem's *Le Devoir de Violence* to the work of "gay writers Jean Genêt and James Baldwin," the latter of whom he depicts "as both victim and perpetrator of European and Euro-American influences." He continued, "Such solemn cadences, extolling the anal salvation of the lonely in the inhuman and indifferent society of Europe, belong to the fictional prose of Baldwin and Genêt and cannot be integrated into the world of iconoclastic literature."

Harry Belafonte disclosed, "While burdened with the problem of homosexuality, Jimmy expressed a gratefulness that in France the climate for such relationships was much more liberal. He frequently compared the French freedom for sexual preference with what he had endured in America. It was Jimmy who brought this into discussion on many occasions. He felt he could openly put it on the table."

Based on letters he had studied, James Campbell concluded that "Baldwin's race and sexuality had provided a double dose of 'difference' — ironically so, considering that all his life he sought freedom from the confinement of color and sexual categorization. He particularly disliked the term 'gay' and refused to identify himself as such.

"Baldwin had his share of labels: 'a Negro,' 'a boy from the ghetto,' 'a holy roller,' 'a bastard,' 'a homosexual.' No label would stretch further than to limit the person so described. Whatever the maze of Baldwin's sexuality, it could not be summed up in the derogatory term 'faggot.' Baldwin was never a closet homosexual; nor did he make his homosexuality into a political stance. He simply insisted on the freedom to be himself, rejecting the orthodoxy that would define him as, variously, a queer, a pervert, a fairy, or the victim of some sort of genetic imbalance, or a disease — or later on, 'gay' . . . definitions which, if one accepted them, corrupted one's experience and understanding of oneself."

Yet in 1982 Baldwin lent his support to Black and White Men Together/New York — a multiracial, multicultural organization of gay and bisexual men committed to addressing and combating racial discrimination in the lesbian and gay male community.

He spoke on the topic *Race, Racism and the Gay Community* at the group's June 5 meeting. "One has to reject, in total, the implication that one is abnormal," he announced to his audience. "That is sociological and societal delusion that has no truth at all. I'm no more abnormal than General Douglas MacArthur. Gays were merely the latest example of America's apparent need to repress difference in the name of morality. Gays were, like blacks, like

American Indians, one more group of prisoners in a society that was not aware that it was itself an emotional and spiritual prison."

Colm Toibin called him a "black writer before the Civil Rights Movement; a gay writer in homophobic mid-century America; a passionate maverick stylist who was swept into the destructive arena of politics." In referring to *Giovanni's Room*, he wrote: "The subject is the flesh and sexual longing, and the closeness of treachery to desire, and the way the truth of the body differs from the lies of the mind.

"Like other gay writers, Baldwin could take nothing for granted. The color of his skin made it necessary for him to watch every word. The sexual desire led to his being told that he should burn his book. His intelligence, the energy of his wit and his longing for love ran up against history and the hardness of the world, against the prejudices which people had about a man who was black and gay. Everything in his fiction is bathed in the sadness which resulted.

"His religious background and his own sexuality gave him the flesh and the devil as a great subject. His position as the eldest of his family, the surrogate father to his siblings, his position as the outsider—the writer, the homosexual, the one with the missing father—may explain his other great subject: the love between siblings. This love in his fiction is all the more fierce and concentrated because it involves the sibling as witness to the other's self-destruction, the other's pain."

These issues continued to dominate his life in southern France. *Mme.* Nelly Poirier, who owned a restaurant, le Morateur, in Saint-Paul until her retirement in 1985, often hosted Baldwin among her guests and received dedicated books from him. She turned out to be one of the few contacted who did *not* claim to have been a good friend or know Jimmy very well. But she knew of two men who had had very close relations with him.

One, a French-American, worked in her restaurant and lived with Jimmy until he was thrown out for improper behavior. Ultimately, after several contacts, he refused to be quoted. In contrast, the other, Patrick Poivre de la Freta, a Frenchman who now lives on the island of Saint Martin in the French West Indies, was eager to recount his experience with Baldwin.

During my phone call to Patric, he recalled, "I knew Baldwin a little bit but not in the conventional way." After his "special" relationship became very clear, I asked him to put his recollections in writing. His email, entitled, *Une Belle Rencontre*, [A Beautiful Meeting], explained: "I was 24 in 1968 when I opened an art gallery in Saint-Paul to show my own paintings. Many people from show business like Orson Wells, Curt Jurgens, Dirk Bogarde, Simone Signoret often came in and some became clients. I'm not sure where I first met James Baldwin. It must have been in 1970 or 1971, possibly at La Colombe d'Or or at the Fondation Maeght, but I remember being very impressed by him. His face was unattractive but his way of looking was luminous and his words unveiled a smoothness bordering on sensuality.

"He spoke to me like he wrote. I was deeply moved. I sensed that he was not indifferent to my youth, nor my appetite to live. I had only one desire: to go to the source itself of this delicate warmth. After the exceptional aspect of this encounter for the young man that I was, I was excited by the invitation to his villa on another day. Nothing happened there since Bernard, his secretary, who was charming, was at home. We made a date to meet at a mutual friend's party in the village a few days later. There was a 'feeling' between Jimmy and me. Obviously I had read all his books which had been translated into French. I appreciated the style and ideas but just as much the human warmth that emerged unobstructed from his writing. Some passages were sensual. Being a homosexual myself, I could hardly not like them. This man understood the soul of men but also their flesh right to the smallest muscles and nerves.

"But I was too shy in front of this 'big man.' I dared do nothing to disturb our fabulous date. Several illicit products ran through the night. I was a big smoker, drank a lot of wine and coffee but I was not into that. But I remember sharing a marijuana joint with him. His words and his desire enveloped me. We started to flirt and left. For me he was an old man but he was so clever, so delicate, so subtle that I didn't see the difference of our years. For him, I represented youth, he was sensitive to that, and the fact that I was white and a humanist gave him hope and encouragement for the future.

"Wonderful kisses, wonderful words. He told me: 'People don't understand that everybody's blood has only one color.' My answer was: The bones too. I prefer the flesh. We saw each other again three or four times, very discreetly. Our adventure was sealed by fleeting love. We talked a great deal and Jimmy understood that I was too turbulent but he helped me in all his wisdom to understand myself. I had been sexually attracted by Jimmy's skin. All my life I have been attracted by black people. Some of my cousins are black. I left Saint-Paul in 1971 with fond memories of Jimmy. It was not by chance that I chose to complete my life in the Caribbean."

While talking to Jere Real for an article entitled *James Baldwin, A Rare Interview with a Legendary Writer* in the gay magazine, *The Advocate* (May 26, 1986), Baldwin expressed his theories concerning attitudes to homosexuality in the Western world. Reprinted with permission.

"The concept of color is the myth of white, European-based supremacy. This myth is coming to an end in our time. It is linked to America's obsession with the perceived threat of homosexuality.

"Americans' concern with homosexuality is all a great waste of time. It won't change anything. It can't change you. The 'threat' posed by the homosexual is similar to that posed by the black man to a culture based on what he terms the myth of white supremacy: It's the idea of heroes. Certainly, it's all bound up in the idea of eliminating other races' sexual threat—the Indian brave, the Negro stud or buck. The myth of the stud is what it's all about—the frontiersman, the pathfinder. When the others are suppressed, it lends to the myth of white supremacy.

"It also has to do with the cowboy idea in our culture as well, the idea of heroes," he explained. "But what's being overlooked is that it is based partly too, on the notion of an all-male environment, men among men.

"However, while American culture liked this myth, it had to be a 'pure' myth, one devoid of any sexuality. It's a combination of a certain kind of New England Puritan virtue linked to a Southern master-slave notion. It's part of that pathfinder, frontier mystique: It makes the male into a hero, and by his being a hero, it also uplifts, creates the myth of the sanctification of the white woman.

"The lack of such a myth in European life explains why Europeans are generally less threatened by the idea of homosexuality and also why bisexuality — or just sexuality — is more easily accepted there as a matter of course in human relationship."

It was primarily in his essays that Baldwin scrutinized and unmasked the clearly obvious — but openly hidden — sexual, racial and class chasm that existed in mid-20th century America and other Western societies. . .Recognizing all the inherent problems, he campaigned, starting at a very early stage, for acceptance, equality and integration not only of blacks but also male homosexuals.

Baldwin's rebuttal to what he judged the contrived, faulty theory espoused by Norman Mailer in *The White Negro* about the mythical American blacks' sexual prowess was simply: "I think I know something about the American masculinity which most men of my generation do not know because they have not been menaced by it in the way that I have been." Baldwin was referring to his own situation as he fought all his life to free himself from the black virility stereotype. He disputed the white liberal writers positioning the black man as "a kind of walking phallic symbol."

When once asked about the roots of homophobia, Baldwin responded: "Terror, I suppose. Terror of the flesh." On another occasion he remarked, "A black gay person who is a sexual conundrum to society is already, long before the question of sexuality comes into it, menaced and marked because he's black or she's black. The sexual question comes after the question of color; it's simply one more aspect of the danger in which all black people live."

Baldwin summarized his theory: "The gay world as such is no more prepared to accept black people than anywhere else in society."

Chapter 11

Black Music:
Gospel, Blues and all that Jazz

Beauford Delaney was responsible for Baldwin's awakening to black music back in 1940. On his barely functional old phonograph, he played scratchy recordings of music that, for the boy preacher, had been associated with sin and degradation. Under Beauford's guidance, Baldwin began to undergo the "religious" experience of jazz and the blues, according to David Leeming.

In Baldwin's introduction to *The Price of the Ticket,* he harked back to his Greenwich Village days and his first visit to the apartment of Beauford Delaney which had such a deep lasting influence on him, his life and his writing. Baldwin wrote, "I walked into music. I had grown up with music, but, now on Beauford's small black record player, I began to hear what I had never dared or been able to hear. Beauford never gave me any lectures. But in his studio and because of his presence, I really began to *hear* Ella Fitzgerald, Ma Rainey, Louis Armstrong, Bessie Smith, Ethel Waters, Paul Robeson, Lena Horne, Fats Waller.

"He could inform me about Duke Ellington and W. C. Handy and Josh White, introduce me to Frankie Newton and tell tall tales about Ethel Waters. And these people were not meant to be looked on by me as celebrities, but as part of Beauford's life and as part of my inheritance. I may have been with Beauford, for example, the first time I saw Paul Robeson in concert and in *Othello* but I know that he bought tickets for us–really for me—to see and hear Miss Marian Anderson at Carnegie Hall."

James Campbell, in his Baldwin biography, commented on the music in Delaney's studio which transformed Baldwin. "He understood how the music also had its roots in spirituals, and that many of these singers and musicians, like him, had a background in the church and had first discovered music there too. When at last he went to dance halls to hear his favorite jazz bands or their local equivalents, he saw how not only the music but the 'dancing. . . and rejoicing' had filtered down from sacred to secular: worshipping at the temple of the spirit or the body. Southern blacks in a Northern street were driven by the same tambourine and piano, the same rhythm and beat."

Wolfgang Binder interviewed Baldwin in Cannes (for the Fall 1980 *Revista/Review Interamericana 10*) when European editions of *Just Above My Head* were coming off the press. Binder asked him, "Why did you write it? What were you trying to say?" Baldwin replied, 'I grew up with music, you know, much more than with any other language. In a way the music I grew up with saved my life. Later in my life I met musicians, and it is a milieu I moved in much more than the literary milieu, because when I was young there wasn't any. I watched and learned from various musicians in the streets.

"'When I was underage I was listening to the very beginning of what was not yet known as bebop. And I was involved in the church, because I was a preacher and the son of a preacher. And all of that has something to do with *Just Above My Head*, with an affirmation which is in that life and is expressed by that music, which I have not found in that intensity anywhere else. The book has something to do with the journey of a people from one place to another, a kind of diaspora which was unrecognized as yet, and in that journey what has happened to them and what has happened to the world as a result of their journey and is still happening to the world.

"'They had brought themselves a long way out of bondage by means of the music which *Just Above My Head* is about. So in a sense the novel is a kind of return to my own beginnings, which are not only mine, and a way of using the beginning to start again. In my own mind come full circle from *Go Tell It on the Mountain* to *Just Above My Head*, which is a question of a quarter of a century, really. And something else now begins. I don't know where I go from here yet.'"

Music had, indeed, become a crucial theme in Baldwin's sixth and longest novel, *Just Above My Head*, in which he probes the lives of a group of friends who are caught up in feverish singing and preaching, rising to religious pandemonium, in Harlem churches. This unveils allusions to traditional African-American sacred music which had a piercing influence on his writing and titles of his books and plays.

David Leeming wrote that "Near the end of *Just Above My Head*, Arthur's lover, tapping into the 'beat' of brotherhood and communion, that Baldwin sought to convey, and thus speaking for his author, says: 'The song does not belong to the singer. The singer is found by the song. Ain't no singer, anywhere, ever made up a song—that is not possible. He hears something. I really believe, at the bottom of my balls, baby, that something hears him, something says, come here! And jumps on him just exactly like you jump on a piano or a sax or a violin or a drum and you make it sing the song you hear: and you love it, and you take care of it, better than you take care of yourself, can you dig it? But you don't have no mercy on it. You can't have mercy! That sound you hear, that sound you try to pinch with the utmost precision—and did you hear me? Wow!—is the sound of millions and millions and, who knows, now, listening, where life is, where is death.'"

W. J. Weatherby, the late prize-winning British journalist and author, was a special correspondent for *The Guardian* in the United States for an extended period. In his biography, *James Baldwin: Artist on Fire*—a perceptive profile based on his 28-year-long friendship with Baldwin—he concluded that in *Just Above My Head* "the style borrows from the excess of black gospel hymns and preaching. . . ."

> The title of that book came from an old song:
> Just above my head,
> I hear music in the air.
> And I really do believe
> There's a God somewhere.

Campbell also quoted from *Just Above My Head*, reflecting on Baldwin's own experience "to listen to the 'sorrow songs'—gospel, blues and jazz—for the history of black people in America is contained in them, as nowhere else." The main character in that book, Arthur Montana, is a famous gospel singer and the vocabulary of gospel and blues constituted a more specific record than most white people realized.

"'Music don't begin like a song,'" Montana says. 'Music can get to *be* a song, but it starts with a cry. It might be the cry of a man when they put the knife to his balls . . . people spend their whole lives trying to drown out that sound." And he says: "'When a nigger quotes the gospel he is not quoting; he is telling you what happened to him today.'"

Further, Campbell writes: "Arthur, the black singer, the essential Afro-American artist, died at the age of thirty-nine. Did Baldwin pluck this figure out of the air? It was in his thirty-ninth year, in 1963, that he began to speak of himself self-consciously in terms of a black singer: 'I see myself as a blues singer; I'm like a jazz musician.'"

Baldwin had contributed an article specially written for *The New Edinburgh Review* (August 1979) at the request of Campbell, who was then editor of this highly-regarded literary magazine, on the creation and the experience of jazz — specifically the black experience. He titled it, "*Of the Sorrow Songs: The Cross of Redemption.*"

". . . I am attacking, of course, the basis of the language — or, perhaps, the intention of the language — in which history is written — am speaking as the son of the Preacher Man. This is exactly how the music called jazz began, and out of the same necessity: not only to redeem a history unwritten and despised, but to checkmate the European notion of the world. For, until this hour, when we speak of history, we are speaking only of how Europe saw — and sees — the world.

"But there is a very great deal in the world which Europe does not, or cannot, see in the very same way that the European musical scale cannot transcribe — cannot write down, does not understand the notes, or the price of this music."

Baldwin goes on to describe how jazz really came about: ". . . The music called jazz came into existence as an exceedingly laconic description of black circumstances and, as a way, by describing these circumstances, of overcoming them. It was necessary that the description be laconic: the iron necessity being that the description not be overheard.

"... That music is produced by, and bears witness to, one of the most obscene adventures in the history of mankind. It is a music which creates, as what we call history cannot sum up the courage to do, the response to that absolutely universal question: Who am I? What am I doing here?

"... The music began in captivity: and is still, absolutely, created in captivity. So much for the European vanity: which imagines that with the single word, history, it controls the past, defines the present: and, therefore, cannot but suppose that the future will prove to be as willing to be brought into captivity as the slaves they imagine themselves to have discovered, as the nigger they had no choice but to invent.

"... It is out of this, and much more than this, that black American music springs. This music begins on the auction block."

Baldwin concluded, "Music is our witness, and our ally. The beat is the confession which recognises, changes, and conquers time.

"... Then, history becomes a garment we can wear, and share, and not a cloak in which to hide: and time becomes a friend."

Ekwueme Michael Thelwell—emeritus professor University of Massachusetts Amherst, where he was the founding chairman of the Department of Afro-American Studies—commented on music in Baldwin's writing: "The best of black American cultural idiom—the blues' earthy ironies, the spiritual's haunting power, the saucy riffs and defiant rhythms of jazz, the awesome moral cadences of King James, the gospel's ecstatic shout and the preacher's God-intoxicated growl—were all synthesized into a prose instrument of remarkable beauty and compelling power. For the first time, and a brief moment, in the history of this sad republic, the distilled voice of three hundred years of African-American moral experience spoke directly to the nation and compelled its grudging attention. That was his power, his gift, and his burden."

Professor Robert O'Meally of Barnard College, in *The People Who Are Dying*, found that "there is little humor in Baldwin's work and the 'transcendence of the blues' is not there. What one does find is harder to take, the nitty-gritty admission that the greatness of Harlem has been challenged by the ugliness and decrepitness of Harlem. Baldwin tells you about the people who are dying there . . . Even though his literature is saturated with references to the blues, there is something more that is more sentimental than tragic, therefore untrue to the blues."

In disagreement with O'Meally's conclusion, E. L. Doctorow—Baldwin's editor at Dial Press who was to write novels himself, including the much-praised *Ragtime*—said, "He seemed to live on music: jazz, the folk music of Black America. Creole began to tell us what the blues were all about. They were not about anything new. He and his boys up there were keeping it new, at the risk of ruin, destruction, madness and death, in order to find new ways to make us listen." (Doctorow died in July 2015.)

While Baldwin at one point was turning away from his early literary mentor, Henry James, he described himself as a "blues singer" or a "jazz musician" and claimed that, while writing, he wanted to "blow" in the way that Miles Davis played jazz. He told an interviewer, "I am not an intellectual, and do not want to be."

Baldwin, reflecting on his literary style, pointed out parallels with a jazz musician and a blues singer: "I would like to think that some of the people who liked *Another Country* responded to it in the way they respond when Miles [Davis] and Ray [Charles] are blowing." He persistently aimed at weaving the life of a performer—actor or jazz musician—into the essence of his own life and writing.

Late in his career, Baldwin's volume of poetry, *Jimmy's Blues*, concerned his intense feeling against racism and oppression with powerful and earthy cadences of the blues, traditionally the blacks' tragic voice.

Unquestionably, David Linx was among the most informed direct witnesses to Baldwin's involvement with music. He recalled that "Jimmy always had music playing in the background. There was music in his soul. Often he would play his favorite Robert Johnson records while typing in the garden.

"The highlight for Jimmy every summer was always the Nice

Jazz Festival. He loved going there for the sound and the guys who were playing. He was greeted like visiting royalty by the jazz greats performing there. But even more impressive than how the great African-American musicians like John Lewis, Wayne Shorter and Herbie Hancock welcomed him was the reception he got from the blacks doing the catering who held out their hands to him in awe."

As a twenty-one-year-old, Linx began work with him on the only CD that Baldwin ever made. On it he recites his poems, narrates and sings a Negro spiritual, *Precious Lord*. It was to become a magical mix of poetry and music—much more than a jazz recording.

"I remember we were sitting in the kitchen in David Baldwin's apartment in New York, at 97ᵗʰ Street and Amsterdam Avenue, where Jimmy had made his favorite peanut butter and grilled bacon sandwich. We discussed the idea of doing a CD together and took up the idea back in Saint-Paul de Vence. Soon after we got started in September 1986, I had to return to the United States. With my Belgian passport, I applied to the American Embassy in Brussels for a visa. I didn't try to hide what they already knew— that I was working on a CD with Baldwin. They stalled for a week without giving any reason. Jimmy had warned me that similar stuff was bound to happen and vaguely grinned at it. At the end of that week, the consul called me at my Belgian address and I could hear in his voice a little embarrassment as he apologized for the 'misunderstanding.' The American officials seemed very concerned and confused apparently about our making a record together.

"When the demo tapes were finished in September 1987, just before we were going to listen to them, Jimmy told me, 'Don't be nervous. It's like a baby, you have to deliver it right and then give it time to grow.' A broad toothy smile spread over his face as he heard the music. A few months later, Jimmy died."

Kalamu ya Salaam, besides directing the NOMMO Literary Society, also launched Runagate Press, which focuses on New Orleans and its African heritage, and runs e-Drum, an informational list service for black writers. He wrote a text for the booklet accompanying the CD, which he sent to me:

"James Baldwin voiced us—articulated black experiences with

a searing intensity. Even if you could not read, once you heard Baldwin, you were convinced of the power of words. His ability to move air was such that it spoke to us, proclaiming what it means to be flesh, and black.

"The gritty texture of Baldwin's voice testified to the realities of black life, the ups, the downs, the terrors, as well as the hard-worn tenderness found in our sometimes brief, but frequent stolen moments of exquisite love. He was no romantic, but oh how he loved. He loved us all and gave his all in the love of us.

"It is easy to think of Baldwin as an Old Testament prophet, raining down fire and brimstone. He was, after all, a professional evangelist as a teen. It is easy to think of Baldwin as a Shakespeare in and of Harlem since his command of language is now legendary. But it is wrong to reference Baldwin solely from outside of black culture. Think of this black voice as a black life-force, as the sound of us, as the sound of living, as a drum. A drum, an insistent beating drum, whose rhythm was synchronous with our heartbeats.

"The fullest appreciation of James Baldwin the writer is not understood until James Baldwin the voice is heard. Once your heart was moved by the way this man moved words can you understand that the power he brought, the fire he brought was no mere mental exercise, that Baldwin was indeed an elemental force of nature. Baldwin was full of passion and the very fire light of life. To reduce him simply to books is to miss the music that this man made of words."

In interpreting the essence of this unique CD, the two-part "A Lover's Question," Kalamu ya Salaam describes "A masterpiece of merging words with music, a precursor to what is now a popular art form . . . In the vein of *The Fire Next Time,* Baldwin questions the citizens of his birth nation as to their desire to hate:

Why
have you allowed
yourself
to become so grimly
wicked

No man can have a

Harlot
for a lover
nor stay in bed forever
with a lie
He must rise up
and face the morning
sky
and himself, in the
mirror
of his lover's eye.

As Baldwin knew, true love is always honest even though honesty is seldom an easy fact to live with a land where lies and commerce replace truth and reciprocity. . . .

"The concluding number, the three-part 'Inventory/On Being 52,' is the introspective of Baldwin fingering his own wounds (some of them self-inflicted). He does not flinch as he cross-examines his own life and realizes the terrible costs of his mistakes, the terrible beauty of embracing both the terrors and joys of being human. Baldwin manages in a stream of consciousness style to encourage us to live the good life, suggesting that we not simply march to the beat of a different drummer, but to be the different drummer."

A poem Jimmy wrote for Linx is reproduced in the booklet:
3.00 am
(for David)
Two black boots,
on the floor,
figuring out what the walking's for.
Two black boots,
now, together,
learning the price of the stormy weather.
To say nothing of the wear and tear
on
the mother-f------ leather.

Two years earlier, in 1985, Jimmy had written a poem which he titled, "Gypsy," as a gift to David on his twentieth birthday.

Chapter 12

Black English: *Own Language*

Besides black music, black language was important to Baldwin. He penned an extensive proposition entitled, "If Black English Isn't a Language, Then Tell Me, What Is?," published with his byline, datelined St.-Paul de Vence, France, on the op-ed page of *The New York Times* on July 29, 1979.

Baldwin expounded on the influence of Black English on American language use. He wondered what white Americans would sound like if there had never been black people. Some of the examples he gave were jazz, like in "jazz me baby," a very sexual term for blacks purified by white people into the Jazz Age. "Let it all hang out" and "right on" phrases used without qualms by whites are actually explicit sexual terms in Black English.

Baldwin remarked also how the term for despairing poverty among blacks, "beat to his socks," turned into the Beat Generation, a group of middle-class white people imitating poverty, doing their thing and trying desperately to be funky. Baldwin said blacks never did that sort of thing. They were just naturally funky.

He went on to say that Black English was the creation of the black diaspora—chained to each other but not able to speak each other's language. Perhaps if they had, the institution of slavery might not have lasted as long as it did. He explained that Black English began with the formation of the black church because language comes into existence by brutal necessity and the rules are dictated by what must be conveyed.

Baldwin recalled that his own family used Black English to warn him of the danger of the white man behind him. They needed a language the white man could not understand and until this day he cannot afford to understand, since this would reveal too much about himself.

Educating black children, Baldwin thought, was not of any interest to white Americans, unless it served their purposes. It was not the black child's language in question and despised, but the experience of being black. The concern of Baldwin was that too many black children had been lost by educators trying to repudiate the fact of the child's blackness and send him or her into limbo where he will no longer be black but can never become white.

Baldwin had once said, "In Harlem, as a boy going to school, I felt myself an outsider. I knew a language different from the one teachers were trying to make me learn—the language of jazz, spirituals, the blues; the language of testifying and signifying; and the language of cool black cats, street kids, holding on to life by their fingernails while they heard their parents screaming up to their God in heaven, asking Him what's going on, and what's going to happen, and, when, oh Jesus, when?"

In one of Baldwin's essays, "This Nettle, Danger. . .," written in early 1964, he remarked, "My quarrel with the English language had been that the language reflected none of my experience. But now I began to see the matter in quite another way. If the language was not my own, it might be my fault. Perhaps the language was not my own because I had never attempted to use it, had only learned to imitate it. If this were so, then it might be made to bear the burden of my experience if I could find the stamina to challenge it, and me, to such a test."

Toni Morrison recognized her friend Jimmy's analysis of Black English, along with other texts, as having been of great significance in her writing, which she again stressed in her eulogy to him.

Chapter 13

Baldwin Anti-Semitic?:
Identification with Jews

James Baldwin was not anti-Semitic, despite remarks such as, "I'm black, I'm a Jew, so what else can you expect?" and other often preposterous comments. Judging by his own actions and attested to by many who knew him well, he often provoked to get reactions — but there was love — not prejudice.

Baldwin insisted all his life that he struggled to keep his heart "free from hatred and despair."

He retained lifelong relationships with his three closest high school pals — Richard Avedon, Emile Capouya, and Sol Stein — all of them Jewish. He always had many Jewish friends, agents, and editors.

At the start of his writing career, his first published full-length essay, *From the American Scene: The Harlem Ghetto: Winter 1948*, appeared in February in *Commentary*, a literary journal of the American Jewish Committee. The publication's editors, Elliot Cohen and Robert Warshow, encouraged him to frankly expose his theory on why blacks were anti-Semitic. The editors were ecstatic about the forthrightness and clarity of the article. Baldwin's text received national attention, which was heralded in future issues of *Commentary*, and led to commissions by other liberal media. *The Harlem Ghetto* was later incorporated in *Notes of a Native Son*.

Baldwin wrote:
. . . The traditional Christian accusation that the Jews killed Christ is neither questioned nor doubted, the term "Jew" actually operates in this initial context to include all infidels of white skin who have failed to accept the Saviour. No real distinction is made: the preacher begins by accusing the Jews of having refused the light and proceeds from there to a catalogue of their subsequent sins and the sufferings visited

on them by a wrathful God. Though the notion of the suffering is based on the image of the wandering, exiled Jew, the context changes imperceptibly, to become a fairly obvious reminder of the trials of the Negro, while the sins recounted are the sins of the American Republic.

"At this point the Negro identifies himself almost wholly with the Jew. The more devout Negro considers that he is a Jew, in bondage to a hard taskmaster and waiting for a Moses to lead him out of Egypt. The hymns, the texts, and the most favored legends of the devout Negro are all Old Testament and therefore Jewish in origin: the flight from Egypt, the Hebrew children in the fiery furnace, the terrible jubilee songs of deliverance. Lord, wasn't that hard trials, great tribulations, I'm bound to leave this land!

"The images of the suffering Christ and the suffering Jew are wedded with the image of the suffering slave, and they are one: the people that walked in darkness have seen a great light.

Underlining how widespread anti-Semitism was in this community, he concluded, "Just as a society must have a scapegoat, Georgia has the Negro and Harlem has the Jew."

Curiously, also in 1948, when Baldwin was contemplating his first escape from America, he seriously considered settling in Israel, the newly-founded Jewish state.

Only much later (in 1972) in an essay, "Take Me to the Water," did he write his reason for not becoming an expatriate in the Holy Land. "If I had fled to Israel, a state created for the purpose of protecting Western interests, I would have been in a yet tighter bind: on which side of Jerusalem would I have decided to live?" He made his position clear that he believed Israel represents imperialism, not Jewish self-determination, and expressed a lifelong support of the Palestinian state. (Note: he chose Paris in 1948 for his getaway.)

When the monthly black magazine, *Liberator,* published an article *Anti-Semitism in the Black Ghetto* (1967), which he had regarded as racist, he wrote a letter resigning immediately as an advisor on the editorial board. He felt the magazine practically instigated "war against the Jews." *Liberator,* founded in 1960, had been building up to anti-Semitism. It had gone from white baiting to baiting of moderate Negroes and finally to Jew baiting.

He described anti-Semitism as "the most ancient and barbaric of European myths, insisting that his name be removed from the masthead and his letter of condemnation published, which was not done. Only later did his letter appear in *Freedomways* in which he wrote, "It is immoral to blame Harlem on the Jews."

When Jews and anti-Semitism came up, Baldwin took bold stands.

The only open attack ever concerning anti-Semitism resulted from a forum he organized February 28, 1984 for over 200 students at the University of Massachusetts at Amherst as part of a course on "The History of the Civil Rights Movement." Baldwin handled questions and objectively led a discussion about the presidential candidate, Reverend Jesse Jackson, who had used the terms "Hymie" and "Hymietown" in referring to Jews and to New York City.

True to form, Baldwin faced the issue head-on, defending Jackson but openly critical of Jackson's use of derogatory terms. Subsequently, he was accused of anti-Semitism by a colleague, longtime friend and supporter, a former black activist, Julius Lester, who converted to Judaism and also called himself Yaakov Daniel Lester. Son of a Methodist minister, with a maternal German Jewish grandfather, he was professor of Afro-American and Judaic studies at the University of Massachusetts.

Curiously, Baldwin had made another provocative remark in the course of that same February forum, saying that Jews are nothing more than "white Christians who go to something called a synagogue on Saturday rather than a church on Sunday." While Lester was also shocked by this comment, it had passed quietly without any uproar.

Baldwin let the media maelstrom provoked by Lester's critical attack for his alleged remarks of anti-Semitism roll off his shoulders. He put the ugly American confrontation behind him and returned to his accustomed Provençal tranquility. He was dead in 1988, when the case was closed with an official university publication underscoring Baldwin's total clearance and the relegation of Lester to the Judaic studies department after being fired from the Afro-American program.

(Baldwin was honored with a Certificate of Recognition from the National Council of Christians and Jews in 1961. Baldwin always identified with Jews. There was never any question of anti-Semitism. However, he frowned upon Zionism and the state of Israel which he viewed as an encroachment that was unjustified for the Arabs.)

Chapter 14

Baldwin Anti-Christian?:
Disenchantment

Had the ex-preacher and stepson of a preacher lost faith?

"There was no love in the church," James Baldwin wrote. "It was a mask for self-hatred and despair. The transfiguring power of the Holy Ghost ended when the service ended, and salvation stopped at the church door. When we were told to love everybody, I had thought that meant everybody. But no. It applied only to those who believed, as we did, and it did not apply to white people at all. " (He was then seventeen.)

Though he was a preacher at the age of fourteen, Baldwin later turned away from the church. James Campbell noted that Jimmy's school friend, Emile Capouya, had told him, when he was sixteen and undergoing a crisis of faith, that it was cowardly to remain in the church only because he was afraid to leave it. "Capouya said that Baldwin was 'in the church but not of it' and 'it was socially impossible for him to leave the church.' When the young minister finally summoned the courage to pry himself away, it was with Capouya's help.

In 1962, Baldwin wrote in *The Fire Next Time*, "Whoever wishes to become a truly moral human being must first divorce himself from all the prohibitions, crimes and hypocrisy of the Christian church. If the concept of God has any validity or any use, it can only be to make us larger, freer, and more loving. If God cannot do this, then it is time to get rid of Him."

Through the ensuing years right up to his death, Baldwin insisted he was not a believer in the traditional manner with a special faith or church. His bible of religious conviction resounded from old black gospel music.

Though Baldwin based much of his style and content of his

work on Baptist theology, he spoke bitterly about Christianity. In an interview he professed, "Much of the scourge of the non-white world has been accomplished under the cloak of the Church. Now, blacks are beginning to understand, beginning to get to the bottom of things." In a reference to the black intellectual's disenchantment with Christianity, he concluded, "We have begun to see the nature of a hoax."

Douglas Field is professor of English, American Studies and Creative Writing at the University of Manchester, United Kingdom. He has written, edited and contributed to numerous books on James Baldwin, his latest being *All Those Strangers: The Art and Lives of James Baldwin,* Oxford University Press (2015). He is a co-founding editor of *The James Baldwin Review,* an annual peer-reviewed online journal published by the Manchester University Press.

In recognition of his Baldwin expertise and specialization, I phoned Douglas Field for his contribution to this book. He proposed citing from *"Pentecostalism and All That Jazz: Tracing James Baldwin's Religion,"* his text in *Literature & Theology* published by Oxford University Press (December 2008). Field insists that "Baldwin's Pentecostal background is central to understanding of his complicated views on Christianity, illuminating the connection in his work between music and the church.

"Baldwin's writing was shaped by key features of Pentecostalism, a marginalized denomination that has actively encouraged a move away from traditional Protestanism, seeking what believers see as a purer or more authentic spirituality. By contextualizing Baldwin's anti-institutional views in a Pentecostal framework, I show that Baldwin, while rejecting religion (the institution), maintained the importance of spirituality, something not predicated or even enabled by the structure of the church.

According to Field, ". . . as late as 1985, in the introduction to *The Price of the Ticket*, Baldwin confessed that 'once I had left the pulpit, I had abandoned or betrayed my role in the community,' a clear indication of the church's continued hold on him. A closer examination of his 'secular' texts, such as *The Evidence of Things Not Seen,* reveal glimpses of his continued fascination with religion.

(The title, *The Evidence of Things Not Seen*, came from the epistle of St. Paul: "Faith is the substance of things he hoped for, the evidence of things not seen.")

Field also mentioned Baldwin's "calling attention to the historical inequality of suffering between white and black Christians.... Writing over twenty years after *Fire* in his last published article ("To Crush the Serpent"), Baldwin again returned to this theme, expressing his 'profound and troubled contempt' for white Christians who invoked the curse of Ham to justify the slavery.... Baldwin's early realisation in *The Fire Next Time* that the 'Bible had been written by white men and that it had been used to justify slavery.' There was the so-called 'white lie' of Christianity that by persuading slaves that 'life on earth was insignificant because obedient servants of God could expect a *reward* in heaven after death,' the (white) church was complicit in attempts to deter and contain black insurrection and rebellion.

"In his last two novels, *If Beale Street Could Talk* and *Just Above My Head*, Baldwin repeatedly criticizes those who surrender agency to what is increasingly depicted as an ineffectual religion. Not only did Baldwin rail against white Christianity, stating that 'I became a Christian by not imitating white people,' but also all institutionalized religion is viewed as hypocritical and ineffectual. Echoing the early Pentecostal ideology, Baldwin told Margaret Mead in their *Rap on Race* that 'the Christian church is meaningless. The Christian church as church'. Field concluded, "In a vehement outburst against the church, Baldwin stressed that 'in order to become a moral human being.... I have to hang out with the publicans and sinners, whores and junkies, and stay out of the temple where they told us nothing but lies anyway.'"

It was evident that in Baldwin's critical stance about Christianity in *Beale Street*, he was simultaneously insisting on a redefinition of the church's role and actions. Even with shades of his earlier fire-and-brimstone preacherly tone in his prose, his relationship with the church remained ambiguous.

Late in his life, during a light-hearted repartee with the TV talk show host, Dick Cavett, Baldwin told him, in all seriousness, that you "can't trust the Christian church."

Chapter 15

The Paris Review: Literary Dialogue

When Jordan Elgrably interviewed Baldwin for *The Paris Review* (Spring 1984) in the house in Saint-Paul he was accompanied by George Plimpton. (Actually, Baldwin was one of the founders of this august literary magazine, along with Plimpton and others, in 1953.)

He wrote: "Saturday, a storm raged amid intolerable heat and humidity, causing Baldwin's minor case of arthritis to pain his writing hand (left) and wrist. Erratic power shortages caused by the storm interrupted the tape machine by our side. . . . Returning Sunday at Baldwin's invitation, the sun was shining and we were able to lunch outdoors at a picnic table, shaded by a bower that opened onto property dotted with fruit trees and a spectacular view of the Mediterranean littoral. Baldwin's mood had lightened considerably since the previous day, and we entered the office and study he refers to as his 'torture chamber.'

"Baldwin writes in longhand ('you achieve shorter declarative sentences') on the standard legal pad, although a large, old Adler electric typewriter sits on one end of his desk—a rectangular oak plank with rattan chairs on either side. It is piled with writing utensils and drafts of several works-in-progress: a novel, a play, a scenario, essays on the Atlanta child murders, these last compiled in *The Evidence of Things Not Seen*. His most recent work includes *The Devil Finds Work*, an attack on racial bias and fear in the film industry, and a novel, *Just Above My Head*, which draws on his experiences as a civil rights activist in the 1960s."

One of the questions *Paris Review* posed: Was there an instant you knew you were going to write, to be a writer rather than anything else?

Baldwin: Yes. The death of my father. Until my father died I thought

I could do something else. I had wanted to be a musician, thought of being a painter, thought of being an actor. This was all before I was nineteen. Given the conditions in this country to be a black writer was impossible. When I was young, people thought you were not so much wicked as sick, they gave up on you. My father didn't think it was possible—he thought I'd get killed, get murdered. He said I was contesting the white man's definitions. He was a pious, very religious and in some ways a very beautiful man, and in some ways a terrible man. He died when his last child was born and I realized I had to make a jump—a leap. I'd been a preacher for three years, from age fourteen to seventeen. Those were three years which probably turned me to writing.

Elgrably: Were the sermons you delivered from the pulpit very carefully prepared, or were they absolutely off the top of your head?

Baldwin: I would improvise from the texts, like a jazz musician improvises from a theme. I never wrote a sermon—I studied the texts. I can't read a speech. It's kind of give-and-take. You have to sense the people you're talking to. You have to respond to what you hear.

Elgrably: Do you have a reader in mind when you write?

Baldwin: No, you can't have that.

Elgrably: So, it's quite unlike preaching?

Baldwin: Entirely. The two roles are completely unattached. When you are standing in the pulpit, you must sound as though you know what you're talking about. When you're writing, you're trying to find out something which you don't know. The whole language of writing for me is finding out what you don't want to know, what you don't want to find out. But something forces you anyway.

Elgrably: If you felt that it was a white man's world, what made you think that there was any point in writing?

Baldwin: Because they own the business. Well, in retrospect, what it came down to was that I would not allow myself to be defined by other people, white or black. It was beneath me to blame anybody for what happened to me. What happened to me was my responsibility. I didn't want any pity. 'Leave me alone, I'll figure it out. . .'

Elgrably: Is there any resistance today to black writers in publishing houses?

Baldwin: There is enormous resistance, though it differs from Wright's time. When I was young, the joke was 'How many niggers you got at your plantation?' Or, more snidely, 'How many niggers you got at your publishing house?' And some had one, most had none. That's not true today.

Elgrably: How does it strike you that in many circles James Baldwin is known as a prophetic writer?

Baldwin: I don't try to be prophetic, as I don't sit down to write literature. It is simply this: a writer has to take all the risks of putting down what he sees. No one can tell him about that. No one can control the reality. It reminds me of something Picasso was supposed to have said to Gertrude Stein while he was painting her portrait. Gertrude said, 'I don't look like that.' And Picasso replied, 'You will.' And he was right.

Chapter 16

Finale: *Last Chapters*

James Baldwin published his conclusive anthology of essays in September 1985.

The Price of the Ticket: Collected Non-Fiction, 1948-1985, along with its tribute to Beauford Delaney, focuses on almost four decades of writing.

Pulling together articles published in magazines during nearly forty years might have appeared to be a cry for literary attention and approval but this compendium of "collected non-fiction" was seen by some critics as a revisiting and a realization of how contemporary his message was in the discourse of race relations in America.

The Price of the Ticket

In *The Price of the Ticket*, there were references to his truth and insight in these prophetic works. He was credited with detailing his hopes, his joys, his bitterness and his feelings about himself and other blacks and especially white America.

In Baldwin's powerful concluding paragraph of the book's introduction, his personal experience dominated his examination of social interaction between the races during that period:

"The price the white American paid for his ticket was to become white—and, in the main, nothing more than that, or, as he was to insist, nothing less. This incredibly limited not to say dim-witted ambition has choked many a human being to death here: and this, I contend, is because the white American has never accepted the real reason for his journey. I know very well that my ancestors had no desire to come to this place; but neither did the ancestors of the people who became white and who require of my captivity a song. They require of me a song less to celebrate my captivity than to justify their own."

Baldwin's late biographer, W. J. Weatherby, headlined his critique, "Art and Struggle/Review of The Price of the Ticket," in *The Guardian* (Books December 5, 1985). His appraisal read:

> If *The Price of the Ticket* had been published in the Sixties, the American book reviews would have been front page news. But Mr. Baldwin—like the civil rights movement whose laureate he was—is no longer fashionable, and the influential *New York Times Book Review* gave this collection of essays written over nearly forty years only a fat paragraph on an inside page.
> Yet this 690-page giant is the closest we will probably get to a Baldwin autobiography. It traces his extraordinary development from boy preacher and teenage friend of a Harlem racketeer to the grim prophet of *The Fire Next Time* and the sombre paternal figure he has now become.
> 'A very tight, tense, lean, abnormally intelligent, and hungry black cat' was the way he described himself in 1961. Now twenty-four years later he is more aware of 'that merciless tribunal I carry around on my own head', which doesn't get you invited on TV talk shows.
> It was a taste of failure in late life that must have been very bitter for that 'abnormally ambitious' black cat. It is greatly to Mr. Baldwin's credit that he persisted along his unpopular course as the messenger with bad news, for it has probably cost him a Nobel Prize.

Following publication of *The Price of the Ticket* critics began to re-evaluate Baldwin's early essays as a significant contribution to the discourse of gender and problematic race relations in the United States. He was lauded for his personal and prophetic writing which in retrospect reflected his eloquence and wisdom in handling at the time those highly sensitive subjects.

The Evidence of Things Not Seen

Six years after his last work of fiction, *Just Above My Head*, had had a disappointing reception, publication of *The Evidence of Things Not Seen* (1985) did nothing to explain the long literary hiatus and the absence of another novel.

Baldwin's 6,000-word article for *Playboy* on his investigation of the unsolved children's murder in Atlanta, was stretched into a 60,000-word book length essays as a padded and not very successful adaptation of that magazine account. There was not much new added.

He had a great deal of difficulty in finding a publisher and he blamed "political sources" for his dilemma. While awkwardly constructed, it did, however, underscore his commitment to seeking racial justice. Press criticism was generally unenthusiastic. The book's title is a reference to the definition of faith from the *Epistle to the Hebrews 11:1*. His dedication of the work reads: "to David Baldwin, the father and the son."

Publishers Weekly (October 31, 1985) wrote, "Often Baldwin is vivid and powerful, as when recalling the terrors of his Harlem boyhood and imagining poor black Atlanta children stepping into strangers' cars: 'To be poor and black in a country so rich and white is to judge oneself very harshly and it means that one has nothing to lose.' Black Atlanta (its officials, the victims and the defendants) provides a point of departure for Baldwin's ruinations on deep and familiar concerns, but this book lacks the impact of his earlier works."

Soon after *Harlem Quartet* was published as a French translation of *Just Above My Head* in 1987, his trusted photographer friend, Alain Cinquini, used the occasion following lunch at the Baldwin house in mid-September of that year, with a dedicated copy in hand, to interrogate him about his writing. This was shortly before the author's decline in health and subsequent death that year. Cinquini gave me a copy of the interview which was conducted in French for publication in *Thémes*. Some excerpts:

Cinquini: Aren't your novels actually your memoirs?
Baldwin: One could say so. You could say that if you wish. One could say, *voilà* Jimmy is in the book. I, myself, could never pinpoint it. I am in all the characters. And in none. I am everywhere and nowhere. Finally it's that. It isn't directly identifiable. There are many reasons which force you to write a novel. It's complex. You are obliged to correct all the time. Everyone has an image of who you are. It's like a mirror, but the image in the mirror is never right. You are obliged to act as if you know much less than you imagine. And if you pretend to know everything, that is false. You just don't know.
Cinquini: Americans compare you to Hemingway. This celebrity

serves you as the activist you are—not a political activist or a sectarian—but more an activist because of who you are.

Baldwin: Yes, it's as simple as that.

Cinquini: Does this international reputation make people listen more to what you have to say?

Baldwin: I don't know if it works that way. It does help no doubt.

Cinquini: Is it dangerous?

Baldwin: There is, of course, some real danger, but it is unavoidable. The danger is being a spokesman, of speaking, of doing lectures, giving conferences. But one must find a way to tell the truth. And you cannot not tell the truth. . . .not lie. And that is very tiring. And almost nothing changes. Within the framework of the Civil Rights Movement, from the sixties until today, not much has changed. We humans don't change much either. There is not only the human nature; there is some type of huge fight.

Baldwin: I have no idea . . . love is what they say.

Chapter 17

Celebrity: *Star Status*

James Baldwin claimed he never wanted to be a celebrity. He made the distinction of being an artist rather than a celebrity. In hindsight, Baldwin felt with all his handicaps, real or imagined, he would not have survived in obscurity. He might not have seen it coming but knew it had to happen.

James Baldwin clearly savored the aura that envelops a celebrity. He enjoyed to the hilt being recognized, photographed, hounded for autographs, hanging out with other celebrities, being fawned over, getting seated in sold-out restaurants and benefitting from all the prestigious perks of being recognizably well-known. This was the glamorous side of the coin. Being a successful author, the spotlight was always on him.

"Jimmy was the kind of celebrity who was made 'famous' by the media," according to Caryl Phillips. "He never turned down an interview or a photo session. The *Time* cover celebrating his fame as a successful author early in his career helped him on the way to instant recognition everywhere in the years that followed. Jimmy was never happier than when he found himself in the company of other 'stars,' particularly actors. His friends included Richard Burton, Burt Lancaster, Marlon Brando, Sidney Poitier and Yves Montand, to name but a handful.

"He talked constantly of helping his younger brother David to 'make it' as an actor, and to this end he even announced that he would be 'adapting' Othello so that David might take the starring role. But David, not Jimmy. The older brother was by this time a different type of actor, the type that the American media creates out of sportsmen, politicians and, of course, writers. He was a star, which involved being in possession of and cultivating all the skills of an actor, in timing, posture and delivery. And in this Jimmy was a natural. There was much his actor friends might have learned from him."

Phillips recalled a wonderful anecdote which underscored Jimmy's laid-back acceptance of his celebrity status. "Perhaps my warmest memory of Jimmy is lunching with him at La Colombe d'Or in Saint-Paul de Vence. It was a beautiful Provençal afternoon. Heads turned as Jimmy walked into the restaurant. We took a table on the terrace. The waitress approached. She knew Jimmy well. After all, he was a local celebrity and this was his regular hangout.

"But she had been asked to put a question to Jimmy, a question which—as it transpired—was being asked by two women seated some tables away, two women who were the highly visible wives of two movie stars. Clearly they were taken with Jimmy. The waitress cleared her throat. She was embarrassed, but she was also trying not to laugh. 'The two ladies, they would like to know if you are the gentleman who played piano in *Casablanca*.' Jimmy smiled broadly. 'Tell them, yes.'"

When Robert Lantz, his former agent, was in Saint-Paul on a visit with Jimmy, he remarked that "he had become a giant figure, a bigger celebrity than a movie star; a man generally admired."

While Norman Mailer, with his characteristic sardonic sarcasm, regularly vented his ambivalent relationship with Baldwin concerning their literary and sexual pursuits, on one occasion he added another poisonous potion in describing his 'friend': "He decided to be a celebrity instead of a writer and that's what he is now."

During the earlier-mentioned "Reflections of a Maverick" interview, Julius Lester also questioned Baldwin's celebrity. The author responded, "The idea of becoming an artist as distinguished from a celebrity was real. I never wanted to be a celebrity."

Phillips also spoke about Jimmy's theatrical character and his penchant for the movies. As a young teenager, he wanted to be a performer, went into the pulpit, retreating to read and write, dreaming of being on stage. He related how excited he had been at the prospect of starring in a proposed documentary about his life. After that project collapsed, he convinced the BBC to honor Baldwin on his upcoming 60th birthday in 1984.

Phillips gave me a copy of *A New World Order*, a collection of his selected essays, which included "The Lure of Hollywood" about Jimmy's fascination for the cinema.

Phillips wrote, "I first met James Baldwin in the summer of 1983 in the south of France. My task was to try to persuade him to participate in a major documentary about his life and work, which would be filmed in the United States, France, Turkey and Britain. Jimmy (it was impossible to address him as James—in fact, he would not hear of it) looked across at me and his eyes lit up. 'The movies, baby. So we're gonna make a picture.' In fact, we never made the 'picture.'

"Some months later we came to film a twenty-minute interview for BBC-TV. When we got together in the main village square in Saint-Paul de Vence, the BBC producer who accompanied me asked him if he thought that he would ever win the Nobel Prize. I was embarrassed by this question but, as generous as ever, Jimmy laughed, then took a languorous draw from his cigarette, smiled and said, 'they'll probably get round to giving it to me some day.' But that smile was a knowing smile. We spent the next three days tape-recording our conversations, the results of which were eventually edited down into a BBC radio documentary.

"It was during the course of this hot Provençal summer that I discovered both the extent of Jimmy's boundless generosity and the fact that my initial hunch was correct. Indeed, Jimmy did want to be in the movies. And, although almost sixty by then, he continued to nurture a long-held desire to see his work on the cinema screen.

"The evidence of Baldwin's writing, in both fiction and nonfiction, suggests a special love for the cinema.... Baldwin's much underrated book on film, *The Devil Finds Work*, makes it clear that Baldwin's love for the cinema was almost as intense as his love for words. In fact, Baldwin discovered the cinema before he discovered books, and he never forgot the impact that these early movies had upon him.

"I knew long before I met James Baldwin that he wanted to be involved in the movies. I don't believe that I ever heard him mention in any interview that he harbored such a desire, but through the public window of his life I espied a man who positively adored the attention of the media. He could, in the early sixties, claim to be one of the most photographed, and certainly one of the most recognizable, men in the world. He peered darkly and mysteriously into the lens of any proffered camera. His face had adorned the cover of *Time* magazine and his eyes beamed out from the dust jackets of his widely translated, best-selling books. But there is a special celebrity which only the movies can bestow and it seemed to me that Baldwin positively yearned for it.

"During the final years of his life, the years when I got to know him, Jimmy's conversation was littered with anecdotes about film. He spoke to me about the time Louis Farrakhan threatened him physically if he were not cast to play Malcolm X in the film of *One Day When I Was Lost*. He spoke about his friend Simone Signoret ['Do you know Simone?']. About Marlon and his neighbor, Donald Pleasence ['Nice men.']. Marlon Brando ['Marlon and I were never lovers. We should have been, but we never were.']. He loved to tell anecdotes about his movie friends, some of which I already knew from the film essay, *The Devil Finds Work*.

"To see his two loves, movies and books, fused together was, I believe, one of the great ambitions of his life. I'm sure that if pressed, Jimmy would have admitted that he craved an Oscar almost as much as he did a Pulitzer. Yet he found a way to participate vicariously in the cinema and he certainly found a way to live the glamorous lifestyle of its leading actors. But—and this is to his great credit—despite his many frustrations and disappointments, not all of which, by any means, could be attributed to his disdain for legal paperwork, Jimmy never lost his innocent pleasure in the cinema."

In late November 1987, the ailing, bedridden Jimmy turned to David Leeming—who had flown over to Saint-Paul from New York to be with his old friend during his last days—and said, "Sometimes I can't believe that I'm famous too." Leeming concluded, "He was seeking confirmation that he had indeed embarked on the road to fame and had successfully reached his destination, though he was heartbroken, recognizing that he had paid a heavy price and bore the indignity of publisher rejections, hurtful reviews and falling sales during the last years of his career. Baldwin died three days later."

Chapter 18

Going Downhill: *Ill Health*

At my request, Dr. Roger Boizard — Jimmy's longtime confidant and general practitioner in earlier days — had asked his colleagues who succeeded him if they would share their personal anecdotes and memories in treating such a special patient like James Baldwin. I assured them that I did not desire any confidential medical information. There were Dr. Joseph Benichou and Dr. Christian Camel, both of whom had treated Jimmy during his last years, as well as Dr. Boizard.

A distinguished cardiologist, Dr. Benichou, who came to France in 1958 from his native Algeria, has his office in the neighboring town of Vence. He made regular calls at Jimmy's house in Saint-Paul during the last two or three years of the author's life to treat him for high blood pressure and heart irregularity.

"On my first visit there, Bernard welcomed me, letting me know with a certain arrogance who I would be treating. 'You know, he's a very important writer.' Whenever I came, there was a certain ritual to be followed. I rang the bell and Bernard opened the gate with great ceremony. He had me wait while he went to Jimmy's room to be certain he was ready to receive me and then accompanied me to his room. I must say Baldwin didn't make a doctor's work difficult. He was, what we call *un bon malade* [a good patient]. He understood I was trying to help him. We only talked about unimportant, everyday things — never about his books. Our relationship remained purely medical, very professional. He was small, thin and realized he was fragile. He wasn't rebellious but accepted the situation as it was."

Baldwin, suffering and frail, felt depressed and insecure. Despite numerous projects on the table, he was not writing. He was keenly

aware that, although not forgotten, he had had his day as the most
eminent black writer following in the footsteps of Ralph Ellison and
Richard Wright. The generation who succeeded him was now in the
spotlight. He was respectfully regarded as a kind of *éminence grise,*
someone who had made his mark but was no longer newsworthy,
more a historical figure.

Besides his cardiac problems, Jimmy's throat irritation had
become increasingly painful. For Bernard and Valérie, his condition
was worrisome. He was not their old Jimmy. With his *joie de vivre*
gone, he had no interest in completing the pending projects or
having a companion, no appetite for food, no thirst for a drink or a
cigarette. He admitted having a great problem swallowing but was
too depressed to see a doctor. Over his continued protests, Valérie
nevertheless phoned Dr. Christian Camel to come immediately.
Besides his throat being obstructed, Jimmy was also suffering from
a severe pain in his back.

The amiable, easy-going general practitioner had arrived in
Saint-Paul in 1977. Dr. Camel spoke with fondness about Jimmy
not only as a patient but as a close family friend. Since Jimmy was
always attracted to creative people, the fact that the doctor was also
an accomplished sculptor fostered a special bond.

"Starting in the early '80s, I was always called by Jimmy to treat
everyone staying in his house but never for himself. That came
later. When I arrived he was always happy to leave his typewriter,
have a drink with me and talk. He often came to dinner and became
part of the family, tenderly embracing my wife and children. They
all loved him as I did. We were also invited to his house for meals
and parties.

"My professional calls for Jimmy himself really only started in
earnest when he began suffering so many aches and pains. On
one visit, I found him in bed with a man but he was nonplussed.
Nothing was said and we proceeded normally. He never flaunted
his homosexual behavior, never hid it, nor spoke about it. He was
not boisterous and didn't talk at all about his alcoholism. He drank
a glass at his own rhythm so he could write. My calls became more
and more frequent. Sometimes he made grim jokes that his heavy

smoking could give him cancer or his heavy drinking would result in cirrhosis of the liver.

"When I got to the house following Valérie's call on April 1, 1987, after examining him, I knew immediately that he required further diagnosis and had him moved without delay to the hospital in Nice. The tests showed that he had cancer of the esophagus. He was given laser treatment which enabled him to swallow and eased his pain. On April 25th he entered a private cancer clinic, the Institut Arnault Tzanck in Saint-Laurent-du-Var. Jimmy was on the operating table for six hours. He was told by the surgeon, Dr. Jean-Claude Bertrand, that he would recuperate but needed one month for each hour under anesthetic. This was a positive prognosis considering that 30 percent of the patients generally don't survive the operation.

"After Jimmy was brought home, I visited him almost every day. Usually he wore a red cap and was wrapped up in a big scarf. He was always cold. He was much more than a patient to me. One of my saddest memories of Jimmy was his birthday party at his home in 1987. There must have been one hundred people there. It was tragic to see this great man, with so many great qualities, very thin and obviously in decline."

Despite the cancer specialist's "good news" to Jimmy, actually his future was grim. The medical team had pulled Bernard aside to tell him frankly that when removing the esophagus they found that the cancer had spread and had also reached the liver which no longer functioned. He had maximum nine months to live—but probably wouldn't make Christmas. They would prescribe light pain killers so he could at least enjoy the summer convalescing in the sun, perhaps with some slight improvement. Bernard wrote to David Baldwin who came from New York immediately to help take care of his brother.

Faced with the somber prognosis, David wanted to level with Jimmy as they had done with each other all their lives. Bernard Hassell, Lucien Happersberger and David Leeming—three of Jimmy's closest friends—convinced him to let Jimmy enjoy what time still remained without his knowing the truth. They would keep the situation secret except for the immediate family to avoid an avalanche of friends and lovers. People could stop by as they usually did so that everything would seem "normal."

David Linx, often at Jimmy's side, recalls, "I never saw him dying. There was always life in his eyes. Since he had arthritis in both arms and hands, and also in his legs, I used to massage his hands so that he could work. He once told me, 'I never had time to take my suffering seriously. Only rich people have time for psychiatrists.' Jimmy was worried that he wouldn't finish his work. Earlier he sensed something was wrong, life in general, but he looked death straight in the eye. When he was sick, he stopped smoking and drinking but in his frustration I saw him throw an orange against the wall when Valérie brought him breakfast in bed. He grew calmer when he listened to Ray Charles and Aretha Franklin singing gospel."

During the summer, Dr. Camel insisted that there should be fewer visitors since Baldwin required rest. Recognizing that he had to use this period to recuperate, Jimmy planned to stay in Saint-Paul. He canceled all travel and other commitments and expected to be fully recovered by the end of the year. But in fact, he became steadily weaker with excruciating pain, using a cane as support when he walked. He talked continually about all the works he still had to finish—a novel, the play and the triple biography of Martin Luther King, Jr., Malcolm X and Medgar Evers. He didn't have the energy to write.

"On July 4, 1987, he penned two important letters, one to Walter Dallas and one to Cynthia Packard," according to David Leeming. "In the letter to Dallas he spoke of his sense of his own life. His 'hopes' had sometimes turned to 'ashes' or 'poison,' but he had no 'real regrets.' The 'awful' thing was the fact that it took so much time 'to learn so little' . . . To Cynthia, Baldwin wrote about the 'journey' that he was undergoing. As he experienced 'the stillness at the center' of the night, he said, he listened to the darkness and felt that 'something' was 'listening to me.'" (Walter Dallas was the black producer of *The Amen Corner* in Baltimore. Cynthia Packard was a teaching assistant and later a lecturer in the African-American

Studies faculty at the University of Massachusetts. She helped Baldwin with arranging things and shared her house in Amherst with him when he was at the school. Theirs was a very special bond—a warm, loving relationship, paramount to being married, or as close as he would ever get to it.)

Leeming continued, "To himself he wrote something less optimistic, a journal entry which he took the trouble to type on a new typewriter that he had bought to be used by a part-time typist during the early summer. He wrote of the 'small cell' which was 'despair' and of how it could be 'the death of love.' He worried that he was 'mean,' even 'spiteful,' that his liver was 'diseased,' and wondered what he should do next.

Leeming said: "Jimmy had written me on August 11 referring to his operation but indicating he would get better; he had, after all, never been told that his tumor was malignant. He spoke of being sixty-three, of having lost weight, and of how much he longed for a drink and a cigarette. Convalescence was possible to bear only when one thought about the 'alternative—Andy Warhol!' It was humbling to have to accept the fact that one's self-image was a myth."

Baldwin had suggested that since it was not possible for him to travel, would Leeming consider going as his emissary to interview the widows of Evers, Malcolm X and King, while he was anxious to get on with *Remember This House*. Not realizing how grave his situation was, Leeming replied that he would come at a later date and Jimmy could do the interviews himself next year.

A friend who lived nearby and came regularly for long talks with Jimmy was the American artist, Fred Nall Hollis, who prefers to be known by his artist's signature, Nall. When Pitou Roux introduced me to Nall, she told me that he had a very special relationship with Baldwin. Indeed, Nall, an unabashed admirer of Baldwin, was at his bedside early in the last evening, massaging Jimmy's feet and conversing in what had become an ongoing mutual confession during the final weeks. Nall had become closest to him soon after having heard of his serious illness.

When Nall was a student of Salvador Dali in Paris in the early

'70s, he was a casual acquaintance of Jimmy's at the Café Flore. "I was young and cute. He bought me drinks," Nall recalled in an interview. The Alabama-born painter and sculptor moved in 1985 to Vence, settling in the studio where Jean Dubuffet had painted. He bought the property housing the Fondation Karolyi, which had been created in 1959 by Catherine Karolyi, widow of the first president of the Republic of Hungary, and it became the Fondation Nall, a residence for writers, painters and musicians. "I named one of the cabins after Jimmy, the James Baldwin Cabin, and placed writers there."

Nall told me there were conversations such as, "Through your books you liberated me from my guilt about being so bigoted coming from Alabama and because of my homosexuality. Jimmy would insist, 'No, you liberated me in revealing this to me.' I remember explaining to him that I was raised as a racist. My grandmother was the campaign manager for George Wallace. My father was an outspoken racist. Only on his deathbed did my father tell me that he had black and Cherokee Indian blood, which was a big burden for him. In retaliation for being ostracized, he managed to marry into the most important family in town. We were brought up with this hatred for blacks in our hearts. My sister married a black from Venezuela just to get revenge on the family.

"Jimmy was so forgiving, so gentle, he had no bitterness personally in contrast to the hardness in his books. He talked about his writing and I understood that he was not an angry man, but one full of love—older, greying, dying. Jimmy remembered going on the Freedom March in Selma, Alabama with his brother David and being so afraid there. He knew the hateful state where I grew up with all the WASP Southern country club privileges and a damaged soul. I was a disgrace in those high circles since I rejected their values and prejudices and had a boyfriend. When I told Jimmy I was living with my secretary, a young Canadian boy, he said, 'In our society we all do what we find normal. There should not be criticism of anyone.'"

Chapter 19

The Last Interview: *A Tribute*

Gloria Baldwin advised my contacting Quincy Troupe, Jr., a well-known African-American writer and old friend of Jimmy. He was helped and encouraged by Baldwin throughout his writing career. He is a journalist, performance artist, professor emeritus at the University of California, San Diego, at La Jolla; and editor of *Black Renaissance*, a literary journal of the Institute of African Studies at New York University.

Troupe is an award-winning author of nineteen books, including ten volumes of poetry, three children's books and six fiction works. He authored the biography, *James Baldwin: The Legacy* and co-authored *Miles Davis: The Autobiography* and *Miles and Me* [translated into French as *Miles, l'Autobiograhie and Miles et Moi*], which had numerous references to the extremely close relationship Davis had with Baldwin.

He came from Harlem to Saint-Paul for an interview when he heard that Jimmy was ill. November 13 and 14, 1987 turned out to be the last interview Baldwin would give, a fortnight before he died.

Troupe recalled: "I conducted my interview with Jimmy over a period of two days, whenever his physical condition allowed, and our conversations ranged over a variety of literary and political topics. He could not finish our last session because of overwhelming pain."

Troupe realized this would be the last opportunity for Jimmy to air his final thoughts and observations. "Although that was what I had hoped to do, I hadn't really expected the situation to be as grave as it was."

The flame went out on December 1st. Troupe. published "Last

Testament: An Interview with James Baldwin" in the *Village Voice* (January 12, 1988). Troupe was amenable to my excerpting from that interview.

"He always invited me to visit him whenever I had the time. I had heard that Jimmy was quite ill, and I wanted an opportunity to see him again. On the way out of the airport David informed me quite matter-of-factly that Jimmy had cancer and the prognosis was that it was terminal. 'At the most,' he said, 'the doctor gave him about a month.' I was stunned, knocked off balance by the finality of the news and by David's casual manner. But he added that he and others close by had decided to have an upbeat attitude about everything so that Jimmy's last days could be as normal as possible.

"David said although Jimmy had not been told that his cancer was terminal, he believed that he probably knew because of the rapid deterioration of his physical condition and was telling me this to prepare me for the way Jimmy looked. As he went on in more detail, I could see the unspeakable grief etched in the mask that was now his face.

"I was shocked by Jimmy's frail and weakened condition. I quickly hugged him and kissed the top of his head. I held him close for a long moment partly because I loved this man and also because I didn't want him to notice the sadness that welled up into my eyes. But remembering that David had admonished me to 'act normally,' I quickly pulled myself together and told Jimmy how happy I was to see him. He smiled that brilliant smile of his, his large eyes bright and inquisitive, like those of a child. He told me in a very weak voice that he was convalescing and tired, but would come out to greet me properly in two or three hours. Then those bright luminous owl eyes burned deeply in mine, as if seeking some clue, some sign that would give him a hint as to the seriousness of his condition. They probed for a moment and then released me from their questioning fire.

"I was relieved when David led me out of the darkened house. I will never forget that image of Jimmy weakly sitting there, the feel of his now-wispy hair scratching my face when I hugged him, the birdlike frailty of his ravaged body and the parting telescopic image of him dressed in a red and green plaid robe that all but swallowed him, his large head lolling from one side to the other as his longtime friend, painter Lucien Happersberger, lifted him to put him in bed. It was a profoundly sad and moving experience that is etched indelibly in my mind. . . ."

The following brief excerpts from Troupe's interview are some of James Baldwin's last words:

Baldwin: It's a great shock to realize that you've been so divorced. So divorced from who you think you are — from who you really are. Who do you think you are, you're not at all. I don't know who I thought I was; I was a witness, I thought. I was a very despairing witness though, too. What I was actually doing was trying to avoid a certain estrangement perhaps, an estrangement between myself and my generation. It was virtually complete, the estrangement was, in terms of what I might have thought and expected — my theories. About what I might have hoped — I'm talking now in terms of one's function as an artist. And the country itself, being black and trying to deal with that.

Troupe: Why do you think it occurred? That estrangement between your generation and the country?

Baldwin: Well, because I was right. That's a strange way to put it. I was right. I was right about what was happening in the country. What was about to happen to all of us really, one way or another. And the choices people would have to make. . . .And watching people make them and denying them at the same time. I began to feel more and more homeless in terms of the whole relationship between France and me, and America and me has always been a little painful, you know. Because my family's in America I will go back. It couldn't have been a question in my mind unless it absolutely really came to that. But in the meantime you keep the door open and the price of keeping the door open was to actually be, in a sense, victimized by my own legend. You know, I was trying to tell the truth and it takes a long time to realize that you can't — that there's no point in going to the mat, so to speak, no point in going to Texas again. There's no point in saying this again. It's been said, and it's been said, and it's been said. It's been heard and not heard. You are a broken motor.

Troupe: A broken motor?

Baldwin: Yes. You're a running motor and you're repeating, repeating, you're repeating and it causes a breakdown, lessening of will power. And sooner or later your will gives out, it has to. You're lucky if it's a physical matter. Most times it's spiritual. See, all this involves hiding from something else—not dealing with how lonely you are. And of course, at the very bottom it involves the terror of every artist confronted with what he or she has to do, you know, the next work. And everybody, in one way or another, and some extent, tries to avoid it. And you avoid it more when you get older than you do when you're younger, still there's something terrifying about it, about doing the work. Something like that. But it happened to Miles sooner than it happened to me. I think for me it was lucky that it was physical, because it could have been mental.

Troupe: It could have been mental?

Baldwin: Yes. It could have been mental debilitation instead of my present physical one. I prefer the physical to the mental. Does that make sense?

Troupe: You mean they wanted you scrubbed and squeaky clean?

Baldwin: Exactly. You have to be scrubbed and squeaky clean and then there's nothing left of you. Let me tell you a story. When Ralph Ellison won the National Award in '52 for *Invisible Man*, I was up for the next year, in 1953, for *Go Tell It on the Mountain.* Then, years later, someone who was on the jury told me that since Ralph won the year before, they couldn't give it to a Negro two years in a row. Now, isn't that something?

(Curiously, Jimmy revealed with astonishing frankness, seemingly for the first time, insight to the bizarre relationship between him and Jeanne Faure.)

Troupe: She decided to sell the house to you? Why do you think she picked you? Do you know to this day?

Baldwin: No.

Troupe: Was it spiritual?

Baldwin: Yes.

Troupe: Cosmic?

Baldwin: I wasn't the best candidate; in fact, I was the worst. Something in her, I don't know. We also had a stormy relationship.

Troupe: Stormy?

Baldwin: Politically speaking we did. In many other ways we did, too. She knew something I didn't know. She knew about Europe, she knew about civilization, she knew about responsibility. . . .A million things that I as an American would not know, that were alien to me. And I was very slow to learn these things. In fact, it was a very expensive lesson, one that I hadn't learned entirely just yet. But she was a valuable kind of guide and a kind of protection. . . .And there was Titine Roux, the old lady who ran La Colombe d'Or, which is a world-famous restaurant and inn. She became my guardian. I never lived in a small town before, which is not so easy, and she protected me. And I didn't realize it at first, that she had picked herself to be my protector.

Troupe: What do you think she saw in you?

Baldwin: I don't know.

Troupe: What do you think?

Baldwin: I knew Titine liked me. Still she must have thought I was crazy, you know, at least a little strange, in any event. But both these women liked me. It was though they recognized where I came from. That I was a peasant, and I am. But I've only found this out over time.

Troupe: Why do you say that?

Baldwin: I'm a peasant because of where I really come from, you know. My background, my father, my mother, the line. Something of the peasant must be in all of the family. And that's where *Mlle.* Faure and Titine come from, too. And the color of my skin didn't add into it at all. Both of these women were watching something else besides my color. And they protected me and loved me. They're both dead now and I miss them both terribly. Because with Jeanne I truly learned a lot from her, from her European optic in regard to others; but she also had an optic that came from Algeria. What I liked about it was that she was willing to be my guide, willing and unwilling. In fact, she was a hard guide. But mostly she was willing. And so it seemed she was my guide to something else.

Troupe: What?

Baldwin: To a way of life, to a potential civilization she had seen only from a height.

Troupe: David told me a story about an incident that happened when her brother died, and *Mlle.* Faure picked you to be at the head of the funeral procession.

Baldwin: Well, she was the last of kin and she made me lead her brother Louis's funeral procession. Yes she did. She put her arm in mine and I had to lead. I had to. It was an incredible scene. I had to lead the funeral procession with her — or she with me. It was fascinating.

Troupe: I think it's a great image. How did you feel?

Baldwin: I was in a state of shock. I didn't know what to do. And of course the people of Saint-Paul were shocked, too. This was in either 1974 or '75. But I was in a state of shock. I didn't quite know what to think; in fact, the town was in a state of shock.

Troupe: What was the reason?

Baldwin: Well, they knew who I was by then, of course, but they couldn't understand why I was representing the family. When we were at the cemetery everybody had to say good-bye to me, too, because I was standing there with her at the head of the family, under the gates of the cemetery. Because what it meant, symbolically speaking, is that I was the next in line, when she died. That's what it meant.

Troupe: Do you think that could have happened in America?

Baldwin: I can't imagine where. I really cannot imagine where.

Troupe: So, in a sense that was a comforting, human experience. A remarkable spiritual connection, bond.

Baldwin: A very great thing, very great. At least for me. I want to write about it one day. Yes, sometime I'll have to talk about it.

In a final comment Troupe wrote: "One of the last things he said to me was that he hoped that I and other writers would continue to be witnesses of our time; that we must speak out against institutionalized and individual tyranny wherever we found it because if left unchecked, it threatens to engulf and subjugate us all — the fire this time. And, of course, he is right. He is right — about the racism, violence and cynical indifference that characterize modern society, and especially the contemporary values that are dominant here in America today."

Chapter 20

Death Vigil: *Final Period*

David Baldwin had moved Jimmy from his lower level "dungeon" quarters during the last period of his brother's life up to the ground floor space formerly used by *Mlle*. Faure as her living room. In his new sleeping area, which was sombre and depressing with its faded fresco walls, Jimmy had hallucinations, imagining that Simone Signoret, who had died two years earlier, and other friends, long dead, were visiting him.

"The Welcome Table" was close by, enabling David to carry Jimmy there for meals. He couldn't leave the house to go to his beloved La Colombe d'Or or anywhere else, but Yvonne and Pitou Roux frequently brought his favorite food from the hotel. Insisting that he needed a place to work, a new "office" was set up in the old kitchen. Despite Jimmy's continuing intention to go there, he never made it.

Just before Thanksgiving, David phoned David Leeming to come as soon as possible since the doctor had indicated that the end was near. He arrived at the house on November 21. Leeming noted, "I found Jimmy in a large bed; he was barely recognizable. He had lost a great deal of weight and had a deathlike, sunken look about him. There was an IV in his arm and some blood on the sheet from the needle. Jimmy woke up, saw me, smiled weakly, and said, 'Hey, baby.' We embraced, and I lay down next to him and conveyed greetings from mutual friends. He had asked for a few things from the States, and I opened the package I had brought for him: Aunt Jemima pancake mix, Aunt Jemima syrup, Brer Rabbit molasses, and some jelly beans. There was a spark of the old laughter, and he whispered, 'We can't escape our culture.' Then the smile faded into a confused, frightened look."

From Baldwin's last week, Leeming recalled, "On the twenty-fifth I went up to the village, lit a candle in the church, and bought the makings of pumpkin pie. Jimmy wanted a 'real Thanksgiving dinner' on the twenty-sixth. That day he spoke by telephone for the last time with his mother and Gloria. 'I'm glad we did that,' he said. Pat Mikell from Mikell's [New York's Upper West Side iconic rhythm-and-blues/jazz club] and Lucien arrived on the twenty-fifth. Lucien had been there earlier in the month and was back to be present at what we all now referred to as 'the end.'"

(When a New York publisher close to the family called Jimmy's mother to ask if she would go to Saint-Paul, she told him she just couldn't fly. Subsequently, Mrs. Baldwin said, "I was happy I was able to talk with him before he passed. David was with him to the last. I don't know if I will ever get over it.")

Leeming continued, "Before he drifted off to sleep again—he was heavily medicated for pain—he talked about feeling 'demoralized' and 'bored.' He complained at some length about how thin he was, how embarrassed he was at looking like 'skin and bones.' Death, he said, did not seem such a terrible idea in the circumstances. We spoke of his accomplishments and his hopes for new projects. Sitting with Jimmy on the first night, I read *The Welcome Table*, and when, at about 3 am, he woke up, we talked about the autobiographical aspects of the play. Then he felt nauseous and I carried him to the commode. My suggestion that it was 'Aunt Jemima's revenge' brought miserable laughter.

"By the twenty-seventh, Jimmy had become much weaker. He slept while the rest of us continued our examination of the past. Jimmy had asked to watch television. Miraculously, one channel was showing a documentary about Bessie Smith with old clips of her singing. Jimmy was moved. These were songs he had listened to on the Swiss mountain with Lucien as he wrote his first novel. Now Lucien was here and Bessie Smith was singing again. The documentary was followed by one of his favorite films, Charlie Chaplin in *The Great Dictator*. Jimmy was fully attentive. It was his last night at the movies; no 'stars' could have pleased him more.

"That night we had our final real talk. He was still preoccupied with the casting of *The Welcome Table*. Would Lena and Ruby like it? He wanted to get well; he had things to do, and his record was 'not bad.'

"We talked about Chaplin, Horne, Bessie Smith, Simone Signoret, and then, after a pause, he said, 'Sometimes I can't believe that I'm famous, too.' We spoke about my leaving the next day. He asked if he could give me something, and I had him sign a copy of *The Amen Corner* to take home to my wife. With great difficulty he signed the book, 'For Pam, with love, Jimmy B.'

"In the morning we embraced and he and David and I talked of my returning in a few days. He rested quietly on the twenty-eighth and on the twenty-ninth the doctor told David that nothing in Jimmy was functioning, that he would die within hours. He woke up during that evening and asked David whether he could see Simone and other friends passing along the wall. On the thirtieth he slept most of the day but was still lucid when he roused from time to time. The doctor said it was almost over.

"Lucien had been sitting with Jimmy all day and into the night. The others were talking at the table when Lucien called David, saying he thought it was time. David sat on the bed and took Jimmy's hands. Bernard squeezed water from a napkin onto his lips. Jimmy looked at them and seemed to drift away. David and Lucien both had the sense that they were taking the journey with him as far as they could go. It was after midnight. They all kissed Jimmy. David said, 'It's all right, Jimmy, you can cross over now,' and Jimmy passed."

———•———

One of the most touching farewells to Jimmy was written by Pat Mikell. On all his US visits, Jimmy had been a regular at Mikell's, the landmark jazz club. His brother David, an aspiring actor, worked there as a bartender. Operated by Pat and her late husband, Mike, on the corner of 97th Street and Columbus Avenue (1969-1991), it was a mecca where major soul, funk and jazz artists showed up to unwind in late night jazz sessions. Wynton Marsalis sat in with Art Blakey's Jazz Messengers. Stevie Wonder and Joe Cocker would show up to sing. Gospel singer Whitney Houston's teenage daughter Cissy was discovered there. It was both a literary and musical magnet. Authors, including Toni Morrison, Amiri Baraka and Maya Angelou were often seen there.

When I phoned Pat in Woodstock, NY, where she had moved with her husband when the club closed, she agreed that I could use the touching account of her adieu to Jimmy, which she called *The Last Days*. This was incorporated in Quincy Troupe's *James Baldwin: The Legacy*.

Pat remembered, "Before Jimmy left New York for the last time, he sat me down and yelled at me. I don't mean he actually yelled, but he was giving me advice on what I should do—I wasn't taking care of myself, so he was getting on my case. David walked by and started to laugh at me sitting there crying. He said, 'Well Jimmy loves you; he only yells at the people he cares about.'

"I think Jimmy knew then that he wasn't coming back. I think he was trying to get people he cared about focused on what they should be doing, and where they were—not where they were messing up. And I think one of the reasons he insisted that David leave New York and move to France was that David needed to get some things together. This was in November 1986.

"A year later, I went to meet a friend of David's for brunch and took along the August issue of *Architectural Digest* because Jimmy had a piece in there on his house in Saint-Paul. I had just looked at the pictures, and I wanted to show this friend where David was, to tell him that he went there with Jimmy and that they were happy. On the way back from brunch, I started reading Jimmy's text, and suddenly it struck me—'He knows he's gonna die.' And as soon as I opened the door, my daughter said a phone call had come and that David was trying to get in touch with me. I was already crying a few minutes later when the phone rang. It was David, and I said—before he even said anything—'I know, Jimmy's gonna die.' And he said 'Yeah, the doctor just said that he doesn't have much longer. There's nothing that they can do at this point.' That's when I said to myself, 'Oh, Pat, you should go over there.'

"Jimmy and David had been trying to get me to France for years, but I'd always have an excuse. Work. This or that or whatever. But I knew what Jimmy's illness was doing to David because they were so close. Jimmy had always said that the one thing he worried about was that David would leave the earth before him and he didn't know how he could stay on earth without David. So I just spontaneously decided to go. A friend got me the plane ticket on a credit card.

"I had no passport, and there I was down in the line at the passport place. You know how crazy it is right before Thanksgiving. But I saw one black man behind an official desk. So I scooted in front of everybody and went directly up to him and said, 'Jimmy Baldwin is very sick and I have to get an emergency passport.' So he took my passport application directly to the supervisor, who still gave me a very difficult time. They—the United States—only gave me one for six months. Then I went to the French consulate. The minute they heard who I was going to visit, I was immediately given a visa.

"When I rang the bell on the gate, nobody knew that I was coming. Bernard—Jimmy's longtime friend—came out, and I could hear— in the house—David yelling out, 'Well, who is it—who is it?' Bernard stood there looking at me in shock. It was raining, pouring rain. David came down, and when he saw me, he screamed, yelling into the house, 'Jimmy, you would not believe who's here!' As soon as I stepped into the room, there was Jimmy looking at me and he just cracked up laughing. He said, 'Look at this, the orphan in the storm.'

"The house was cold and damp, and it was rough. David was exhausted, he had been crying—almost everything was on his shoulders. But some help had just come. One of the people used to be Jimmy's secretary, a wonderful man named David Leeming. And Lucien was there.

"Before Jimmy left New York we had a long talk about the love of his life, but he never mentioned the name. So the whole time I was in Saint-Paul I had no idea that Lucien was the one he was talking about. I didn't know. But Jimmy had told me the whole story of how he had gotten sick and Lucien had taken him up to the mountains and that's how he wrote *Go Tell It on the Mountain.* Afterwards he told me that 'one has to learn to let go' and that one of the most difficult things in his life was to let go of Lucien. But he told me he had to let go of that, told me that 'unless you let go, you know, you'll just never be free.'

"So all I tried to do was just cheer up everyone. It was raining constantly. That first night, I went downstairs and wandered around and found wood and lit fires everywhere. I think I got on everybody's nerves lighting fires, but it did warm up the house. There is something very peaceful about fire. I lit one in Jimmy's room, which has a huge ceiling. I'd go in through the night and turn the fire up. When I tiptoed in, he would open his eyes and smile at me and then close them and curl up so he would be facing the fire.

"On Thanksgiving Day, he did get up. We came into the dining room and all had the Thanksgiving dinner. It was a *mishmash*, you know. Somehow they managed to find a few traditional American things, actually Southern—things like orange cup and sweet potatoes. Valérie was the cook. Valérie did everything. Valérie, Bernard, David, Lucien, David Leeming, a lawyer named Bill, an opera singer named Sophia, others were there, too, I think—I lost track; one day just went into another after a while. After dinner, we went into Jimmy's room. David got a bottle of champagne; everybody had a drink in front of the fire and talked. Jimmy had a drink too.

"He said, 'I hear you're leaving tomorrow; will you stay three or four more days?' And I said, 'Well, I'll speak to David.' But he kept insisting. (I was so happy he asked me.) 'I just want to thank you for having me here,' I said. 'It has been beautiful, it was just what I needed.' And he replied, 'No, I thank you. But please, promise me you'll stay three of four more days.' And then the thought passed through my mind, 'Oh, my God, don't tell me he knows that he's going to die.'

"People are into this New Age thing now—spiritualism and crystals; but Jimmy was into all of that way back. He was one of the most spiritual human beings I ever met. And I think that really there is no way he would be afraid of death—I think he dealt with that: life and death were one. Lots of people are afraid of dying but then again, that's how they are and how they live their lives and what kind of spirit they are. I don't think he was afraid of death at all. There was no fear there at all. No complaint. He was courageous.

"The night that Jimmy died, three or four doctors were there. David said that Jimmy was lucid right up to the end. He knew he was passing, and he had seen his past positions on the wall, and he talked till the end. Then he just smiled and closed his eyes. Lucien ran into the room. David put on 'Amazing Grace,' and it resounded throughout the house. Everyone then knew that he had passed. They went into their own little corner and cried, went up individually, into the room, and then came back and sat down at the table.

"David said I could stay in the room with Jimmy. His face had an unbelievably beautiful smile—absolutely peaceful. It was almost like he was still there; his spirit was still there. So I knelt down next to him and held his hand. His arm stayed warm for the longest period as if he were alive, just sleeping. I wasn't watching time, I don't really remember how long I knelt there. But Lucien came in at one point—and I took his hand and put it on Jimmy's still warm arm. It was actually pulsating. Then I noticed that Jimmy's face seemed different. I said, 'Look, Lucien—his expression,' and he said, 'Yes, his expression has changed.' It was actually more of a smile. Later David came back in and sat with Jimmy through the night, in a chair.

"During the final days, people were calling from all over the world. Guests were coming from all over. At that point my leaving would have just caused more confusion. And Valérie was not there at night. So at least I could help by serving people and cooking dinner and just basically being someone that everybody knew. One night I slept on the floor next to the phone so everybody could get some rest."

Among those who appeared at the house in the period before Jimmy passed was Rodolphe "Rudi" Ankaoua. He remembered in an interview: "I came from Paris to see Jimmy three or four times after his operation," he recalled. "I was at his bedside, holding his hand and talking to him, two days before he died. He was very weak so I kept my visit short. I am reminded every day of my great friend, who I dearly miss, when I am in my living room and look at the framed poem he wrote for me."

> Time is a game
> We play with sorrow:
> Win, or lose,
> You bet,
> Tomorrow.
> for Rudi A.
> from Jimmy B.

Philippe Bébon had also returned from his hamlet in the mountains to be at Baldwin's bedside. "When someone in Saint-Paul phoned me to advise that Jimmy was critically ill, I came immediately," he remembered. "It was three days before he died. I hadn't seen him for several years. He was very happy to see me. David, Bernard and Lucien, *le grand amour de sa vie,* the greatest love in his life, were there and we talked and drank red wine through the crazy night until morning. Jimmy was very important for me. It's difficult to say why. He was like a father. I had lost my own father when I was very young. Jimmy taught me everything."

Chapter 21

Jimmy's Passing (December 1, 1987):
Death in Saint-Paul

You don't die in Harlem, you pass. This expression has echoes from slave days of a release from bondage to somewhere better.

Baldwin was conscious when he died. Bernard Hassell commented, "Jimmy had a quiet and painless death. That is to say, he died with great dignity and the world will never be quite the same without him. You know he encouraged and inspired so many people. I had a serious problem a couple of years ago and I was depressed. He said, 'I have seen you go through a lot, but I have never seen you in despair. You are going to be all right.' I will never forget that."

Pitou Roux, who had been there that evening with her mother and brother, remembered Jimmy saying to her mother, 'I'm bored — so bored.' He was dead hours later. Wrapped in a sheet, his brown nude torso was so young for an old man. I stayed there all night drinking wine in the kitchen with David, Lucien and Bernard."

"I came ten minutes after he died," Dr. Roger Boizard recounted. "I cried. The image of him laying there was something I will never forget. To lose Jimmy was terrible, heart-breaking. He was lying in his bed in the middle of the room, surrounded by four big candles. Negro spirituals were playing loud on the old record player and friends were singing at the same time.

"Early the next morning word buzzed through the village. Throngs crowded the gatehouse to gain entry to the house in order to see Jimmy for the last time and pay their respects as he lay there in the large coffin with one red rose and a bouquet of white lilies. He was dressed in a grey suit with the cross of Commander in the French Legion of Honor in the buttonhole of his jacket. I was there to say good-bye to my dear friend before his body was taken to New York."

When I went to see Caryl Phillips in his Manhattan apartment, he referred to his account (*The Guardian,* July 14, 2007, used with permission) of returning to Saint-Paul to pay his last respects to his emaciated friend in the coffin, before he would fly to New York to attend the Baldwin funeral.

"The day after Baldwin died, I remember standing in the entrance hall to the house in Saint-Paul de Vence and looking at his body as he lay in an open coffin. In the living room, his Swiss friend of nearly forty years, Lucien Happersberger, his brother David Baldwin and his friend and secretary, Bernard Hassell, were talking quietly. I sat down next to Jimmy and stared into his now-peaceful face. I remembered that I had challenged him on a snowy night in Amherst, Massachusetts, and asked him why he was wasting his time in 'this dump of a town,' instead of buckling down and producing another Jimmy Baldwin novel.

"The folly and stupidity of youth. He heard me out, then smiled gracefully and said, 'One day you'll understand, baby.' As I looked at him in his coffin, I wanted to apologize for not understanding that night in Amherst. He had given me friendship and warmth, and in return I had nothing to give back to him.

"Twenty years after his death, I still have nothing tangible to give back to him, except some increased understanding of the price that he paid to become the extraordinary man that he was. By returning to the US in 1957, he found what he called a 'role,' and he found fame, but in order to achieve these goals he had to live a life that in the end could only prove injurious to him as a writer.

"I now understand that behind the clever title, *The Price of the Ticket*, there was courage, sorrow and pain. There was no self-pity. I now understand that the 17-year-old boy already knew something profound about the man that he would become. The boy had already intuited the price of the ticket. 'Fame is the spur and — ouch!'"

(In the 1941 DeWitt Clinton High School yearbook, Baldwin had indicated this ambition for fame next to his photo.)

Before I left the apartment, Phillips added a footnote describing an unforgettable experience in Saint-Paul. "The night after Jimmy died, Bernard and I went into the village to drink. We left Lucien and David with Jimmy's coffin. One drink led to another but at the end of the evening when we went to pay, there was a most touching moment. The bar owner wouldn't take money from us. 'No question,' he said. 'This is for Jimmy.'"

César recalled, "You can imagine my shock after those years of silence to hear that Jimmy had died. I was at an opening in Istanbul when a journalist sitting with Elia Kazan came over to give me the news. When his brother David called me the next morning, we were both crying on the phone. It made me so mad and so sad that I couldn't say good-bye. I tried on that weekend to get a visa for the United States since his body was being taken there. I pleaded, explained that a very dear friend had died, but I was talking to deaf ears. On the night he died, little David told me, Jimmy asked him to read from the screenplay he had written from the Turkish novel, *The Swordfish*."

François Roux added, "I had gone to the hospital to see him after his operation and brought him what he had requested, vanilla ice cream. He was in good spirits, full of plans for the future. On the night he died, I accompanied my mother to his house. Jimmy was a legend for American blacks. Soon after he died, Danny Glover came to La Colombe d'Or and asked me to take him to Jimmy's house. It's a pity that his family didn't pay the taxes to the French government. If they had followed legal procedures, they would have kept the house and, perhaps, could have made a home for young writers in Jimmy's memory."

Wanda van Dijk said, "Dick and I had always respected Jimmy as a complete man, a total entity who was small—but big. When I went to New York with my daughter a few years ago, we carried stones from Saint-Paul to put on his grave."

Alain Cinquini choked up as he told me, "We celebrated the date of Jimmy's first arrival in France, which was on Armistice Day in America, just the two of us, at lunch in the bar of La Colombe d'Or every year—it was our tradition. This time he was visibly very weak and David had to help support him but Jimmy insisted on getting together there. He hadn't been out of the house for a long time. Jimmy barely nibbled at some of the tapas. That was November 11, 1987—just a few weeks before he died. When Jimmy passed away, David phoned to ask me to photograph him. I refused. I wanted to retain the still-beautiful image I had of my dear friend."

Nall said, "I was there with Jimmy during the evening, and left the house about four hours before he died. David Baldwin phoned me in the middle of the night asking me to come over right away to do some drawings and take photos before the press would arrive the next morning. I documented Jimmy lying in his coffin. At 8 am, a huge crowd of journalists and photographers were gathered outside the house. I returned home to start working on these coffin pieces as an homage to Jimmy. Before I left, David said, 'Here's a piece of paper I think Jimmy wanted you to have. It's the last thing he wrote.'

Nall said: "This is the poem Jimmy left for me:"

'Safety and Honor both adore each other, but are doomed to discover that they cannot find a way to live, or sleep, together. Honor's demands are brutal, and so are those of Safety, one, or the other, must give way. One, or the other, must surrender.'

By summer 1988, Nall had completed two paintings based on photographs of Jimmy in his coffin with the sun coming up over the foothills of the Alps and the window making a cross over his body. He offered one to David but he refused it, saying the pain of the memory was still too fresh. Nall gave one work to the Birmingham Museum of Art which felt its home should rightfully be the Civil Rights Museum in Birmingham, Alabama, where it is now in their permanent collection. Nall kept the other painting at home in Vence as his own memorial to his friend.

On the back of the painting, Nall wrote: "Given in loving memory to the family and many friends of Jimmy Baldwin from a Southerner who has suffered the same pains and frustrations in trying to bring a small ray of light to a sun-blinded world."

Nall's last words to me when we met for his recollections were, "I played a small role in Jimmy's life but he played a very big one in mine."

Annie Terrier recalled in an interview, "A year after my first visit to the house, I returned to Saint-Paul to pay my last respects to Jimmy. His brother David was at the door. I remembered all of his books and all of the characters in them as I peered into the casket. He looked so tiny whereas in life his personality was so overwhelming you never thought of him being physically small. He was actually attractive in an unorthodox way with his very special, thin physique. I had understood his latest revolt—against dying—and the pain he suffered until the end. 1987 was a very sad year for me. I lost two good friends: Jimmy to stomach cancer and Simone to leukemia. Jimmy never saw the wonderful photos of the three of us together taken by Simone on that unforgettable day we spent at his house."

A final recollection from Pat Mikell: "It was after midnight and continually raining when Jimmy died, cold and raining. The next day the rain stopped. I don't know what that means but it must mean something heavy because he was a beautiful, spiritual man. I'm very grateful that I got to meet and know him. Jimmy was one of the greatest gifts that I have gotten in life. It means a lot to me to remember that he really did like me, you know, because he really could see through people.

"In Saint-Paul, they loved him too. They were so sad. The village people had besieged the stores for newspapers, to read about Jimmy's death. They don't sell a lot of newspapers there. But when Jimmy died, you could barely find one. Knowing the family would want a paper, I had to snatch one from a little old lady. She stared at me until someone else said. 'Oh, she's with Jimmy. She's staying there.' And the old lady said, 'Take the paper, take the paper.'

"The people of the town had seen me going back and forth to get coffee and cigarettes and whatever was needed at the house. Even when I was in the kitchen preparing trays of food, they would come in and cry and hold me. Everyone, even the village bocce players, came to the house, to Jimmy's house, to pay their last respects. They loved Jimmy over there. The president of France, the French diplomats were calling, were all sending flowers and telegrams. Now I think of all those people who said, 'Who does he think he is, living in France, he doesn't like America?' But once you've been there, you understand completely why he was there," Mikell said.

"The next day they came with the casket. It was made in France and beautiful, unlike any ever made in this country. Police officers, all in uniform, performed the ceremony of sealing the casket with such formality, dignity, drama, and respect. The head *gendarme*, a sergeant, stood there, very formally. Then they all surrounded the casket and put their hands on it, or their fingertips. Then they tightened the screws and carried it out in a procession. Later we all went to the airport and gathered in one room to say the last good-byes.

"As it turned out, I think I left France on the same plane with Jimmy's casket. At the security check, I was so hysterical I could not say a word. I couldn't stop crying, didn't know where I was. David had given me a beautiful ashtray—all hand-painted—picturing a particular white bird that was very prevalent in Saint-Paul. And on it was written 'Happy Birthday, Jimmy.' I had put it in my bag. So I pulled it out. All I did was show the ashtray. That's all I had to do. The next thing I knew, I had people escorting me on the plane. I only showed the ashtray because I couldn't stop crying. And all of a sudden guards were there. They took me on the plane and didn't check anything. They didn't bother to ask. The guards also must have told the stewardesses, because they really looked out for me the whole ride back."

Beside Jimmy's deathbed, there was a letter from Cynthia Packard, his housemate in Amherst, and a ring she had given him. David wore the ring to his brother's funeral and subsequently gave it back to Cynthia.

Ekwueme Michael Thelwell recounted, "At one point in late fall 1987, I phoned him and was contemplating going to Saint-Paul to see him. I thought he would be coming back in the spring. Life came into his voice and he said we'll be together before long. Subsequently I heard he was very ill.

"Alive or dead, James Baldwin seems to pose for certain writers—these days, mostly men and mostly white—a constant challenge: for them he is a source of unending mystery and provocation. And yet

Baldwin's life and career, though admittedly complex, are neither so ambiguous nor so troubling to most of us in the black world.

"And slender, gay James Baldwin taught a generation of us how to be black men in this country, and he gave us a language in which to engage the struggle. Which is why if the generation of black writers see and reach any further, it is because we stand on those narrow but durable shoulders.

"In a eulogy I delivered in 1987, I said Baldwin's power came from a style and a vision both of which were firmly and irrevocably anchored in the soul of black folk. The remorseless clarity of his vision lay in a perspective on American reality forged in the fiery crucible of the black experience. And the wisdom and insight of that bitter and ennobling history was simply not negotiable. And further, that magnificent prose, at its finest, was a near perfect instrument for its expression. Because the nuances and poetry of that style were informed by centuries of the rich cultural expression of black America," said Thelwell.

February 20, 1988

To The People of St. Paul:

Dear friends and neighbors of my son James Baldwin, who passed December 1, 1987. My family and I want you to know that we are deeply grateful to all of you for your kindness and support demonstrated through his illness.

Jimmy came among you as a stranger, and it was your friendliness that made him feel at home and made St. Paul his second home. He never stopped trying to get me to visit St. Paul, but my fear of flying kept me from making the trip. The members of my family who have visited, speak fondly of your village and its people.

My family and I want the people of St. Paul to know, you will always have a place in our hearts. May love and peace abide in your village.

Sincerely,

Mrs Berdis Baldwin

Mrs. Berdis Baldwin

Mrs Berdis Baldwin

Berdis Baldwin thanked the people of Saint-Paul de Vence in 1988.

Chapter 22

New York Cathedral Funeral:
Celebrity Cemetery

It was in the imposing Cathedral Church of St. John the Divine where the oversized French mahogany casket bearing Baldwin's tiny, frail body was brought for his funeral service on December 8th, his brother David's birthday. Started in 1892, but never completed, this is the world's largest cathedral. (St. Peter's and Notre Dame are basilicas.) Located on Amsterdam Avenue extending from 110th to 113th Streets in New York's Morningside Heights bordering on Harlem, it was jammed with over 5,000 mourners in the crowded pews, with many more standing against the walls beneath the soaring vaulted ceiling and high stained-glass windows. Huge throngs jammed the sidewalks as far as one could see.

There were family, friends from across the United States, France and all over the world; admirers, politicians, show business celebrities, high school classmates, ex-lovers and fellow champions of the Civil Rights Movement who came to honor Baldwin, as they had in earlier times mourned the slain Martin Luther King, Jr. , Medgar Evers, and others.

In 1974, in this cathedral, Baldwin had been awarded its centennial medal for being an "artist as prophet." A commemorative plaque had been placed on the sidewalk. Multitudes have unknowingly walked over it in the intervening years. It had virtually been forgotten.

Now his body lay there near the high altar in the black-draped casket with a glass window for mourners to have their final look at Jimmy's serene face. Family arrangements assured this would not be the usual church funeral for "our son, our brother, our uncle, our father — our Jimmy — now ancestral." The title on the cover of the program proclaimed, "A Celebration of the Life of James

Arthur Baldwin." It was a pageant unfolding, first with one drum reverberating through the great space. Suddenly eight drummers of the African Babatunde Olatunji, dressed in white, short-sleeved *akbadas* [tunics], played "Drum Salute" during the opening procession.

A monumental crucifix was carried between two candle-bearers, followed by priests, pastors, acolytes, cathedral choirs, the Baldwin family and the pallbearers moving slowly along the aisles. For over three hours, there were psalms chanted, prayers offered, folk singing, a jazz trumpet and spiritual solos of "Sometimes I Feel Like a Motherless Child," "Glory, Glory, Hallelujah," and "Let's Break Bread Together." During the service conducted in Baldwin's two languages—"Black English" and "White English"—the King James Bible was read against the backdrop of the African drumbeat.

Three of Baldwin's black writer friends—Toni Morrison, Maya Angelou and Amiri Baraka—delivered lengthy, powerful eulogies talking to him or about him. This drew amens and applause from the spellbound mourners. Author and journalist Herb Boyd, in his book, *Baldwin's Harlem: A Biography of James Baldwin*, published notes he "had scribbled" as those writers spoke during the service. He wrote:

Toni Morrison said, "You made American English honest. You stripped it of ease and false comfort. . . . You went into that forbidden territory and decolonized it. No one powered or inhabited the language the way you did for me. In your hands, language was handsome again. We saw it as it was meant to be. . . . You brought us to ourselves."

Maya Angelou called Baldwin her brother in a time "when black women had a crying need for brothers."

Amiri Baraka was at his rhetorical best during some forty minutes at the podium. He spoke of Baldwin's "righteous anger," insisting that "he lived his life as a witness."

The French ambassador to the United States, Emmanuel de Margerie, likened Baldwin to the great French writers. "He was regarded in the land of Voltaire and Zola as a man of principle and dedication. He was a spokesman for his people."

His friends and admirers came from all over France and from many other countries. French president François Mitterrand sent a condolence telegram to the Baldwin family. It read, "France has lost a friend and the world a great writer. In his life, his work, he never ceased to be a witness for what he knew of the American black community's suffering and hope."

Unquestionably, the star of the service remained Jimmy himself. Toward the end, even though a tape recording was indicated in the program, most people in the cathedral were jolted to hear Baldwin's own gentle baritone voice singing the gospel hymn, "Precious Lord, take my hand, lead me on." One could hear a pin drop in the cavernous space as the overflowing crowd listened to each word, every syllable, as if Jimmy was there himself singing his own farewell to all those who knew and loved him. There was nary a dry eye amidst the people.

Several of Jimmy's friends in the cathedral to take leave of him—Hélène Roux, Sol Stein and Caryl Phillips—were asked for their personal memories.

Hélène Roux, working in New York as a dancer at the time, remembered, "My mother phoned me from Saint-Paul to tell me that Jimmy's brother, David, had just come into the hotel to ask her to attend the funeral. She explained that she couldn't make the trip and asked me to represent the family. When David was back in New York, he asked me to come to the house on 71st Street. I went to the funeral home and cathedral with the Baldwins and then in the cortege to the cemetery.

"In the limousine someone asked me who I was. When I identified myself as 'Yvonne's daughter,' I was treated like royalty. Mrs. Baldwin stroked my cheek. Upon our return from the cemetery, David said, 'I have something for you.' He handed me a bag containing pointe shoes which I had worn dancing when I was twelve. Jimmy had saved them. We finished the evening drinking at Mikell's, where Jimmy's brother David worked."

Sol Stein reflected, "I am remembering five thousand people crowded into the cathedral for James Baldwin's funeral, and I imagine my lifelong friend Jimmy and me watching that event, an elbow poking the other's rib for attention, as in the old days when our lives intersected.

"In the Cathedral of St. John the Divine, the place of my formal good-bye to my friend of a lifetime, my wife and I were asked by David Baldwin, Jimmy's closest brother, to sit with the family, which we did until an usher came over and asked us to move to a different section, facing the rear of the cathedral, not quite the back of the bus. We were seated next to a white woman Baldwin had known in Paris. People who watched the funeral on television said our white faces were conspicuous in a sea of black. Our presence had somehow survived, and if Jimmy had been there to witness it, he would have laughed."

Caryl Phillips, who attended the service with his friend, James Campbell, said, "I found it very moving, but it was a little too theatrical, too Hollywood, with the African drummers and Jimmy singing. Though I was not particularly enamored of the three speakers, Toni Morrison was excellent. It was strange to hear LeRoi Jones [Amiri Baraka], who was extremely homophobic and hurtful to Jimmy during all those years, up there eulogizing him. The family had chosen him. Afterwards, James Campbell and I walked all the way down Broadway to Greenwich Village and ended up that evening at Mikell's for the wake where Jimmy's presence was felt."

At the culmination of the service, the Babatunde Olatunji played a recessional called, "Continuum Drums," until the great cathedral had emptied. Countless numbers, many simple people who had skipped going to their jobs or other appointments, waited patiently outside during the long ceremony so they could say good-bye when the casket was brought to the funeral hearse.

During the last drive through the streets of Harlem, the forty-car cortege with police escort was thronged as Jimmy returned to his roots and his people. The procession, passing close to where Jimmy had once lived and gone to school, weaved its way at a snail's pace hindered by mobs blocking the route.

Finally, it reached the freeway leading to Ferncliff Cemetery and Mausoleum in Hartsdale, Westchester County, about twenty-five miles from Manhattan. A number of Baldwin's good friends chose to avoid the burial, preferring to drink to Jimmy's memory at Mikell's.

"At my death," Baldwin had once said, "I will pass on the torch to the young. They are all my children." Likewise, he had remarked, "You don't tell life, life tells you."

Befitting his celebrity status, arrangements were made for Jimmy to be interred at Ferncliff, the last resting place of the famous. Ferncliff is like an expansive, peaceful park with neat, winding paths and well-trimmed lawns. There are no upright gravestones. All plots have discreet flat bronze markers flush with the lawns to identify the graves. James Arthur Baldwin lies in plot Hillcrest A, number 1203. His mother, Berdis Baldwin, who died in 1999, was buried next to him in this double plot. There is one marker in memory of both.

Here he would be amidst other well-known people like Jerome Kerns, Judy Garland, and Diane Sands. Close by are fellow witnesses from the Civil Rights Movement, Paul Robeson and Malcolm X. Next to him a plaque identifies the grave of Toots Shor, owner of the bar-restaurant in the heart of the Broadway theatre district, famed for his celebrity clients. Someone joked that Jimmy would be assured of a drink in the hereafter.

Chapter 23

Posthumous Lawsuit (1989):
Unwritten Books

Baldwin's acceptance of a large advance sum for a contracted book never written resulted in a lawsuit after his death. This threatened the solvency of his family and might have caused the dispossession of his eighty-nine-year-old mother from the home he had bought her in New York City.

Baldwin had agreed in 1979 to revisit the American South to write an extended article for *The New Yorker* magazine, which would serve as a prelude for a book commissioned by McGraw Hill—memoirs, history and biography of the Civil Rights Movement interwoven with his personal recollections of the three assassinated leaders: Martin Luther King, Jr., Malcolm X, and Medgar Evers.

Baldwin signed a contract and received a $200,000 advance payment on January 9, 1980 for the work, tentatively titled, *Remember This House*. It was to be delivered by January 1, 1982, which was extended by mutual consent to July 1982. The arrangement was amended twice, with the last one on December 21, 1984 calling for a September 1, 1985 delivery date.

When David Leeming came to Saint-Paul in the early '80s, he was well aware of Jimmy's commitment. He recalled years later when Baldwin was terminally ill, "Most of all, he tried to work on *Remember This House*. It was proving an almost impossible task, and he realized he did not have the strength to do the necessary research. Before he died, he managed to complete thirty or forty pages."

In the suit filed in October 1989 in New York's Surrogate Court, McGraw-Hill insisted it had been left no choice but to file because Mr. Baldwin's family refused repeatedly to discuss the issue. "We are not looking to cause hardship or set a precedent, but we have a duty to our shareholders to account for that money," Betsy Rousso, a spokeswoman, said. Joseph L. Dionne, the chairman and chief executive officer of McGraw-Hill, wrote: "Mr. Baldwin effectively received an interest-free loan of $200,000 to write a book as to which together we await evidence that he ever wrote more than a very rough eleven-page draft. As a publicly owned company, McGraw-Hill is not in a position to waive repayment of that sum."

The company demanded "the sum of $200,000, plus interest at the legal rate from the date of Mr. Baldwin's death."

However, the Authors Guild, a writers' organization that intervened on behalf of the Baldwin estate, succeeded in their plea to have the suit abandoned. Rousso said, "The Baldwin estate had a duty to reimburse us. That is still clear. But we did not want to cause distress to his family. That is why we dropped the suit."

James Silberman, the president of Summit Books, an imprint of Simon & Schuster, said, "I have never heard of a publisher filing suit in such a situation. It is very unusual that they did so. On the one hand, a contract is a contract. On the other, since time immemorial, publishers in certain situations have found ways to work things out. Jimmy was an enormously important writer."

His comment was typical of publishers' reactions to the filing of the suit. Several publishers confirmed that they had sued authors — but never a dead one.

Chapter 24

House Legacy Battle (1987-2007):
Decades Ownership Dispute

After James Baldwin died in 1987 another legal dispute broke out, this time concerning inheritance of the Saint-Paul house and property. The Baldwin estate was pitted against a slew of *Mlle.* Faure's remote family members who suddenly emerged and ·claimed descendancy from her. The judiciary proceedings were concluded in December 2007—twenty years later.

In the interim two decades, the abandoned once-splendid residence and beautiful sprawling gardens had fallen into total ruin. Thieves had stolen windows and doors, resulting in total interior degradation due to penetrating rain and wind. The decorative, old frescoes painted by Italian artisans became marginal segments barely hinting at their former colorful, rich splendor. Holes appeared everywhere in ceilings, walls, and floors during the forsaken two decades while the legal battle was being waged. Jungles of overgrown weeds had killed all the cultivated plantings. Some majestic trees had grown wildly into haunting shapes and others had become infected or simply withered and died.

Based on his purported purchases, room by room through the years, and his landlady's assurances that she wanted him to have it, James Baldwin was certain that he was the rightful heir. So did his estate. It proceeded with the claim when he died precisely one year after *Mlle.* Faure. The plot thickened when some very distant Faure relatives appeared out of the blue with a claim, as did *Mme.* Josette Bazzini, housekeeper and companion in the small village home where *Mlle.* Faure lived the last decade of her life.

Presumably, *Mlle.* Faure had considered selling the big house to an outside interested party but rescinded in favor of Jimmy who promised to pay the balance still due. She obviously wanted him to keep the house.

Pitou recalled that her mother and Simone Signoret had at an early stage accompanied Jimmy and Jeanne Faure to sign a paper ascertaining that *Mlle.* Faure had ceded the house to Baldwin while retaining the right to live there until her death in a French legal arrangement known as *viager.* The alleged paper has disappeared.

Hélène added, "Jimmy had entrusted the keys to the house to my mother who kept them in the hotel safe but the house became a real problem after Jimmy died. David came and squatted there with his Welsh companion, Jill Hutchinson, in the crumbling building until he was diagnosed with cancer. Some of his sisters came over to bring him home. They didn't understand why he had gone back to Saint-Paul. They thought the house was haunted because of the two deaths there. Black crosses appeared on the doors as the house was 'exorcised.' Jill was treated appallingly by the family like she was a thief.

"When a lengthy legal case developed over ownership, the Baldwin estate insisted on recouping the money Jimmy had paid but lost the appeal and that wonderful property went to her housekeeper. Where were all his black writer friends like Maya, Toni and the others who could have saved the house as a shrine to Jimmy?"

When I spoke to Gloria Baldwin Karefa-Smart, executor of the Baldwin estate, at her home in Washington, DC, she told me she had become "fed up" during the long struggle and finally withdrew.

Jill Hutchinson gave me her firsthand account: "When I first got to know David, he was intent on keeping the house in Jimmy's memory. It was only in 1991 that he decided we would live together permanently in the house. When he was diagnosed with stomach cancer in 1996, he had no insurance here or anywhere else. Yvonne Roux offered to arrange the best surgeon to help him and was ready to take care of all the costs to save him, keep him in France, but he went back to the States to a veterans hospital in Washington, DC for an operation. When he returned, he was emaciated, looked exactly like Jimmy. Subsequently, after his scar opened up, he went into a French hospital, where he was told that death was imminent. It was terrible to see him suffering. His son, Daniel, was here with me. David wanted to live his last days in the house.

"Not respecting his wishes, Gloria and some of his other sisters came over to take him back. They insisted he couldn't be properly looked after in France and didn't want him to die in the house. They felt there was a curse on it, a voodoo, since both Jimmy and Bernard died there. They came with an official-looking document from a woman he had married when he was twenty years old but never divorced, supposedly empowering them to take him back to the US. David said, 'I have no choice, I have to go.' I had no authority to insist that he stay.

"He spent the rest of his life on machines in an American hospital where he died in 1997 of stomach cancer just like Jimmy. The last thing David said to me before they took him away was, 'Here are my keys. Whatever you do, look out for the house.' I spent ten years in that house, which was crumbling in desperate need of repair. I had the roof fixed and tried to interest the authorities to turn it into a foundation for young writers honoring Jimmy. But finally I was forced out after getting veiled threats from some strange people with commercial interests in the property."

———•———

Dr. Véronique Larcher, a general practitioner in the village, went into many homes and heard countless stories, gossip, and rumors about the Baldwin home. There was speculation from all sides as to who should be the heir: the very distant relatives on *Mlle.* Faure's paternal side who suddenly appeared from out of the blue with their claim; the estate of James Baldwin, who Jeanne wanted to continue living in her house; or the housekeeper, Josette Bazzini, who faithfully cared for Jeanne.

Dr. Larcher treated Jeanne Faure during her final years, as well as having Josette Bazzini as a patient. She also knew Jimmy and Bernard very well since they had been her patients when they first arrived.

I had the pleasure of meeting this highly-respected, tall, elegant woman during several visits to Saint-Paul and getting some objective clarification on the muddled claims and disclaimers from the various parties seeking to inherit the house and property. On one occasion, she told me that everyone in town had a theory on who should justifiably get ownership of the house. In her clear view of the situation, she declared, "There's no point listening to everybody's opinion. Since Madame Bazzini got the house after twenty years of litigation, you should go talk to her."

With an introduction from Dr. Véronique Larcher, I phoned *Mme.* Bazzini to request an interview. I suggested that she might bring along the court papers, normally accessible in the public domain, so the court ruling would be clear to me. She agreed.

I proposed the popular Café de la Place, where I had interviewed most of the other locals, but she refused, saying, "I don't like that place." She suggested instead the terrace of le Tilleul, a restaurant situated high on a hill close to the medieval walled fortifications. Since the terrace was jammed with tourists having lunch, we retreated to stone benches hugging the ancient walls. *Mme.* Bazzini showed up precisely at the appointed hour, with a granddaughter as chaperone, but without the promised papers.

As we sat across from each other, I could sense a certain hostility and suspicion. She quickly advised me, "My attorney said I should not bring the papers and not say too much." In her right hand, she clenched a piece of paper which would serve her with the points she wanted to make.

She began with, "I want you to know that I was a distant cousin on her mother's side and a companion to Jeanne Faure—not a *femme de ménage* [housekeeper] as everyone says. I didn't come to clean her house. I came there to help her every day since she was old."

Repeating with great emphasis once again, she said, "I was not a cleaning woman. I helped her move into her small village house and put everything away in the closets. She became very close to me because she needed company. She was all alone. In the morning, I would shop for her, make meals at home and bring them in the afternoon and then stay with her for a while.

"Jeanne was eighty-one years old when she moved into her village house in 1976 because she was afraid to stay in the big house after someone had forced her door and tried to break in. As soon as she had left and Baldwin had the big house to himself, Bernard called in some dealers and sold off all of Jeanne's antique furniture.

"I knew that Baldwin wanted to buy the property but he never paid it off. Jeanne called Baldwin every morning but he was always sleeping late and she would get Bernard on the phone. Baldwin appeared one day when I was there. Jeanne thought he had come to regulate the debt but, no, he was just charming her to ask for more time. Bernard used to come crying for money when the fuel was delivered or to pay gas and electric, water bills. She was too good and paid everything for them.

"Baldwin was traveling a lot. Whenever he came back to Saint-Paul, she invited him for lunch and it was always exactly the same menu: purée, roast beef or chicken. She never forgot to buy a bottle of whiskey and some red wine. They were actually very close. He called her *Jeanne* and she called him *Jimmy*.

"I worked for her during the ten years she lived in the village. It was only on the last day when she died that I wasn't there in the afternoon because I had to take my daughter to the airport. I had seen her early in the day and she didn't seem sick. Jeanne phoned Baldwin around 2 am the next morning and he came with Bernard. They called Dr. Larcher who stayed all night with her. She died at 7 am. The doctor phoned me to come quickly at 7:30 am.

"Baldwin had bought a duty-free pearl necklace which he had given Jeanne as a gift. The day after Jeanne died, Valérie phoned me to say that Baldwin wanted her to have the necklace and would I see that she got it." (Whether or not she actually did give her the necklace was not clear.)

"Some time before, Jeanne had told me she wanted to give me the village house. I explained there would be too much inheritance tax which I could not pay so I couldn't accept it. So instead she sold it to a man from Paris for 500,000 francs [roughly $81,000]. That was several years before she died in December 1986. I guess she arranged with the notary that the sale was *en viager*. That meant that she could stay in the house until her death. After she received payment, she wrote out a *chèque au porteur* [bearer's check] which she was going to give me. Baldwin heard about the sale and came crying to Jeanne that he needed 500,000 francs to pay his taxes. She gave him the check.

"After Jeanne died, I found papers in the village house. One of them was for two debts, each for 350,000 francs, a total of 700,000 francs, [roughly $121,000] which Baldwin had signed as a promise to pay on the house and property. And I found another paper saying that whatever money remained in the bank account at the post office should be given to the *Sécours Catholique* [a charitable organization for the poor] and everything I would find within the four walls of her house was for me. Before long I gave the money in the bank account to the charity.

"The legal battle for the inheritance of the big house started with Baldwin's death in December 1987. It was between the Baldwin estate, some cousins on *Mlle.* Faure's father's side and me. I don't know where her father came from or where those far-off cousins lived. I was related to *Mlle.* Faure on her mother's side through my mother. She, like all my family, was born in Saint-Paul. I won the court case in December 2007 after twenty years of this upsetting dispute."

Back to Dr. Larcher for her account: "I would see Jimmy at La Colombe d'Or, house parties, and on other occasions. During lunches Jeanne arranged at the big house, my mother and I, as well as Jeanne, were always shocked when he got drunk at those meals. Jeanne was always talking to me about Jimmy. He had great respect for her and came often to see her but she was always disappointed because she expected that he had come to settle what he owed.

"While it was always, *demain, demain* [tomorrow, tomorrow] with him, she remained patient but she liked money and wanted to be paid. Jimmy assumed no one would know he had paid only one-third, though he had committed himself to pay the remaining two-thirds within a year. This only came out when *Mme.* Bazzini found papers showing what he still owed.

"When Jeanne was dying, and she knew it, Jimmy came very often to visit her. In the last year of her life, Jeanne was completely obsessed by him but still she felt he had to pay. She kept his *reconnaissance de debt* [his signed IOU] close by—pinned to her nightgown—a reminder to herself of what she was determined to collect from him.

"Jimmy and Bernard came on the last night and spent part of the night there with her. She was alone, lonely, and cherished their being there. I arrived soon after their call and stayed with Jeanne until she died in the early morning. Jimmy returned the next day. He truly loved her.

"After Mme. Bazzani inherited the house, it was sold to a Dutch property developer. He presented plans to the municipality to restore the eighteenth century *bastide* [country house] as a boutique hotel and also build several houses on this magnificent property. He was threatened by another interested and influential party that he would never get to build there.

"The Dutchman subsequently sold the property to the owner of the luxury hotel located just outside Saint-Paul. Rather than propose another top hotel for the area, a plan was submitted for circa twenty-five dwellings. The city rejected this at the end of the summer 2009, indicating that a new plan for urbanization would be drafted over the coming four years, while the mayor advised that he was not issuing any permits for such a grand scale project.

"When *les Architectes des bâtiments de France*—a state organization for the protection of buildings important to the national heritage—became aware of the prospect of the three centuries old mansion being demolished, an architect was delegated to study its historic importance and advise on its protection. Its findings and recommendations are mandatory and must be followed. But the house and property was not classified and listed as a monument. Shortly thereafter signs went up on the property offering the possibility to build houses on three small plots."

Two wings of the magnificent *bastide* have been razed, while the main residence has been spared until now from becoming the bulldozers' victim. This is due to Baldwin's prominent friends and admirers in France and the United States who launched a fundraising campaign, *James Baldwin's House*, to honor the great author, while establishing a residence for young writers.

Chapter 25

Recognition, Accolades:
Honors, Disappointment

James Baldwin had a great deal of support and recognition early in his career. Besides the Julius Rosenwald Fellowship which enabled him to flee to Paris in 1948, there were Guggenheim, MacDowell Colony, *Partisan Review* fellowships, as well as National Institute of Arts and Letters (now the American Academy of Arts and Letters) and Ford Foundation grants.

Among the numerous awards and university honorary degrees, Baldwin received the Martin Luther King, Jr. Memorial Award for his "lifelong dedication to humanitarian ideals" along with an honorary degree from the University of Massachusetts in 1978. *Playboy* magazine recognized him with its Best Nonfiction award in 1981 while the Université Nice Sophia Antipolis named him a *Docteur Honoris Causa* [Honorary Doctorate title] in 1982.

There were many other forms of support and recognition but Baldwin never received any awards commensurate with his contribution to 20th century American literature. He was bypassed for the Pulitzer Prize. Though nominated for the National Book Award, he lost out on that as well.

A humorous note: *Le Canard enchaîné,* a satirical weekly French institution since 1915, published an editorial (October 9, 1985) titled, "The Foreigners Who Enchant Us." The tongue-in-cheek commentary decried that among some 200 books published in the fall season, so many are foreign translations since the choice is vast and contains so many wonderful works. The article singled out six outstanding foreign titles, including James Baldwin's *Meurtres à Atlanta* [*The Evidence of Things Not Seen*], described as "Not happy, but incredibly ferocious with texts to make your head spin." This editorial was illustrated with a cartoon figure of a bulbous man exclaiming, "Nous Supprimerons le Prix Médicis Etranger" ["We will abolish the Medicis prize for foreigners"]. In any case, the Medicis judges passed over Jimmy's nomination.

While Jimmy lay terminally ill in Saint-Paul, his novel, *Harlem Quartet* [translated from *Just Above My Head*], was shortlisted in 1987 for the *Prix Femina Etranger,* a French literary award initiated by a female jury. This prestigious prize rewards foreign writers, male or female, published in French. Baldwin died a few days after being notified, once again, that the prize was not going to him. As for the Nobel Prize, the committee never even listed him for consideration. The prize must be awarded during a writer's lifetime—it was too late for Jimmy.

Without doubt the most significant acknowledgment during his lifetime came with the convocation in June 1986 by President François Mitterrand for the distinction as Commander in France's Legion of Honor, the highest recognition of service to the country. Josephine Baker was the only other African-American before him who was recognized with this distinct recognition.

Jimmy was accompanied to the ceremony by his brother David, Lucien Happersberger, Valérie Sordello, and Jeanne Faure. He was delighted to see that Leonard Bernstein was also there being decorated. To an interviewer, Jimmy had explained why his housekeeper and landlady accompanied him to the ceremony: "Because they had seen me through so much and I'd promised to take Jeanne and Valérie to Paris one day. Jeanne had been to Paris but she hadn't been there for a long time. I thought that would be nice for her to go. So I took them and because I owed it to them, but especially to Jeanne Faure." (*Mlle.* Faure died in December of that year.)

France also recognized Baldwin with a posthumous homage, the literary prize of French-American Friendship, for his entire oeuvre.

In the period of over two decades since the Baldwin's demise, there have been a number of manifestations underscoring his importance—and proving he has not been forgotten.

An homage was rendered during a ceremony in November 1998 to James Baldwin in Saint-Paul. It was the 150th anniversary of the abolishment of slavery, under the patronage of UNESCO and the French government. The exhibition included objects and documents, including his well-known *Open Letter to Angela Davis.*

On that occasion, those who had been close to him, including Valérie, Nall, Dr. Boizard and André Verdet, reminisced about "their Jimmy." Verdet read a poem created for the occasion and later published a tribute, *James Baldwin Rhythms: Sa vie, sa lutte, sa mort.* [His life, his fight, his death]. Madame Catherine Trautmann, Minister of Culture, and her predecessor, Jack Lang, sent messages, as did the sculptor Arman with a touching letter to "Dear James" sent from New York.

Although during his lifetime he was not awarded some of the literary prizes he craved, Baldwin continues to be honored in a myriad of ways. His books are read and discussed in schools and colleges around the world. One of his richest short stories, *Sonny's Blues,* appears in many anthologies of short fiction used in introductory college literature classes.

Kevin Brown, a photojournalist in Baltimore, Maryland, is just one of many devotees in the United States and globally who work to keep his memory alive. Brown founded the National James Baldwin Literary Society in 1987 to organize free public events celebrating Baldwin's life and legacy.

Dr. Rosa Bobia, emerita professor, department of foreign languages and former director for African and African Diaspora Studies at Kennesaw State University, is president of the International James Baldwin Society which she founded in 2006. She is also associate editor of the *James Baldwin Review.*

In February 2001, eight prominent writers assembled in Manhattan's Lincoln Center to pay homage to Baldwin.

Dr. Molefi Kete Asante in 2002 included James Baldwin in his biographical dictionary, *100 Greatest African-Americans.* He is the most-published African-American scholar, with over sixty-five books, some three hundred articles, a cultural theorist in history and language and founder of the first doctoral program in African-American studies.

In 2004, the United States Postal Service issued a stamp—the

20th in the Literary Arts series—honoring James Baldwin. This 37-cent stamp features a portrait by the artist Thomas Blackshear, II, based on a black-and-white photograph of Baldwin taken around 1960, probably in New York. The stamp background is evocative of Baldwin's semi-autobiographical novel, *Go Tell It on the Mountain*, set in Harlem. The back sheet affixed to the stamp reads: "James Baldwin (1924-1987) was a leading American writer of the 20th century and an influential figure in the Civil Rights Movement. He explored race relations, love, and other subjects in works such as *The Fire Next Time* and *Giovanni's Room*."

Dr. Michael Eric Dyson, writing in *Ebony* in November 2005 on "What America Would Be Like without Sixty Years of Black Contributions," singled out Baldwin as the first person he cited.

The New York Public Library on Fifth Avenue in Manhattan organized *A James Baldwin Tribute* with a number of well-known authors as speakers in 2008. Universities everywhere regularly schedule seminars honoring Baldwin, such as Suffolk University did in 2009.

Professor Toni Morrison keeps his legacy in the forefront with her organization of the Princeton University Program in African-American Studies Annual James Baldwin Lecture series which she launched in 2006. "This celebrates the scholarship of a distinguished faculty member reflecting on the issue of race and American culture, while honoring the extraordinary legacy of the late James Baldwin, one of America's most powerful and cultural critics and essayists."

It was close to twenty-five years after his death before Baldwin's name even came up in Oslo in a Nobel Prize context. Thorbjorn Jagland, the chairman of the Norwegian Nobel Committee, made the presentation on December 10, 2011 to three female activists and political leaders "for their nonviolent struggle for the safety of women and for womens' rights" as peacemakers invoking gender equality and the democratic strivings of the Arab Spring. Jagland concluded his remarks by citing "the American writer James Baldwin who wrote, 'The people that once walked in darkness are no longer prepared to do so.'"

In 2012 James Baldwin was inducted in Chicago's Legacy Walk, an outdoor public display which celebrates LGBT history and people.

The city of New York honored Baldwin in 2014 in what would have been his ninetieth birthday declaring the Year of James Baldwin with a New York Live Arts celebration from April 2014 through June 2015. This multi-disciplinary festival had extensive programming of concerts, dance, lectures, theatre, poetry, and other events.

To further honor the writer, a James Baldwin Place was created in August 2014 between Fifth and Madison Avenues, facing 22 East 128th Street, where the school he attended still stands, now called the Harlem Renaissance High School. A ceremony with great fanfare was attended by many family members and throngs of friends and people from the neighbourhood — but there was no street sign! A makeshift text was used since a city councilwoman had neglected to arrange signing of the official resolution in time. The authentic street sign was quietly put in place in April 2015. The *James Baldwin Review* was launched in 2015. This annual online journal brings together a wide array of peer-reviewed critical and creative work on the life, writings, and legacy of James Baldwin. It's published by Manchester University Press.

At the State Hermitage Museum in Saint Petersburg, Russia, the Manifesta 10 exhibition in 2014 included an ink and pencil paper portrait titled *James Baldwin 2014* from *Great (Gay) Men*, a cogently, beautifully-drawn single series by Marlene Dumas, a South African-born artist living in Amsterdam. It was subsequently shown in the Fondation Beyeler in Basel, Switzerland in 2015.

The American University of Paris organized in May 2016 the International James Baldwin Conference, "A Language to Dwell In: James Baldwin, Paris and International Visions."

The honors and recognition continue. James Baldwin has not been forgotten.

%

Chapter 26

The French Connection:
Critical Success

Well aware of French recognition of Baldwin as a literary figure and adoration as a celebrity, I looked at his publishing success.

As a young writer in Paris in the late 1950s, his first two novels, *Go Tell It on the Mountain* and *Giovanni's Room*, were subsequently published in French as, respectively, *Les Elus du Seigneur*, and *La Chambre de Giovanni*.

He was seen as the heir apparent to Richard Wright, the established, older African-American author who lived in the French capital. These were followed by various other works written by Baldwin back in the States including: *Another Country*, [*Un Autre Pays*], and *The Fire Next Time* [*La Prochaine Fois le Feux*].

In the first five years after Baldwin settled in Saint-Paul, his popularity was evidenced by the publication in France of five of his books. *Tell Me How Long the Train's Been Gone* appeared as *L'Homme Qui Meurt* in 1970. Two years later, *Rap on Race* came out as *Le Racisme en Question*, while *No Name in the Street* was translated with the title, *Chasssés de la Lumière*. In 1973, *Notes of a Native Son* became *Chroniques d'un Pays Natal*. And in 1975 the French version of *If Beale Street Could Talk* went into the bookshops as *Si Beale Street Pouvait Parler*. Later translations included his last novel, *Just Above My Head*, published as *Harlem Quartet* in 1985. *The Evidence of Things Not Seen*, a collection of essays, also came out the same year as *Meutres à Atlanta*. Marguerite Yourcenar translated *Amen Corner*, her friend's three-act play, as *Le Coin des Amen*.

Seeking more information about Jimmy's success in France, I contacted Dr. Rosa Bobia. She authored, *The Critical Reception of James Baldwin in France* (1997), and had interviewed the writer in 1985 on the subject of his reputation in France. In her book, she recounted the many reasons for Baldwin's singular critical success in his adopted homeland. While she examines the large body of commentary by French-language critics, she adds to the knowledge not only of Baldwin, but also the French response to African-Americans and African-American artists who reside in the country. Prior to her work, James Baldwin's reputation was essentially analyzed as an isolated American phenomenon.

Dr. Bobia concluded that James Baldwin was the most intensely-studied author in France among the postwar group of African-American authors since Richard Wright.

"Known by a select group in the fifties and by the general public since the early sixties, Baldwin's reception had developed into a fairly stable tradition by the early seventies. Lucien Guissard expresses the opinion of many French critics when he says the French reader 'would not really understand the soul and ideology of black Americans without reading Baldwin or Richard Wright.' This kind of statement, coming after the Black Power Movement, indicates in a significant way Baldwin's place in France at the start of another decade of criticism." Dr. Bobia was obviously referring to the seventies.

Another reason for Baldwin's popularity she pointed out "is that the political Baldwin resurfaced in an overt way in 1972 with the publication of *Rap,* a dialogue on racism with the respected anthropologist Margaret Mead, and to a lesser degree, with *No Name in the Street.* African-American writers who attacked Baldwin's *Notes of a Native Son* helped to increase his popularity. The publication of *Notes* in France may be seen as a direct result of the attacks. The critics wanted to examine the work which had caused such dissension between Baldwin and the young generation of black American writers.

"Added to the above reasons, one needs to consider the increasing number of documents devoted to the literary analysis of Baldwin's work granting him a canonized status in France. An important manifestation of this aspect of the reception (and of the mutually stimulating process of political and literary reception) is the dissemination of his works in universities.

"At the end of the seventies, there were at least ten doctoral dissertations on Baldwin in progress or completed in France. All of this academic work on Baldwin in the seventies indicates that his reception was a process relatively independent of the media. In bringing Baldwin and other African-American writers to the attention of the Francophone public, the media emphasized the political.

"Lastly, Baldwin's popularity in France gained impetus when he purchased a home in southern France. Several influential newspapers published the news. The fact that Baldwin bought the house in France made a statement about the country. It was all the more important because the French public helped in the success of this African-American writer," Dr. Bobia said. (The purchase actually was never effected.)

Among Dr. Bobia's conclusions: "Baldwin's reception by French academic and journalistic critics revolves around some forms of 'appropriation' that may well be typical for the French reception of African-American writers in general. The association of the African-American with esotericism, entertainment, questions of racism and political protest we have found to be a fairly consistent frame of reference and therefore a system of assumptions which 'prestructured' the reception of individual authors and works."

Chapter 27

The Oeuvre:
Saint-Paul Era

In the period 1970-1987 when James Baldwin lived in Saint-Paul, he produced the following works, besides numerous articles and other writing.

1971   *A Rap on Race* (collaboration with Margaret Mead)

1972   *One Day When I Was Lost: a Scenario based on Alex Haley's The Autobiography of Malcolm X*

1972   *No Name in the Street* (essays)

1973   *A Dialogue* (collaboration with Nikki Giovanni)

1974   *If Beale Street Could Talk* (Chosen for the Best Young Adult Book List by the American Library Association)

1976   *Little Man, Little Man: A Story of Childhood* (children's book)

1976   *The Devil Finds Work* (essays)

1979   *Just Above My Head* (novel)

1983   *Jimmy's Blues: Selected Poems*

1985   *The Evidence of Things Not Seen* (essays)

1985   *The Price of the Ticket: Collected Nonfiction 1948 – 1985* (essays)

1988   Toni Morrison edited two books for the Library of America: *James Baldwin: Early Novels & Stories* with the complete texts of *Go Tell It on the Mountain, Giovanni's Room, Another Country* and his short story collection, *Going to Meet the Man.*

James Baldwin: Collected Essays, a memorable array of Baldwin's nonfiction including nine essays never before collected, some dating as far back as 1947.

2004   *Native Sons* by James Baldwin and Sol Stein, One World/ Ballantine (Random House). A posthumous book by Baldwin, edited by Stein.

2010   *The Crossroads of Redemption: Uncollected Works* by James Baldwin. Edited by Randall Kenan for Pantheon Books (Random House).

2014   *The Critical Reception of James Baldwin, 1963-2000* by
Consuela Francis (Camden House).

2015   *James Baldwin: Later Novels* edited by Darryl Pinckney for
the Library of America. It contains *Tell Me How Long the Train's
Been Gone, If Beale Street Could Talk, Just Above My Head.* Library
of America heralded this work as the stirring and provocative
final three novels by the literary voice of the civil rights era.

Chapter 28

Literary Positioning:
Writers' Evaluations

I again contacted Kalamu ya Salaam in New Orleans after learning that he had interviewed Baldwin during his 1979 stopover in the US. I sought recollections from his meeting with Baldwin. He referred me to his piece, "James Baldwin: Looking Towards the Eighties," published in *The Black Collegian* 10 (1979).

Citing Kalamu: ". . . His complex prose style has often been favorably compared to the King James version of the Bible [primarily the fire and brimstone Old Testament.] Although books such as *The Fire Next Time* have earned Baldwin a reputation for being a harsh critic, James Baldwin is actually most concerned with the problems and possibilities of finding and holding love.

"While he had not found it easy to live and work in this country, Baldwin continues to prolifically produce novels and essays. Most often he writes from a small town in France. The important thing is that he is not running away but rather searching out a rock, a desk, a stone table from which he can find the needed moments of silence and rest out of which will come rushing full force another letter, or a new nerve-jangling essay, or perhaps a huge and rich novel (such as his latest, *Just Above My Head*, which some critics think is his best since his first novel, *Go Tell It on the Mountain*)."

Fred L. Standley noted in the *Dictionary of Literary Biography* that Baldwin's concerns as a fiction writer and dramatist included "the historical significance and the potential explosiveness in black-white relations; the necessity for developing a sexual and psychological consciousness and identity; the intertwining of love and power in the universal scheme of existence as well as in the structures of society; the misplaced priorities in the value systems in America; and the responsibility of the artist to promote the evolution of the individual and the society."

Carolyn Wedin Sylvander, in her book, *James Baldwin*, concluded that what emerges from the whole of Baldwin's output is "a kind of absolute conviction and passion and honesty that is nothing less than courageous. . .Baldwin has shared his struggle with his readers for a purpose—to demonstrate that our suffering is our bridge to one another."

In *The Black American Writer: Poetry and Drama,* Walter Meserve wrote that "Baldwin's greatest achievement as a writer was his psychological perspective, exploring the ability to address American race relations from implications of racism for both the oppressed and the oppressor, while repeatedly underscoring that whites as well as blacks suffer in a racist climate.

He noted: "People are important to Baldwin, and their problems, generally embedded in their agonizing souls, stimulate him to write. . . . A humanitarian, sensitive to the needs and struggles of man, he writes of inner turmoil, spiritual disruption, the consequence upon people of the burdens of the world, both white and black."

Chinua Achebe, a Nigerian author, said: "Principalities and powers do not tolerate those who interrupt the sleep of their consciences. That Baldwin got away with it for forty years is a miracle. Except, of course, that he didn't get away; he paid dearly every single day, every hour of those days. What was his crime that we should turn him into a man of sadness, this man inhabited by a soul so eager to be loved and to smile? . . . The words of James Baldwin will be there to bear witness and to inspire and elevate the struggle for human freedom."

In Caryl Phillips's ode to Baldwin marking the two decades since his death (*The Guardian,* July 14, 2007), he remarked, "The passion and purpose of his writing, his early work in particular, had long ago ensured the permanence of his place in the literary canon. And, of course, more than any other mid-20th century American writer, he had set the stage for the debate on race that was needed then, and is still desperately needed today. The journey was complete. The price paid. The pain and frustration fully absorbed. Baldwin used to say, 'A life was a journey and you had to pay the price of the ticket. . . . What an incredible journey it has been.' He knew he had paid the price."

Though a fervent admirer and devoted friend, Phillips remained objective: "Even the most trenchant supporter of Baldwin's work will find it difficult to argue that the two novels of the 70s, *If Beale Street Could Talk* (1972) and *Just Above My Head* (1978), would, if they were not part of the Baldwin oeuvre, be much spoken of today. They are excessively rhetorical, structurally confusing and lacking in any coherent characterization. There are passages in both novels, particularly in *Just Above My Head*, which soar with a familiar eloquence, but all too often such moments quickly give way to longueurs where one feels as though the impatient author, Baldwin, has decided to elbow his way past the gallery of assembled characters and speak directly to us — witness to congregation.

"Again, Baldwin's nonfiction of the 70s and early 80s is more successful than his fiction, because the form itself is more forgiving of his rhetorical habits. However, while *No Name in the Street* (1972) and *The Devil Finds Work* (1976) have much of his familiar perception and wit, the sinewy prose appears to have atrophied and the liturgical rhythms have lost some of their skip and their beat. Sadly, *The Evidence of Things Not Seen* (1985), Baldwin's report on the Wayne Williams trial for the Atlanta child murders, is a book that appears to have been, from the beginning, badly conceived. As it proceeds it feels increasingly padded with irrelevant autobiographical asides that continually lead the reader away from, rather than towards, the central subject matter."

Sol Stein in *Native Sons* (2004) commented, "The fact that Baldwin's writings during his later public career lack some of the power of his earliest work does not diminish his accomplishment. Neither Hemingway nor Fitzgerald got better with every book. *Notes of a Native Son* has not dated the way so many books of its period have. Its insights are relevant today when separatism sometimes threatens the image of America as harbor and sanctuary. Baldwin the ex-preacher taught best when he preached least."

D. Quentin Miller, associate professor of English, Suffolk

University, Boston, edited *Re-Viewing James Baldwin: Things Not Seen (2000),* a compilation of ten essays by perceptive Baldwin specialists appraising his disregarded later work. The contributors elucidated Baldwin's accomplishments as an experimental writer who routinely questioned cultural norms and daringly examined the controversial, sensitive sphere of racial identity, social justice and sexuality.

The David Leeming foreword to Miller's compilation, underscored, "In this much-needed collection we finally find a serious consideration of this late, angry, and still articulate James Baldwin, who understands that the fire is smoldering under the brush of complacency, who knows that 'he who collaborates is doomed, bound forever in the unimaginable and yet very common condition which we weakly suggest as Hell.'"

Andrew Shin and Barbara Judson, who teach English at the University of Minnesota, published *Beneath the Black Aesthetic: James Baldwin's Primer of Black American Masculinity* in the *African American Review* (Volume 32, Number 2, 1988): "James Baldwin's voice has been both silenced and lost—silenced by the sexual politics of an emergent black left, lost because critics like Irving Howe decried Baldwin's putative aestheticism in favour of Richard Wright's militancy. But from our perspective, Baldwin's is a voice ahead of its time, one that explicitly addresses the implication of race and gender and, even more, attempts to articulate a gay ethic well before 'gay' entered common parlance and certainly before other writers and scholars legitimated 'queer theory' as a critical discourse. Baldwin's career strongly suggests the influence of feminism on his gay aesthetic, the insights of which he subsequently recontextualized in the struggle for black liberation."

X. J. Kennedy and Dana Gioia collaborated on *Literature: An Introduction to Fiction, Poetry and Drama* (2007). Excerpts from their *Critical Overview* of Baldwin's work:

> The complexities of response to Baldwin's writings reflects his own complexities as an artist and a human being. As is the case with virtually any "ethnic" writer in America, Baldwin treated themes of the individual's quest for personal identity in terms of the

complicated and often painful tangles of relationships to one's own ethnic group and to the larger culture.

From the beginning of his career, as indicated most directly by the novel *Giovanni's Room* and the essays on Richard Wright, Baldwin refused to be categorized as a protest writer or a cultural commentator who happened to employ fiction as one of the modes of expression. Instead, he insisted of being taking seriously as an artist and being judged by the same assumptions and evaluative concerns as would be applied to any other writers of fiction.

In some of his later work, Baldwin, in the opinion of many, substituted rhetoric and propaganda for the subtlety and the honesty of his earlier essays. Despite poor reviews, neglect and widespread assumption that his time had passed, he was a productive writer of fiction and especially nonfiction to the end of his life.

Ta-Nehisi Coates — author of *The Beautiful Struggle* and *Between the World and Me* as well as national correspondent covering culture, politics and social issues for *The Atlantic* — headlined his article in the magazine (September 24, 2013) *Is James Baldwin America's Greatest Essayist?* The reply in the subhead was *Baldwin's genius increases as we grow older*.

Coates spoke of Baldwin's writing about the Civil Rights Movement as not one of hope and goes on to say that Baldwin was a realist who didn't believe love conquers all. He continues by describing Baldwin as a clearheaded humanist not someone trying to change the world, flatter or inspire. Coates said Baldwin just wanted to write and for that he loved him.

When *T Magazine,* a *New York Times* supplement, (July 31, 2015) asked Coates to rate his 10 favorite books, *The Fire Next Time* was number one. He found it the finest essays he had ever read, direct and beautiful, not written to convince you but to go beyond.

Actually, also in July 2015 when *Between the World and Me* was published, there was an endorsement of "required reading" by none other than America's greatest living black author, the Nobel and Pulitzer Prize winner Toni Morrison. Upon receiving an advance copy of the book, she had replied, "I've been wondering who might fill the intellectual void that plagued me after James Baldwin died. Clearly it is Ta-Nehisi Coates."

A longtime, faithful devotee, Coates is becoming the heir apparent of the great Baldwin writing tradition. He acknowledged that after re-reading *The Fire Next Time*, he was inspired to write *Between the World and Me*. Coates had asked himself, "Why don't people write books like that anymore?" So he did.

Shortly after publication of *Between the World and Me*, it rocketed to the top of *The New York Times* hardcover nonfiction best seller list. He received the National Book Award for Nonfiction in 2015.

Chapter 29
Barack Obama and James Baldwin:
Parallel Paths

Though there is a generational gap between Barack Obama (born 1961) and James Baldwin (1924-1987), they follow parallel paths in their respective writing, speeches, career development and philosophy on life as blacks in white America.

President Barack Obama, as a boy growing up in Indonesia, learned about the American Civil Rights Movement from books his white American mother gave him. In his own first autobiographical book, *Dreams from My Father*, written before he entered politics while he was a community organizer in Chicago, he recalled as an adolescent reading James Baldwin, among other African-American authors, in an effort to come to terms with his racial identity. In his book, Barack Obama revealed his seeking to understand his roots—a quest in search of his father and in search of a home.

There was a schizophrenic positioning during their youth which set both of them apart in their own familiar surroundings while they sought to find out where they truly belonged.

Obama, raised by a single mother, with an absent father, was born on American soil but spent his early years in foreign lands. He was half-black, half-white. Baldwin—son of a single mother and an unknown father—was despised and cruelly treated by a stepfather who sired eight children. Jimmy was burdened with caring for his eight step-siblings while his mother was absent every day cleaning houses and the stepfather was in church preaching. Outside the house, Baldwin faced problems of acceptance, even in Harlem, as a black who was homosexual.

Obama—reconciled to being black, forged ahead with a fervent belief in the American Dream—had a good education, was successful as a community organizer and gained recognition in political circles. Baldwin, on the other hand, had limited schooling but early on was singled out by a white teacher for extra-curricular reading, theatre-going and other activities which were formative for his lifelong intellectual search and development. The two men endured racism, prejudice and conflict with blacks and whites, but they surmounted these problems with an optimism as they developed each in his own chosen direction.

President Obama's autobiography indicates that he has turned to books throughout his life to acquire insight and information from others. Baldwin once observed, "Language is both a political instrument, means and proof of power" and "the most vivid and crucial key to identity; it reveals the private identity, and connects with, or divorces one from, the larger, public, or communal identity." President Obama has demonstrated that his command of the magical power of language and his passion for reading have endowed him with a rare facility to communicate his thoughts to millions of Americans while treating complex ideas about race and religion.

The two men wrote about their fathers' blackness. Books by Baldwin and Obama both started with the death of their fathers. Baldwin's *Notes of a Native Son* opens with: "On the 29th of July, in 1943, my father died." He was almost nineteen at the time.

Barack Obama's *Dreams from My Father* also relates to his father's passing. "A few months after my twenty-first birthday, a stranger called to give me the news."

I again contacted Colm Toibin at his Brooklyn home since I recalled his writing about similarities in the lives of Barack Obama and James Baldwin. He began by recounting that "both men had established a distance from their fathers which caused them sharp grief and loneliness. But this had given them strength, confidence and the right to speak with authority. Neither had been trained by any other man. It was through their own force of will and strong character that made them the men they became."

Toibin went on to say that "Baldwin had not known his father very well. They did not really get on, probably because they shared the vice of a stubborn pride." He related how Badwin had hardly ever spoken to his father when he was alive and how long after his death he wished he had.

Comparing the relation of Obama with his father, Toibin told me that "Obama had written that his father remained a myth both more and less than a man. Since his father left Hawaii when he was only two years old, Obama only knew this father through stories his mother and grandparents told him."

After reading Baldwin's essays and Obama's speeches, which he felt were high on inspiration and short on policy, Toibin remarked, "I was struck by the connection between them." Both men, he felt, were trying to remake the world in their own images against all odds, unafraid to face the future of America represented by its children, a question alien to most politicians. He concluded our conversation using Baldwin's wonderful phrase: 'What will happen to all that beauty?'

Their travels abroad made them recognize how American they actually were. It would be difficult to find an American writer other than Baldwin who was so "adopted" by a foreign country, as he was during those seventeen years in France, and still felt foremost American. Or, Obama, who sought his roots in Kenya during his first visit in July 2015, when he identified himself as the first Kenyan-American president of the United States.

The church played determining roles in their development but they turned from the pulpit to take on other challenges. Baldwin as a teenage preacher became disenchanted and fled the restrictive church. Obama, in turn, rejected the ecclesiastical trappings which he had earlier embraced.

Both Baldwin and Obama surmounted their inherited legacy. Each did it in his own manner. Baldwin called on his childhood poverty and adolescent struggle to create enduring literary works which furthered understanding in a white society and served as a powerful tool in the civil rights movement. Obama gained recognition and respect as he moved upward through education, public service and forthright determination to achieve landmark gains.

Amazingly, during an early stage in the fiery civil rights battle, in the dark period of 1951 with little basis for optimism, Baldwin predicted that our "fantastic racial history" might ultimately take a positive turn. In an essay he voiced his hope, "Out of what has been our greatest shame, we may be able to create one day our greatest opportunity."

Even before Baldwin vented his vitriolic disappointment at governmental laxity in combating blatant racism and improving conditions for the blacks during his 1963 controversial encounter with Robert Kennedy, he recalled the attorney general's still-earlier speculation about the prospect of a black president. In a 1961 speech given for the Liberation Committee for Africa, he said, "Bobby Kennedy recently made me the soul-stirring promise that one day — thirty years if I'm lucky — I can be president too. It never entered this boy's mind, I suppose — it has not entered the country's mind yet — that perhaps I wouldn't want to be. And in any case, what really exercises my mind is not this hypothetical day on which some other Negro 'first' will become the first Negro president. What I am really curious about is just what kind of country he'll be president of."

Baldwin further speculated that even if such an unlikely development could take place, the United States itself must first be "revised" and, subsequently, the imagined "Negro problem" would have to be conjured up and re-evaluated as a problem of the classes in power. "The confusion in this country that we call the Negro problem has nothing to do with the Negroes." Baldwin emphasized that he could not envision a black man in the White House unless the nation's standing order was completely reversed.

In an essay in 1965, he reverted again to the prognosis of an African-American occupying the highest office in the land. "I remember when the ex-Attorney General, Robert Kennedy, said it was conceivable that in 30 years in America we might have a Negro president. That sounded like a very emancipated statement to white people. They were not in Harlem when this statement was first heard. They did not hear the laughter and bitterness and scorn with which this statement was greeted. We were here for 400 years and now he tells us that maybe in 30 years, if you are good, we may let you become the President."

During the American Bicentennial and presidential election year in 1976, James Baldwin wrote, *How One Black Man Came to Be an American: A Review of Roots (The New York Times,* September 26). Using Alex Haley's book as his sword, he revealed a foresighted political acumen.

Baldwin saw that America as the center of a troubled world now had not only recognized the power of the black vote but respected it. Never in living memory was this so before.

He continued saying that in the twenty-four years left of the 20th century, the black presence on the country's political scene would change forever the influence and significance of blacks in the world.

Warning that black people now bore a great responsibility facing a future totally different from where they had been, Baldwin talked about the end of the black diaspora. It would be the beginning of the end of their world of suffering.

One might presume that Barack Obama, fifteen-years-old at the time—who later acknowledged reading Baldwin in his quest for clarification of his own special situation—undoubtedly would have read Baldwin's indignant reaction to Bobby Kennedy's prophecy. With his fight for civil rights, essays and books, teaching and preaching, Baldwin played a substantial role in preparing America to elect a black president. (It actually happened eight years later than the predicted three decades.)

Barack Obama started his run for the presidency in February 2007—some forty-six years after Kennedy had broached the then-unthinkable prospect. Baldwin had mocked the three decades as being too long. Earlier, Obama was already on his way, after serving three terms in the Illinois Senate from 1997 to 2004. He was elected to the United States Senate in 2004.

In "A More Perfect Union" speech on race on March 18, 2008, Obama condemned the still-existent problems a half century after Baldwin's essay decrying the blacks' status-quo inheritance as second class citizens. He said, "That legacy of defeat was passed on to future generations—those young men and increasingly young women who we see standing on street corners or languishing in our prisons, without hope, or prospects for the future. Even for those blacks who did make it, the question of race and racism, continue to define their world in fundamental ways."

Further, on the issue of what he referred to as the black hostility to whites, he alerted the country to this wrath, "The anger is real; it is powerful; and to simply wish it away, to condemn it without understanding its roots, only serves to the chasm of misunderstanding that exists between the races . . . race is an issue that I believe this nation cannot afford to ignore right now. . . ." On the subject of his possible candidacy, he remarked that "some commentators have deemed me either 'too black' or 'not black enough.'"

Obama echoed Baldwin's lifelong struggle to resolve the chasm and strife without blacks reverting to violence.

On the forty-fifth anniversary of Martin Luther King, Jr.'s legendary "I Have a Dream" speech, August 28, 2008, Obama was nominated as the Democratic candidate for the office of the president of the United States. For his acceptance speech, throngs of people turned out, in number comparable to the 250,000 who had marched on Washington in support of civil rights legislation and an end to segregation on that blistery late fall day in 1963. Among those who marched was James Baldwin whose career as a preacher, civil rights spokesman, lecturer and writer centered on the enigma—and problem—of being black in the United States one hundred years after president Abraham Lincoln signed the Emancipation Proclamation which brought an end to slavery.

Baldwin died at the age of sixty-three. He would have been eighty-four had he lived to witness Obama's inauguration as president of the United States. He would have been justifiably proud that his civil rights agitation, essays and novels, teaching and preaching all were important contributing elements that led to a crucial evolution in American society.

Index